Canadian Painting in the Thirties

Charles C. Hill

The National Gallery of Canada, Ottawa

© The National Gallery of Canada
for the Corporation of the National Museums of Canada,
Ottawa, 1975

ISBN 0-88884-285-6

ITINERARY
The National Gallery of Canada, Ottawa
The Vancouver Art Gallery
Art Gallery of Ontario, Toronto

A reduced version of this exhibition to be circulated by the
National Programme of The National Gallery of Canada,
Ottawa
Glenbow-Alberta Institute, Calgary
The Edmonton Art Gallery
The Mendel Art Gallery, Saskatoon
Musée d'art contemporain, Montreal

FRONTISPIECE
26. PRUDENCE HEWARD, *Dark Girl* (1935)

Lenders to the Exhibition

Mrs Charles S. Band, Toronto
Jules Bazin, Montreal
Dr and Mrs Raymond Boyer, Montreal
Estate of M.A. Brooker
Morley Callaghan, Toronto
Canada Packers Limited
Paraskeva Clark, R.C.A., Toronto
Maurice Corbeil, Montreal
John H. Creighton, Vancouver
Dr and Mrs Albert Fell, Kingston
The Honourable Milton Gregg and Erica Deichmann
    Gregg, Fredericton
Mrs Jack Weldon Humphrey, Saint John
Kastel Gallery, Montreal
Mrs Leslie J. Kerr, Vancouver
Dr G.R. McCall, Montreal
McCready Galleries Inc., Toronto
Miss Isabel McLaughlin, Toronto
Mr and Mrs W.A. Manford, Toronto
Reta and Max Merkur, Toronto
Louis Muhlstock, C.G.P., Montreal
Mr and Mrs T.E. Nichols, Dundas
Power Corporation of Canada, Limited
Roberts Gallery, Toronto
St. Hilda's College, University of Toronto
Mrs Carl F. Schaefer, Toronto
Mrs Ninel Schuman, New York
Frank H. Sobey, Sobeys Stores Limited, Stellarton,
    Nova Scotia
Philip Surrey, Montreal
University College, University of Toronto
Mr Stuart H. Wallace, Vancouver
and other private collectors
Art Gallery of Hamilton
Art Gallery of Ontario, Toronto
The Art Gallery of Windsor
Beaverbrook Art Gallery, Fredericton
Hart House, University of Toronto
The McMichael Canadian Collection, Kleinburg
The Montreal Museum of Fine Arts
Musée du Québec, Quebec
The National Gallery of Canada, Ottawa
The Sir George Williams Art Galleries and Collection of
    Art, Concordia University, Montreal
The Vancouver Art Gallery
The Winnipeg Art Gallery

Preface

This is the first occasion on which The National Gallery of Canada has examined intensively a particular decade of Canadian art in an exhibition and in a publication. To many of us it may seem curious that such a study should have begun with a decade that, because of the Depression and the beginning of the Second World War, we would prefer to forget. Nevertheless, with fashion recently directing our attention to the thirties through films, revivals in dress, music, and literature, it seems appropriate now to examine this period in the exhibition *Canadian Painting in the Thirties* – with a seriousness that has little to do with fashion.

The thirties were a time in which The National Gallery was, through various circumstances, less closely allied to the more progressive movements in Canadian art than it had been since the beginning of the First World War. One reason was that during the Depression its appropriations inevitably were far from generous. For all its purposes, including staff salaries and acquisitions, its income ranged from $130,000 in 1930 – 1931 (the highest) to $115,000 in 1939 – 1940, with a low of $25,000 in 1934 – 1935. Added to these difficult circumstances, was the distress of the Director, Eric Brown, when more than a hundred artists petitioned the Government, protesting the Gallery's support of certain artists, essentially the Group of Seven, through acquisition and exhibition. Eric Brown expressed his disillusionment in a letter to a friend in 1932: 'I am getting rather doubtful of the wisdom of trying to push Canadian art forward as much as we do . . . . I think it would be wise to withdraw from current art activities gradually or at least temporarily so as to give us time for more study and some peace of mind at least.' As the author of this publication shows, these circumstances meant that The National Gallery between 1932 and 1936, very uncharacteristically, acquired only one work – Varley's *Self-Portrait* in 1936 – by any of the artists shown in this exhibition, whom it had previously enthusiastically supported and who were among the nearly 300 artists who rose to Brown's defence in 1933.

In spite of these problems, The National Gallery did buy a few major works, aside from contemporary Canadian art, during those years. One of these was *Sister Saint-Alphonse* by Antoine Plamondon (1802–1895). Another was the great *Vulcan and Aeolus* by Piero di Cosimo (1462–1521), bought, like the Plamondon, in 1937. One of the artists in this exhibition, David Milne, was particularly enthusiastic about the acquisition of the Piero di Cosimo. He made a detailed analysis of the painting in words and drawings in a letter (now in the Public Archives) to his friend Graham McInnes.

Despite the period of four years between 1932 and 1936 when The National Gallery appeared to have withdrawn its support of the artists represented in this exhibition, it should be noted that one of them, Lawren Harris, served on the Board of The National Gallery from 1950 to 1962 and that another, Charles Comfort, became its Director from 1960 to 1965. In addition, solo exhibitions of eighteen of these artists' works, not always necessarily organized by The National Gallery itself, have been shown at The National Gallery.

When the time came to study this period with both respect and detachment, it is interesting to note that the young Assistant Curator, Charles Hill, who applied himself to this task with so much enthusiasm and scholarly apparatus, should have been born well after this decade ended. Dennis Reid, the Curator of Post-Confederation Art, under whom Mr Hill began this project and to whom he has owed much for guidance and advice, was born after 1940. Consequently, in his work Mr Hill has every reason to be grateful to the artists, their friends and their descendants who have talked with him so generously about the period and its paintings.

Jean Sutherland Boggs
DIRECTOR

Acknowledgements

This exhibition has taken a year and a half to prepare and during that time I have been assisted by numerous people who have very kindly given of their time and memories. To those who allowed themselves to be interviewed, I would like to express my deepest gratitude. My thanks go to Harry Adaskin, Sylvia Bercovitch Ary, Robert Ayre, André Biéler, Mrs Fritz Brandtner, Ted Campbell, Paraskeva Clark, Dr Charles Comfort, Mrs Louise Comfort, Lawren P. Harris, Allan Harrison, Edwin Holgate, Yvonne McKague Housser, John P. Humphrey, Louis Muhlstock, Lilias T. Newton, Carl Schaefer, Frank Scott, Marian Scott, Jack Shadbolt, Hazen Sise, Jori Smith, Doris Spiers, Philip Surrey, Jacques de Tonnancour, and Isabel Wintemute.

I would also like to thank those who patiently answered my questions and kindly supplied information: Mrs Marcelle Abell, Mrs Anna Vanderpant Ackroyd, Hedwige Asselin, John Aveson, James Borcoman, Mrs Nan Cheney, Stanley Cosgrove, Mr and Mrs Gordon Davies, Ann Davis, Dr Paul Dumas, Mrs Regina Goldberg, Dr Naomi Jackson Groves, Howard Harris, Mrs J.W. Humphrey, Ruth Humphrey, Rick Kettle, Mrs James Knox, Peter Larisey, Norah McCullough, Mrs Barbara Macdonald, Donald Mackay, Mrs Pat Morrison, Mrs Vera Mortimer-Lamb, Kathleen Munn, Jean-René Ostiguy, Allison Palmer, Marian Robertson, David Silcox, Frances Smith, Dr and Mrs Paul Toomik, Peter Varley, and Margaret Williams.

During my research I have been assisted by the staff of galleries across Canada. I would especially like to mention Juanita Toupin, Librarian, and Ruth Jackson, Registrar, at The Montreal Museum of Fine Arts; Charles McFaddin, Registrar at the Art Gallery of Ontario; Wylie Thom, Registrar at The Vancouver Art Gallery; Miss Jacqueline Hunter, Librarian at The National Gallery.

For their assistance in indexing periodicals of the decade, I would like to thank Andrée Lemieux and Karen Love, summer students at The National Gallery; for their patience and help, I would like to thank Peter Smith and Donald Mowat, editors of the English text, and Jean-Claude Champenois, Hélène Papineau, and Louis Arial, editors of the French text.

Lastly I would like to express my sincere gratitude to the Director of The National Gallery of Canada, Dr Jean Sutherland Boggs, and to Dennis Reid, Curator of Post-Confederation Art, for the opportunity to work on this exhibition.

Charles C. Hill
ASSISTANT CURATOR
POST-CONFEDERATION ART

Table of Contents

Introduction

The thirties in Canada lack a definite image in the history of Canadian art. While the twenties are dominated by the success of the Group of Seven and the forties by the explosive development of the Automatistes, the thirties only raise the names of a few isolated artists. In fact when the exhibition was first considered, it was felt to be an arbitrary chronological imposition on actual artistic developments. Yet as the research began certain characteristics did develop: reaffirmations of earlier trends and the beginnings of other developments that were to find their fruition in the next decade. The dominant theme of Canadian art in the thirties can be broadly defined as a movement between polarities: from nationalism to internationalism, from the Group of Seven to the Contemporary Arts Society, from Toronto to Montreal.

THE NATIONAL SCHOOL

The Toronto-based Group of Seven was the embodiment of the nationalist cause, and A.Y. Jackson remained its leading spokesman. He believed that an art determined by geography and created by artists 'with their feet in the soil'[1] would naturally be a true expression of Canada and that the revitalization of Canadian art would come about through the continued exploration and interpretation of its landscape.

To a degree this attitude was shared by Lawren Harris, another member of the Group, who believed that art was a universal expression created through the interplay of the personality of the artist, time, and place and that one could reach the universal only through concentration on the particular or national.[2] However, unlike A.Y. Jackson, Lawren Harris believed the artist should move from the necessities of time and place to an art beyond time and place.

The influence of the Group continued in Toronto throughout the thirties. They had their copyists, followers, and loyal disciples: Paraskeva Clark, trained in a formalist tradition in Russia, even turned to landscape painting under this influence. However, younger artists, while recognizing their debt to the Group of Seven, were seeking new resources and new directions and these came mainly from the United States.

THE DEVELOPMENT OF INTERNATIONALISM

The rapid development of American art during the previous two decades had attracted the attention of many young Canadians. They now went to New York instead of studying in the open academies of Paris. The American Government's sponsorship of art and artists during the Depression and the strong Social Realist school also interested many Canadians seriously concerned about their

rôle in times of social unrest. Miller Brittain in Saint John was seeking a form of expression similar to that of New York's Fourteenth Street School. Charles Comfort was attracted to the machine-like Precisionism of Charles Sheeler, and Carl Schaefer to the regionalism of Charles Burchfield. David Milne, returning to Canada in 1929 after almost twenty-five years in the United States, produced landscape studies in colour and line totally different in intent and character from the epic grandeur of the Group.

Montreal, which had never been won over by the Toronto artists' work, already had a strong figurative school in Edwin Holgate, Lilias Newton, and Prudence Heward. André Biéler developed this tradition in directions paralleling the Social Realist art of the Works Progress Administration (W.P.A.) in the United States. Jean Paul Lemieux incorporated into his work qualities of native folk art and social comment.

While in Toronto these new developments could harmoniously coexist with or develop from the Group of Seven, among some Montreal artists internationalism was a conscious rejection of the Group's nationalism. The most articulate spokesman for this point of view was John Lyman. Having lived in France for almost eighteen years, he returned to Canada in 1931 to find Canadian art dominated by what he felt to be a self-conscious nationalism bordering on artistic xenophobia. Lyman especially identified with another expatriate Canadian, James Wilson Morrice, whom he had known in France and whom he considered Canada's finest artist. The nationalist legend of the Group placed Tom Thomson at the source of a 'Canadian' art and relegated Morrice to the rôle of a French artist for not having painted in Canada.[3] To this Lyman replied, 'The talk of the Canadian scene has gone sour. The real Canadian scene is in the consciousness of Canadian painters, whatever the object of their thought.'[4] To Jackson's concentration on landscape or the object he opposed the subjective vision of the artist expressed in plastic terms of design, colour, and structure. To the 'native school' of painting he opposed Cézanne, Matisse, Lurçat, and Derain. Through his writing and organizing efforts he sought to create a greater appreciation of the 'subjective' qualities of art and support newer Canadian artists working in this vein. Goodridge Roberts, Jori Smith, Marian Scott, Eric Goldberg, and Paul-Émile Borduas were all among the founding members of Montreal's Contemporary Arts Society whose aim was to foster 'contemporary trends in art,'[5] specifically, in John Lyman's eyes, those trends deriving from a European tradition.

For younger Canadian artists, the thirties were the decade of the British aestheticians Clive Bell and Roger

Fry. 'Significant form' and 'pure art' replaced the 'Canadian' subject matter. James Wilson Morrice replaced Tom Thomson as their predecessor. New methods and attitudes brought new themes. Figure studies, nudes, still-lifes, industrial scenes, social comment, and abstraction slowly displaced the predominance of landscape.

CRITICAL SUPPORT FOR NEW DIRECTIONS

Though opposed by some, these new directions found support among many Canadian critics. Donald Buchanan, author of the excellent biography of James Wilson Morrice, was especially sensitive to the aesthetic qualities of art. Writing in *The Canadian Forum* and university journals he offered some of the most intelligent observations on the contemporary scene in England, France, and the United States as well as in Canada. He was the first Canadian writer to discuss the work of David Milne and did much to bring him to public attention.

Graham McInnes, newly arrived from Australia via England, began writing for *Saturday Night* in 1935.[6] While a fervent champion of the Group of Seven, he came to criticize the predominance of landscape painting among the Group's followers to the exclusion of any consciousness of the contemporary scene.[7] He championed the newer figurative artists as well as the aesthetic studies of David Milne, and was the first Toronto critic to publicize the work of the newer Montreal artists, including Alexandre Bercovitch, Fritz Brandtner, Marian Scott, Jori Smith, Louis Muhlstock, and John Lyman.

Walter Abell, American-born and a Quaker, had spent several years at the Barnes Foundation in Pennsylvania before taking a teaching position at Acadia University in Wolfville, Nova Scotia, in 1928.[8] Familiar with contemporary art in France and the United States, he too championed those artists working in more international directions, especially Jack Humphrey in Saint John. He also was the sole Canadian critic to enter the realm of aesthetics.[9] He not only wrote about art but also was the prime mover in the formation of the Maritime Art Association and the publication of *Maritime Art*, Canada's first art magazine.

While Graham McInnes and Walter Abell wrote about the newer developments with insight and faith, they both favoured specific directions for Canadian art. McInnes's social sympathies made him especially interested in an art of social comment and at the same time prevented his appreciation of Abstraction. He wrote, 'More than anyone else, the cubists are responsible for the frantic rush of the younger artists of the twenties up a blind alley, and the divorce of art from the people.'[10] Abell also rejected abstraction, not on political grounds, but in the belief that

'visual elements reduced to an abstract state are limited in the range, the variety and the subtlety of the relations to which they can give rise . . . . Its aesthetic effect is limited to . . . the "decorative" level.'[11]

Robert Ayre, a native Winnipegger, alternating between Montreal and Toronto during the thirties, wrote in *The Canadian Forum*, *Saturday Night*, and the Montreal *Gazette*. Less committed to any particular school of art than McInnes and Abell, he reported current developments in Canadian art with a judicious sense of balance and direction.

EXHIBITION OUTLETS: TORONTO

While the artists forged into new territory and were supported by intelligent writers and critics, the more practical problems of exhibiting and selling their works remained. The exhibition system was still dominated by artists' societies ranging from the progressive to the conservative. The Canadian Group of Painters, a national body, supported those artists creating a living art that would reaffirm the Canadian identity won by its parent group, the Group of Seven. Liberal in its jurying, supportive of progressive trends, it remained nonetheless in the control of Toronto artists and in its statements continued to express the Group's nationalist bias. Artists from the rest of Canada recognized its importance as an exhibiting group though they had little say in its direction or policies.

The Canadian Society of Painters in Water Colour rose to greater prominence during the thirties. At the time of its formation in 1926 it had a membership of twenty-four, mostly more conservative artists.[12] By 1940 the Society had grown to forty-three[13] and had become one of the leading exponents of progressive Canadian art. Watercolour was an attractive medium for many artists since it was more economic than oils. For various reasons there also was a shift away from the large salon canvas. Artists were less concerned with the production of an object for the homes of the wealthy or for exhibition purposes and more concerned with art as process, as the expression of a subjective vision that could be more rapidly laid down in watercolour than oil. The preferential status of oil over watercolour remained, nonetheless: as Lawren Harris wrote Carl Schaefer, 'Each medium has its own virtues but oils seem capable of a deeper, a profounder and a more exhaustive expression.'[14]

Due to the more democratic nature of the medium, as well as for reasons of economy, artists also began seriously to explore and recognize the qualities of the graphic arts, especially drawing and lithography. The greater number and quality of such works brought about an increase in importance of the Canadian Society of Graphic Art.

While some societies prospered during the thirties, others declined in importance. After the conflict in 1932 between The National Gallery and senior Academicians, both the Royal Canadian Academy and the Ontario Society of Artists ceased to play any progressive rôle in Canadian art. The Ontario Society of Artists grew to be more and more dominated by commercial artists repeating in slick and superficial work the 'Canadian' themes of the Group of Seven. The Royal Canadian Academy, by its continual rejection of contemporary works and by its concentration on technique and 'tone' at the expense of expression, killed itself. However, the Academy's social importance remained great. Especially in Montreal it remained so strong that John Lyman made membership in the Academy cause of rejection for membership in the Contemporary Arts Society.

Apart from the societies' annual exhibitions, Toronto artists could exhibit at Hart House at the University of Toronto – a tradition originally begun by the Group of Seven to expose the students to contemporary art. The exhibitions were, however, closed to the public and sales were almost non-existent. Similarly the Women's Art Association organized regular exhibitions, being especially effective in sponsoring the work of women artists from across Canada.

Private galleries exhibiting contemporary Canadian art did slowly emerge in Toronto, though they were only to rival the societies in the forties. The Galleries of J. Merritt Malloney held infrequent exhibitions of some of the younger artists, though its artists were predominantly members of the Ontario Society of Artists and the Royal Canadian Academy. Mellors Galleries (which later became Laing Galleries) opened its doors to contemporary art with an exhibition of the work of David Milne sponsored by Vincent Massey. From Milne they moved into such 'blue-chip moderns' as J.E.H. MacDonald, A.Y. Jackson, Arthur Lismer, and Lawren Harris.

EXHIBITION OUTLETS: MONTREAL

Montreal artists had far fewer exhibition outlets than their Toronto counterparts. The annual Spring Exhibitions at the Art Association of Montreal and the appearance of the Royal Canadian Academy once every two years were the highlights of the season. The Academy consistently rejected works by younger Montreal artists, and the Spring Exhibition was a conservative mixture of amateur and professional work. For the graduates of the École des Beaux-Arts there were the annual exhibitions of the conservative Anciens des Beaux-Arts. Certainly Montreal artists could, and did, send works to the Toronto societies. Nevertheless, there remained a need for a strong

Montreal-based organization under local control. The Eastern Group and the Contemporary Arts Society were both formed to meet that need.

Several important exhibitions took place at the Arts Club of Montreal during the thirties; however it was a private club rarely open to the public. More important were the commercial galleries such as W. Scott & Sons or Henry Morgan & Company. W. Scott & Sons handled the estate of James Wilson Morrice and sponsored a series of important exhibitions of nineteenth- and twentieth-century French art as well as solo exhibitions by members of the Group of Seven, David Milne, John Lyman, and members of the Eastern Group. Henry Morgan & Company through the influence of John Lyman, a cousin of Cleveland Morgan (of the store's executive and an active board member of the Art Association of Montreal), opened its galleries for several important exhibitions including the work of the staff of the Atelier, Fritz Brandtner's exhibition sponsored by The Canadian League Against War and Fascism, an exhibition of Soviet art in 1935, and the Contemporary Arts Society and Les Indépendants in 1941. The Montreal branch of the T. Eaton Company, for a short period, under Jeannette Meunier, André Biéler's wife, held annual exhibitions of works by Canadian artists.

Outside Canada's two major cities exhibiting opportunities were fewer. Vancouver artists exhibited with the B.C. Society of Fine Arts and in the annual exhibitions of British Columbian art held at the Vancouver Art Gallery. Many also sent works to the Annual Exhibition of North-West Artists in Seattle. The Maritime Art Association was also influential in organizing annual exhibitions of works by Maritime artists. There were, of course, local art societies in most towns and cities across Canada, usually dominated by amateur or academic artists.

ART SALES IN THE THIRTIES

While artists were able to bring their works to the attention of the public, purchases were rare. Sales from the spring exhibition of the Ontario Society of Artists in 1929 totalled $923. Three years later there was not a single picture sold, and it was not until 1940 that more than two works were purchased from that annual exhibition.[15] Artists with established reputations saw their incomes drastically reduced during the Depression. Younger or unknown artists never had a chance to get off the ground. Carl Schaefer earned twelve dollars from the sale of his works in 1930 and absolutely nothing the following year. By 1934 his sales had improved to the figure of $145, hardly enough to support a family.[16] Jack Humphrey in 1937 was selling his watercolours for $5 and even at that, if it had not been for the continuous efforts of Walter

Abell, he would have become totally destitute.[17] Even so, David Milne could comment wryly, 'Artists stand depressions quite well, depressions look so much like their regular brand of prosperity.'[18]

Public galleries, some of which had previously been important purchasers of contemporary Canadian art, had their budgets slashed. The National Gallery of Canada's budget went from a high of $130,000 in 1929 to $25,000 in 1934.[19] From 1932 to 1936 only two contemporary Canadian paintings were purchased.[20] However, the Gallery's continued allegiance to the Group of Seven biased its purchases even after the annual grants increased. Works by members of the Group and their immediate followers in the Canadian Group of Painters were acquired to the exclusion of the newer Montreal artists.

The Art Gallery of Toronto, a private organization, was less severely limited by the Depression. Nevertheless, from 1931 to 1933 not one contemporary Canadian work was acquired. Later purchases leaned heavily to the Group of Seven and its followers, though after 1939 a series of group exhibitions by artists from across Canada were held from which liberal purchases were made.[21]

The Art Association of Montreal, an extremely conservative private institution, began only modestly to buy contemporary art in 1939. The Musée de la Province de Québec was more generous in its sponsorship of local artists, purchasing works by Jean Palardy, Jori Smith, Marc-Aurèle Fortin, and Jean Paul Lemieux.

MAJOR COLLECTORS

Private patronage of the visual arts, never great in Canada, was similarly limited during the thirties – confined to Ontario. Vincent Massey had been an important and early patron of the Group of Seven. He and Mrs Massey purchased works annually, and in at least one case, offered an artist financial assistance.[22] Massey's major purchase of five years' work by David Milne capped his career as a collector of Canadian art: after he left for England as Canadian High Commissioner in 1935 he virtually ceased to purchase Canadian art.

Charles S. Band, a native Torontonian, had collected paintings by members of the Hudson River School while living in New York. Returning to Canada and finding Canadians totally ignorant of the American works, he sold his collection and through Lawren Harris, a childhood friend, turned to Canadian art. From the mid-thirties he began to develop his Canadian collection, beginning with works by Emily Carr and Lawren Harris.

In Ottawa Harry Southam built up an important collection of French nineteenth- and twentieth-century art, including works by Courbet, Corot, Ingres, Van Gogh,

Cézanne, and Matisse. From the mid-thirties he also began purchasing works by members of the Group of Seven as well as by Emily Carr, Prudence Heward, and Sarah Robertson.

The sole major collector to purchase works by the newer Toronto artists was J.S. McLean, then president of Canada Packers Limited. He too began by collecting works by the Group of Seven, advised by A.Y. Jackson.[23] Later, with the advice of Douglas Duncan and through his friendships with the artists, he turned to the work of Carl Schaefer, Paraskeva Clark, and David Milne. As a member of The Art Gallery of Toronto's acquisition committee after 1939 he was influential in directing the purchases of works by newer Canadian artists.[24] He also was a generous contributor to the Kingston Conference in 1941.[25]

Douglas Duncan cannot actually be defined as a collector. As he himself said, his collection was actually an 'accretion.'[26] However, his purchases of Canadian works from 1936 on offered crucial financial assistance and encouragement to many artists.

ALTERNATIVE EMPLOYMENT

Without sales or bursaries, artists sought other sources of income. Many turned to teaching either at public schools or art colleges, or in children's art programmes. Among others, Arthur Lismer, Jack Humphrey, Fritz Brandtner, Paul-Émile Borduas, Anne Savage, and Jock Macdonald were all involved in the 'children's art crusade,'[27] as David Milne called it.

Artists not involved in teaching turned to commercial work, either setting up their own studios or working freelance. René Cera at the T. Eaton Company in Toronto employed quite a few artists in window display. In fact, of all the Toronto artists, A.Y. Jackson was the only one able to live off his painting. A bachelor, living frugally in the Studio Building, and with an established reputation assuring sales, he alone avoided the diversion of time and energy to other work.

Montreal artists were more severely hit by the Depression than Toronto artists. There was less commercial work available in Montreal and there were fewer teaching jobs. Alexandre Bercovitch had been evicted from his apartment and was about to have all his paintings confiscated by his landlord when Sidney Carter offered him an exhibition at his gallery.[28] Louis Muhlstock worked for his family's fruit-importing firm delivering goods to stores and keeping accounts. Rarely having enough money to buy canvas or decent drawing paper, he painted on washed potato sacks and drew on wrapping paper.[29]

The Maritimes offered nothing in the way of commercial

art or teaching for non-academic artists. Jack Humphrey did teach children and adults in his studio for a few years, but with little success. Miller Brittain worked at odd jobs all through the thirties. Sales were out of the question.

The most striking effects of the Depression occurred in British Columbia where the three leading artists all had physical breakdowns to a large extent attributable to their financial situation. Emily Carr, overworked and consistently having to make financial shortcuts, had a heart attack in 1937. (The sales of that year, however, enabled her to carry on.) Fred Varley and Jock Macdonald left the Vancouver School of Decorative & Applied Arts when their salaries were cut by sixty per cent, as both had families to support. Their new school, the British Columbia College of Arts, went under after two years, just avoiding bankruptcy. Varley had severe personal and financial difficulties after that, and had to be assisted by The National Gallery in the spring of 1936 and brought east. Overworked and undernourished, Jock Macdonald had a physical breakdown in the spring of 1937. Many established artists suffered greatly, but one can only guess at the number of younger, less well-established artists who, unable to sell their work or earn a living, gave up art entirely for other careers.

ART AND SOCIETY

In the face of such widespread economic and social dislocation, many artists felt the need to re-evaluate both their art and their relation to society. They felt isolated in their studios, cut off from a public that either ignored or misunderstood them, or purchased their works merely as luxury goods. They wanted to reintegrate themselves and their art into the moving forces of their age.[30] However, there was a wide divergence of opinions as to what rôle the arts should play in society, the attitude taken being partly dependent upon generation and partly on the financial situation of the individual. Quite a few of the artists in Montreal and Toronto came from wealthy or socially prominent families – a circumstance which to a certain degree cushioned the full impact of the Depression. More important than their own personal financial situation was their concept of art, to a large extent determined by their training in art.

Lawren Harris, Arthur Lismer, and Fred Varley had all gone to art school in Europe prior to the First World War in an environment still strongly influenced by Symbolist art theories, oriental religions, and Theosophy. For these artists, as well as for Emily Carr and Jock Macdonald (who inherited their concepts from the Group of Seven), art was synonymous with religion, the highest expression of a society; its rôle was to raise the spiritual awareness of

the community. In a talk to the Theosophical Society in 1933, Lawren Harris outlined the preparations for war, the research into chemical warfare, the corruption of the orthodox churches; yet he saw this as a spiritual crisis, not a political or economic one. The solution to this crisis lay in Theosophy and its manifestation in art which would create 'a living spiritual identity of all mankind, true brotherhood, and the immortality of the soul.'[31]

Arthur Lismer saw art as a social responsibility whose extension into all facets of life would combat ugliness and 'make man a socially minded, creatively alive and peaceful citizen of a larger community . . . .'[32] He wrote, 'Of the forces existent in the world today which can give to man self-knowledge and self-respect, the greatest is art.'[33]

While these artists did believe in a spiritual, and, by extension, social rôle for art, there were others who totally denied it any non-aesthetic purpose. Like the artists who organized the Armory Show and the Society of Independent Artists in the United States, Bertram Brooker and David Milne saw art as an expression of personality and inner feeling, concerned with the formal expression of the individual's reaction to reality. Milne, especially, was a staunch individualist who consistently denied any extrinsic rôle for his art. 'The painter', wrote Milne, 'must get his when he paints. If anyone else gets anything out of the product that is no concern of the painter's or if he doesn't just the same.'[34]

Bertram Brooker also denied that art had any 'useful' purpose or meaning beyond the artist's own individual aesthetic expression: 'Great art is essentially useless, in the practical sense. It appeals purely to the spirit.'[35] These concepts were initially stated by Brooker to counteract the influence of Victorian anectdotal art as well as public incomprehension of his own abstractions. However, by the mid-thirties the demand for a social purpose for art was coming from the Left and from younger artists.

Most of these artists had grown up or received their art training after the First World War. The disillusionment that followed that war had been accentuated by the economic and political crisis of the thirties. Many of them had studied at the Art Students League in New York where the influence of the Ash Can School and its Social Realist derivations was strong. Others had come from socialist backgrounds or became involved in left-wing politics in Canada. Certain of the newer critics, such as Graham McInnes and Walter Abell (both strongly influenced by developments in the United States), supported the younger artists in their questioning of the social rôle of artists and art.

The three sides of the issue were debated in a series of articles between Bertram Brooker, Elizabeth Wyn Wood, and Paraskeva Clark. In his essay 'Art and Society,' in *Yearbook of the Arts in Canada* (1936), Brooker again decried the 'demand for meaning or moral in a work of art' as well as 'propagandistic art in the service of a cause.' He reaffirmed his belief that art's concern was solely with perfection and 'the holiness of beauty.'[36]

Reviewing the *Yearbook* in *The Canadian Forum*, Frank Underhill, the *Forum*'s editor, criticized this attitude, commenting, 'European artists have been compelled to rethink the whole question of the relation of the artist to society, and the finer spirits among them . . . are deciding one after another that in our troubled generation the artist must be red or dead.'[37]

This review raised a blistering attack from the sculptor and Group associate Elizabeth Wyn Wood, who characterized Underhill's attitude as a 'mild epidemic of the Early Christian Martyr – Communist – Oxford Group fever which demands the consecration of all talent to the services of a readily recognizable cause . . . . What should we do instead? Paint castles in Spain – crumbling? Paint the Russian proletariat standing on the fallen Cossack, a modern Saint George and the Dragon? . . . Such things are not authentic stimuli to the Canadian Artist . . . . Let us [instead] camp for awhile on our northern pre-Cambrian shield . . . [so that] we may offer [the refugees from a smouldering civilization] the spiritual sustenance of an art which grows on the bare rock and bare chests.'[38]

To this, Paraskeva Clark cried, 'Come out from behind the Pre-Cambrian Shield,' denouncing Elizabeth Wyn Wood's 'exaltation of the individual [which blinds] an artist to the forces which approach to destroy that relative security in which he is permitted to exercise his individuality.' She affirmed that 'those who give their lives, their knowledge and their time to social struggle have the right to expect great help from the artist,' and finished with an impassioned plea that artists leave the unreality of the barren rocks and identify with the struggle of their fellow men.[39]

ARTISTS AND POLITICS

Paraskeva Clark was not alone in her commitment. Many artists contributed cartoons and articles to socialist and Marxist periodicals. *The Canadian Forum*, mouthpiece for the League for Social Reconstruction and the C.C.F. (Commonwealth Cooperative Federation, forerunner of the New Democratic Party), included articles on Marxism and art and on Mexican and Soviet art. Drawings and cartoons were contributed by Gordon Webber, Pegi Nicol, Fritz Brandtner, and Louis Muhlstock. *New Frontier*, a Marxist publication, gave extensive coverage to the arts and was liberally illustrated with drawings and cartoons by Ernst Neumann, Laurence Hyde, Fritz Brandtner, Louis Muhlstock, and Harry Mayerovitch.

Through Dr Norman Bethune, an amateur artist and well known among Montreal artists, quite a few people became actively involved in the Committee to Aid Spanish Democracy, the organization set up by Bethune to supply funds and volunteers for the Loyalist cause in Spain.[40] Artists designed posters and leaflets for the cause, and auctions of donated works were held in Toronto[41] and and Montreal[42] to raise money.

Other artists were actively involved in the League for Social Reconstruction and the C.C.F. and an exhibition of Soviet art[43] was brought to Montreal by a committee of artists and critics in the face of anti-Communist opposition. As Robert Ayre commented, Montreal survived the Bolshevik onslaught: 'the safety vaults under Saint James Street are still inviolate, and Mayor Houde sits in his aplomb like a chicken in aspic.'[44]

The political situation was actually more severe in Montreal than Toronto. Duplessis' Padlock Law and Adrien Arcand's Nazi Party were real threats to liberty in Quebec in the thirties. Anti-semitism became manifest to the point where hotels in the Laurentian resort area displayed anti-semitic slogans. As a result Jewish artists were especially sensitive to the oppression and suffering about them. Harry Mayerovitch's lithographs were strongly influenced by the Mexican 'proletarian' artist Diego Rivera, and Louis Muhlstock's drawings expressed his concern for, and identification with, the unemployed and other victims of society.

In spite of the high degree of political activity among artists, surprisingly little overt political or social content appears in Canadian painting at this time. There was definitely a bias against 'propaganda' in art, and the primacy of landscape painting remained strong. Nonetheless both Paraskeva Clark and Louis Muhlstock produced works with reference to current political events in Spain and China. Surprisingly, even Bertram Brooker painted a dramatic work of an unemployed man entitled *Derelict*.[45] Edwin Holgate and Philip Surrey exhibited works in a social-comment vein which they later destroyed.[46] Jean Paul Lemieux depicted the plight of the farmers[47] and Fritz Brandtner's watercolours, stimulated by the work of George Grosz, expressed the horrors of chemical warfare and the misfortunes of the unemployed.[48] Miller Brittain's paintings depicted the life of the urban poor and labourers.

Other artists' social sympathies are reflected in their choice of subject matter – Louis Muhlstock's abandoned houses and slum streets, Marian Scott's workers, or André Biéler's rural families raised to the level of modern saints.

Social or political comment was more common in the

graphic arts as painting was an expensive medium for impoverished artists and there was no market for paintings in this vein. Marxist theory also militated against the production of objects for private consumption. Prints were more democratic as they could be more widely distributed and were less costly. Drawings reproduced in magazines also could reach a far wider audience.

ARTISTS' COOPERATIVES

In light of events in the United States, the lack of co-operative activity among artists to better their own situation is a bit surprising. While Canadians were aware of the w.p.a., there were no petitions to the Canadian government from artists' societies to initiate such programmes. The only contact with the government appears to have been a polite letter from Frances Loring on behalf of the Sculptors' Society of Canada to the Minister of Public Works, suggesting that all sculptural work on public buildings be done by Canadian artists.[49] The only notice of cooperative political activity directed toward the interests of artists appeared in an article in New Frontier announcing the formation of an artists' union;[50] however no painters appear to have been involved.

Geographical isolation hampered contacts between artists in Canada, hindering any effective organization on a large scale. At its peak, in New York City alone there were three thousand artists employed on the w.p.a. projects,[51] but it is doubtful there were that many artists in all of Canada. Moreover the whole w.p.a. programme had been initiated by the government and artists unionized after its formation when they were receiving wages for time and production. Canadian artists, with a government that had absolutely no interest in the arts, didn't even get that far. Moreover the leaders of most of the already existing art societies in Canada were economically secure and apolitical, and had no real identification with fellow artists.

One of the few successful cooperative ventures at this time was the Picture Loan Society in Toronto. Recognizing the difficulties younger artists were having in the exhibition and sale of their work, a group of artists and their friends initiated the project, modelling it on Picture Hire Limited in England. By this scheme artists would receive an income from the rental of their pictures (based on two per cent of the purchase value) and increase the possibility of eventual sales.[52] Douglas Duncan put up the initial capital, and together with Rick Kettle, Erma Lennox, Norah McCullough, Gordon MacNamara, Pegi Nicol, and Gordon Webber, found space and arranged for exhibitions. The new gallery opened on 14 November 1936 with a group show of pictures by younger artists.[53] During the first year three hundred works were rented, fourteen exhibitions held, and special exhibitions sent to towns outside Toronto.[54] For quite a few artists the opening of the Picture Loan marked the first upswing in their careers in seven years.

While there were no cooperative galleries in Montreal, a group of architects, artists, and their sympathizers organized the Seven Arts Club in February of 1940.[55] Its aims, as stated in the introductory leaflet were to:

(1) Promote understanding of the arts, always stressing their interdependence and their roots in human experience;
(2) Endeavour to bridge the existing gap between the artist and the public;
(3) Enquire into methods of widening appreciation . . . [and] of marketing and promoting more effective art education.

During its very short existence (a little over a year) the club sponsored talks on the rôle of the arts, modern theatre, and contemporary architecture, the latter by Serge Chermayeff of the Modern Architectural Research Group in England. As well, an auction of donated objects was held to raise money for Canadian Aid to Russia.[56]

The most productive, long-range programme to try to bridge the gap between artists and society was initiated by André Biéler. In a talk he gave in 1937 to the Conference on Canadian – American Affairs he praised Mexican and American artists for their social consciousness and for making the public aware 'that the artist can, and should, function as a normally necessary member of national life.'[57]

w.p.a. projects got more publicity in the spring of 1940 when studies for murals commissioned under the Administration toured Canada,[58] and Edward Rowan, Assistant to the Director of the Fine Arts Projects, lectured in Ottawa and Montreal.[59] Government sponsorship of public works of art interested many artists concerned about their rôle in the social issues of the day, especially now that Canada was at war.

Teaching at Banff in the summer of 1940, André Biéler was struck by the isolation of many Canadian artists.[60] Resolved to do something to bring artists together, and with the aid of Harry McCurry, Director of The National Gallery, he organized the Kingston Conference in June 1941, a conference attended by artists from across Canada. Out of that conference came the Federation of Canadian Artists, whose main task for several years was to define the rôle of artists in society. Ironically, a government that had done nothing for artists during ten years of economic crisis was able to support an artists' organization in the forties, primarily because it enhanced the war effort, a politically popular struggle.

NOTES TO THE INTRODUCTION

THE RISE OF A MONTREAL SCHOOL

While the Federation of Canadian Artists developed active organizations across Canada, most notably in Vancouver, the most dramatic development of the forties occurred in Montreal – independent of the Federation. The Contemporary Arts Society and the Automatistes, while dealing with some of the same issues, operated on a philosophy quite alien to the w.p.a.-like purpose of the Federation. The transfer of focus from Toronto to Montreal also entailed the decline of strength in the Toronto community.

The Canadian Group of Painters, from its outset, suffered from the strength of the Group of Seven. During the first three years of its existence, from 1933 to 1936, control remained in the hands of the senior artists who, for various reasons, no longer acted as a body. Though the Canadian Group's statements consistently reiterated its allegiance to the Group of Seven, the younger artists had in fact rejected its nationalistic formula but were unable to unite in the expression of one coherent ideology. Moreover, defections to the Royal Canadian Academy weakened its strength. The older group had consisted of a few people intimately involved with each other and united by a single faith in the creation of a national art. The Canadian Group was dispersed across Canada and contained such a diversity of interests that it could never act as a collective, creative force.

The Contemporary Arts Society was never as unified as the Group of Seven had been, though its leaders, specifically Lyman, Borduas, and Maurice Gagnon, shared a common goal during its early years. Opposition to the conservative academicism which predominated in Montreal added strength to the constructive struggle to foster contemporary art in line with international trends. The victorious return of Alfred Pellan and the creative activities of French emigrés in North America during the War acted as catalysts to artistic developments in Quebec which were to dominate Canadian art in the forties.

1. A.Y. Jackson, Toronto, to H.O. McCurry, Ottawa, 9 June [1938]; in The National Gallery of Canada.
2. Lawren S. Harris, 'Different Idioms in Creative Art,' Canadian Comment, vol. II, no. 12 (December 1933), p. 6.
3. Frederick B. Housser, A Canadian Art Movement (Toronto: The Macmillan Company of Canada, Limited, 1926), p. 21.
4. John Lyman, 'Art,' The Montrealer (1 February 1938).
5. 'Contemporary Arts Society Constitution' [1939]; private property.
6. For an autobiographical account of McInnes's career as an art critic during the thirties, see Graham C. McInnes, Finding a Father (London: Hamish Hamilton Ltd., 1967).
7. Graham C. McInnes, 'The World of Art,' Saturday Night, vol. LII, no. 14 (6 February 1937), p. 6.
8. Conversation with Mrs Walter Abell, Ottawa, 12 June 1974.
9. Walter Abell, Representation and Form (New York: Charles Scribner's Sons, 1936).
10. Graham C. McInnes, 'The World of Art,' Saturday Night, vol. XLI, no. 52 (31 October 1936), p. 11.
11. Walter Abell, 'The Limits of Abstraction,' The American Magazine of Art, vol. XXVIII, no. 12 (December 1935), p. 738.
12. The Canadian Society of Painters in Water Colour (exhibition catalogue) (Toronto: The Art Gallery of Toronto, 1926), p. 43.
13. Catalogues. Canadian Society of Painters in Water Colour. Annual Exhibition (Toronto: The Art Gallery of Toronto, 1939 and 1940).
14. Lawren S. Harris, Hanover (N.H.), to Carl Schaefer, Toronto 15 August 1936; property of Carl Schaefer, Toronto.
15. Ontario Society of Artists, Toronto, President's Annual Report(s), 1929 to 1940.
16. Carl Schaefer, Toronto, to Charles Hill, Ottawa, 18 December 1973; in The National Gallery of Canada.
17. Walter Abell, Wolfville, to Jack Humphrey, Saint John, 5 January 1937; property of Mrs J.W. Humphrey, Saint John.
18. David Milne, Palgrave, to H.O. McCurry, Ottawa, 7 January 1932; in The National Gallery of Canada.
19. The National Gallery of Canada, Annual Report(s), 1929 and 1934.
20. Fred Varley's Self Portrait (1919) was purchased from the Group of Seven retrospective in 1936 to enable him to leave British Columbia. Mountain River (1932) by Homer Watson was purchased in 1934.
21. The Art Gallery of Toronto Bulletin and Annual Report(s), 1929 to 1941.
22. Vincent Massey gave Alexandre Bercovitch funds to enable him to visit the Gaspé to paint in return for a promised future work. Alexandre Bercovitch, Montreal, to Mrs Massey, Ottawa, 22 November 1935; in The National Gallery of Canada.
23. J.S. McLean, 'On the Pleasures of Collecting Paintings,' Canadian Art, vol. x, no. 1 (Autumn 1952), p. 4.
24. Ibid., p. 6.
25. A.Y. Jackson, 'Introduction,' Paintings and Drawings from the Collection of J.S. McLean (exhibition catalogue) (Ottawa: The National Gallery of Canada, 1952).
26. Alan Jarvis, 'Douglas Duncan,' in Pierre Théberge, Gift from the Douglas M. Duncan Collection and the Milne-Duncan Bequest (exhibition catalogue) (Ottawa: The National Gallery of Canada, 1971), p. 26.
27. David Milne, Severn Park, to H.O. McCurry, Ottawa, 15 February 1934; in The National Gallery of Canada.
28. 'Eviction of Artist Brings Recognition,' Montreal Daily Herald (7 April 1933).

29. Taped interview with Louis Muhlstock recorded at Montreal on 15 September 1973, by Charles Hill; in The National Gallery of Canada. All interviews will be referred to by the name of the person interviewed, the place, and the date. All recordings are by Charles Hill and are in The National Gallery of Canada.

30. Marian Scott, 'Science as an Inspiration to Art,' *Canadian Art*, vol. I, no. 1 (October–November 1943), p. 19.

31. Lawren S. Harris, 'Theosophy and the Modern World: War and Europe,' *The Canadian Theosophist*, vol. XIV, no. 9 (15 November 1933), p. 286.

32. Arthur Lismer, 'Art and Child Development,' *Canadian Comment*, vol. IV, no. 3 (March 1935), p. 16.

33. Arthur Lismer, 'Art in a Changing World,' *Canadian Comment*, vol. IV, no. 2 (February 1935), p. 23.

34. David Milne, Big Moose (N.Y.), to James Clarke, Yonkers (N.Y.), 13 November 1927; in the Public Archives of Canada, Ottawa.

35. Bertram Brooker, 'The Seven Arts,' *The Ottawa Citizen* (9 December 1929).

36. Bertram Brooker, 'Art and Society,' *Yearbook of the Arts in Canada, 1936* (Toronto: The Macmillan Company of Canada Limited, 1936), pp. xiv, xxii, xxviii.

37. Frank Underhill, 'The Season's New Books: *Yearbook of the Arts in Canada*,' *The Canadian Forum*, vol. XVI, no. 191 (December 1936), p. 28.

38. Elizabeth Wyn Wood, 'Art and the Pre-Cambrian Shield,' *The Canadian Forum*, vol. XVI, no. 193 (February 1937), pp. 13, 14, 15.

39. Paraskeva Clarke [sic] (as told to G. Campbell McInnes), 'Come Out From Behind the Pre-Cambrian Shield,' *New Frontier*, vol. I, no. 2 (April 1937), pp. 16–17.

40. Roderick Stewart, *Bethune* (Toronto: New Press, 1973), p. 88.

41. A.Y. Jackson, Toronto, to H.O. McCurry, Ottawa, 20 February 1939; in The National Gallery of Canada.

42. Montreal *The Gazette* (15 March 1938) and Montreal *The Gazette* (10 December 1938).

43. Montreal, Henry Morgan & Co., 15 May–1 June 1935, *The Art of Soviet Russia, under the Joint Auspices of the Pennsylvania Museum of Art and the American Russian Institute 1934–1935.*

44. Robert Ayre, 'Soviet Art Comes to Canada,' *The Canadian Forum*, vol. XV, no. 177 (August 1935), p. 320.

45. *Derelict* (1939), Estate of M.A. Brooker.

46. Edwin Holgate, *Unemployed*, exhibited Toronto, The Art Gallery of Toronto, December 1931, *An Exhibition by the Group of Seven*, no. 76; Philip Surrey, *Idle Hands*, exhibited Montreal, Art Association of Montreal, January 1940, *The Eastern Group*, [no. cat].

47. Jean Paul Lemieux, *Le colon et sa famille* (1938), exhibited Toronto, The Art Gallery of Toronto, October 1941, *Charles Goldhamer, Jean Paul Lemieux, Peter Haworth, Tom Wood*, [no cat. no.].

48. Fritz Brandtner painted numerous watercolours in this vein. One series was entitled 'The Other Side of Life.'

49. Frances Loring, Toronto, to The Hon. Mr P.J.A. Cardin, Minister of Public Works, Ottawa, 20 November 1935; copy in The National Gallery of Canada.

50. A.T. Vivash [President, Local 71, Artists Union, Toronto], 'Trade Unions for Artists,' *New Frontier*, vol. II, no. 1 (May 1937), pp. 22–23.

51. Audrey McMahon, 'A General View of the W.P.A. Federal Art Project in New York City and State,' in Francis V. O'Connor, ed., *The New Deal Art Projects/An Anthology of Memoirs* (Washington, D.C.: Smithsonian Institution Press, 1972), p. 56.

52. Rick Kettle in Alan Jarvis, ed., *Douglas Duncan: A Memorial Portrait* (Buffalo, Toronto: University of Toronto Press, 1974), p. 50. The original prospectus is reproduced on pp. 52–53.

53. 'Artists Exhibit Many Pictures for Loan Plan,' *The Toronto Telegram* (14 November 1936).

54. Graham C. McInnes, 'The World of Art,' *Saturday Night*, vol. LIII, no. 7 (18 December 1937), p. 12.

55. Robert Ayre, 'Seven Arts Alive to Relation of Arts to Society,' Montreal *Standard* (10 February 1940). The organizing committee consisted of Dr L. Hamilton Stilwell, Charles Rittenhouse, Harry Jacoby, Henry Eveleigh, Henry Finkel, Peter Dawson, and Hazen Sise.

56. *The Seven Arts Club is on a 'Treasure Hunt'*. Pamphlet, n.d.

57. André Biéler, 'National Aspects of Contemporary American and Canadian Painting,' *Conference on Canadian American Affairs Held at Queen's University, Kingston, Ontario, June 14–18, 1937: Proceedings* (Montreal: Ginn & Company, 1937), p. 136.

58. *Exhibition of Mural Designs for Federal Buildings from The Section of Fine Arts, Washington, D.C.* (exhibition catalogue) (Ottawa: The National Gallery of Canada, 1940).

59. Robert Ayre, 'Art Project Here a War Casualty,' Montreal *Standard* (27 April 1940).

60. André Biéler, 'The Kingston Conference – Ten Years Afterwards,' *Canadian Art*, vol. VIII, no. 4 (Summer 1951), p. 150.

1. Formation of the Canadian Group of Painters

Canadian art of the twenties is dominated by the rise and growth of the Group of Seven. It is the story of a struggle to develop an art inspired by the Canadian landscape, of a brotherhood, united by the mystical number seven, working to open up the creative channels of Canadian art. By 1930 the Group of Seven was Canada's 'National School,' dominating the image of Canadian art abroad, either through shows the members organized themselves,[1] or through their inclusion as Canadian representation in international exhibitions.[2] Articles in foreign art journals[3] also confirmed the impression that the only living Canadian art was that of the Group of Seven and its followers.

Opposition had always played an important rôle in the Group's development;[4] however this opposition had temporarily lost credibility. The dangers of widespread acceptance soon became apparent, and were commented upon by Bertram Brooker, a close friend of the Group:

So long as the Group of Seven operated to release young Canadian painters from the stuffy ties of Victorian atmosphericism, and encouraged them to find new ways of seeing and expressing the Canadian scene as honestly as they could and as 'individually' as possible, their influence . . . can only be regarded as a healthy and helpful one. But already – although the Canadian public has by no means accepted the Seven – the influence of their work shows signs of hardening into a formula which a good many painters are adopting as being, so to speak, the 'fashionable' native school of painting.[5]

Reviewing the Group's exhibition in 1930,[6] Brooker pinpointed some of the problems:

The present show at Toronto rings the deathknell of the Group of Seven as a unified and dominant influence in Canadian painting . . . . They have themselves ceased to experiment. Moreover, they are much less productive . . . . MacDonald and Varley have been too much engaged in teaching, and Lismer in educational work at the gallery [The Art Gallery of Toronto], to spare much time for painting. Casson and Carmichael have a roomful of watercolours – extremely capable things but not experimental – and no oils. Jackson and Harris, the only two of the Group who have much time for painting, are represented mostly by smaller paintings than usual, all landscapes, and of a type that one has learned to expect from them. The experimentation is over, the old aggressiveness has declined.[7]

Generous sponsorship of younger artists accentuated the crisis the Group was undergoing. The exhibition of 1931 included eighty-five works by twenty-six invited contributors to the sixty-three works by the Group members.[8] Varley was not represented at all. The uneven quality of the newer work caused one observer to comment, 'If the Group intends to be a nursery for incompetent painters, then all right, but if they aim to raise the standard of painting in Canada and to increase the love and understanding of our country, then something different must be done.'[9]

Finally, at a party at Lawren Harris's house after the opening of the exhibition of 1931, A.Y. Jackson announced, 'The interest in a freer form of art expression in Canada has become so general that we believe the time has arrived when the Group of Seven should expand, and the original members become the members of a larger group of artists, with no officials or constitution, but held together by common intention of doing original and sincere work.'[10] However, as Brooker noted. 'The announcement was very intangible. No name was suggested . . . .'[11]

It appears, in fact, that the Group was at an impasse. The members were not willing to give up their control, partly, perhaps, for reasons of prestige but also recognizing that there were no other artists of their stature or ability in Toronto to take over. It also appears that there was disagreement as to how the Group should expand and who should be brought into a new organization.[12] Edwin Holgate had become a member in 1930,[13] expanding the Group's geographic range to Montreal; and in May 1932, to reach westward, LeMoine FitzGerald (from Winnipeg) was invited to join,[14] an invitation he accepted gladly.[15] He was told to prepare works for a Group exhibition for the following winter.[16] However, other events intervened.

Certain members of the Royal Canadian Academy had never accepted defeat after the Wembley exhibition conflict over the control of The National Gallery and Canadian representation in international exhibitions.[17] Criticisms of The National Gallery's rôle and, by consequence, of the Group of Seven, were voiced at the time of the Philadelphia Sesqui-Centennial Exhibition in 1926[18] and the Canadian exhibition in Paris in 1927. This latter attack included denunciations of Eric Brown, the Gallery's Director, to Government Ministers,[19] newspaper attacks and counter-attacks and petitions from artists in Montreal, Toronto, and Ottawa in support of Eric Brown.[20]

In January 1932 Franz Johnston, ex-Group of Seven member, wrote to the Prime Minister, R.B. Bennett, complaining of discrimination in his representation in National Gallery exhibitions.[21] This was followed in March by a letter from Arthur Heming[22] who also brought in the issues of control of the Gallery by the Royal Canadian Academy, the composition of juries for international exhibitions, favouritism to the Group in Gallery purchases and annual exhibitions, and supposed gross errors in the purchase of 'Old Master' works. In the meantime, Academicians and their supporters were circulating a

1. In the Arts and Letters Club, Toronto, 1929.
Clockwise from lower left: Merrill Denison, Bertram
Brooker, A.Y. Jackson, J.E.H. MacDonald, Lawren
Harris, Arthur Lismer.

petition criticizing The National Gallery for 'extreme and flagrant' partisanship.[23] First rumours of the petition with sixty-five signatures[24] emerged in the press in May and June,[25] but the issue climaxed in December when one hundred and eighteen petitioners stated they were going to boycott all National Gallery exhibitions and demanded a government investigation.[26]

While the Royal Canadian Academy never actually took an official stand on the issue, it was obvious that it was an attack directed by the senior Academicians. A.Y. Jackson felt he could no longer support the Academy and resigned, accusing the petitioners of trying to control other artists not in accord with them and trying to influence National Gallery purchases, which he felt would result in 'patronage and politics.'[27] The next three months saw Canadian papers full of articles and letters for and against The National Gallery. In the meantime, a Toronto group consisting of Frances Loring, Louise Comfort, and Elizabeth Wyn Wood circulated a counter-petition across Canada in support of Eric Brown; it was signed by two hundred and eighty-two artists and sent to the Gallery at the end of January.[28] The press debate died out by the spring, though meetings with government ministers and lawyers for the anti-Gallery petitioners continued until December 1934.[29] Eric Brown retained his directorship and the Academy attacks ceased. It was a decided victory for the Toronto artists; however there were casualties. Eric Brown had little to do with Canadian art after this débâcle, and The National Gallery's annual exhibition of Canadian art was discontinued. Some of the artists' societies had been badly split. Lawren Harris resigned from the Ontario Society of Artists,[30] as did all the sculptor members.[31] It was against this background that the Canadian Group of Painters was formed.

A small Group of Seven exhibition was being organized for Hart House at the University of Toronto[32] when J.E.H. MacDonald died.[33] Ten days later news of the boycott hit the press and A.Y. Jackson resigned from the Academy. MacDonald's death affected the artists greatly, for with him died the Group of Seven. There was no going back. Circumstances had forced the Group to act. The threat of Academy control of The National Gallery would mean the younger, more progressive artists would be left out in the cold. Lawren Harris quickly wrote to FitzGerald: 'We feel it is essential to form a society of the so-called modern painters in the country, secure a charter and make ourselves felt as a country-wide influence in terms of the creative spirit. We propose to call the society "The Canadian Group of Painters." '[34]

Before publicly announcing the formation of the new organization, the Group of Seven, for the first time, issued

a manifesto refuting the criticism the Group was receiving in the National Gallery controversy, and with the future Canadian Group in mind:

> The group of seven has always believed in an art inspired by the country, and that the one way in which a people will find its own individual expression in art is for its artists to stand on their own feet, and by direct experience of the country itself . . . to produce works of its own time and place . . . . The group has always . . . maintained for themselves and others the right to freedom of expression, believing that only in diversity of outlook will there ever be a widespread interest in the arts of this country. While it believes that faction is a healthy sign, it has no quarrel with any individual artist, critic or society of artists. Its members are a group of serious workers imbued with a creative idea and seeking to practice it.[35]

In late February, after the height of the controversy had passed, formation of the Canadian Group was announced.[36] The original Group of Seven never actually disbanded but was absorbed instead into the larger society whose twenty-eight members included most of the progressive English-speaking artists from across Canada.[37]

With Lawren Harris as president and Fred Housser as secretary it was evident the new group would follow a nationalistic path, a direction not accepted by all the new members. Brooker wrote to FitzGerald:

> I am a little afraid that a strong nationalistic bias, which always gets into the utterances of the old Group, either public or private, is going to continue very strongly in the new Group. Comfort and I were the only ones at the meeting who raised our voices in protest against this rather insular attitude. We both felt, for example, that the very name of the new Group – Canadian Group of Painters – puts undue emphasis on the word 'Canadian.'[38]

However, the majority of the new members felt a great debt to the Group for supporting them and were honoured to be invited as members.

The first exhibition was being prepared for November[39] when the new group was invited to exhibit at the Heinz Art Salon in Atlantic City.[40] The Group of Seven had always put great stress on foreign exhibitions to project their particular image. It did not seem incongruous, apparently, that a new nationalistic Canadian group should have its first exhibition outside of Canada.

The Atlantic City exhibition[41] was limited solely to members of the Canadian Group of Painters – with two works by J.E.H. MacDonald[42] as a tribute to that deceased member of the Group of Seven. The foreword to the catalogue pointed out that 'Modernism in Canada has almost no relation to the modernism in Europe . . . in Canada, the main concerns have been with landscape moods and rhythms . . . . Their work is strongly redolent of the Canadian soil and has a distinctly national flavor.' Some reviewers appreciated this aspect of the art,[43] while others did not. The American critic Carlyle Burrows, for example, commented: 'In spite of the full-flavored quality of their work, the Canadians are seldom painters of robust and telling vitality. Too much seems dependent upon a decorative formula which is repeated rather obviously by most of the painters in the exhibition.'[44]

The first exhibition to be held in Canada opened in November at The Art Gallery of Toronto. The scope of the Group's aims was expanded in the Foreword to the catalogue: 'Hitherto it has been a landscape art . . . but here and there figures and portraits have been slowly added to the subject matter, strengthening and occupying the background of landscape. Here also more modern ideas of technique and subject have been brought into the scope of Canadian painting . . . .'[45] Paintings by twenty-five invited contributors supplemented the works of the 'group of twenty-eight.'[46]

The exhibition was met with some good-natured bantering (fig. 2).[47] Augustus Bridle, a leading Toronto journalist and early friend of the Group of Seven, pointed out, 'this is the third phase in Group psychology. The first, in 1919, was Whoopee. The second, about 1925, was Family Compact, with occasional associates. This is New Democracy.'[48] Robert Ayre made the most intelligent comments on the exhibition:

The Seven are not interested in imitators; it is the spirit they recognize, what they gave these new members was support and stimulus; the newer bearers of the revolutionary spirit have not had to fight alone against prejudice . . . . The canvases of the original members of the Group are not the most interesting part of the show. The younger men and women have brought a new energy and a new vision. Not only are we moving toward human life, away from landscape . . . but in growing up we are beginning to show the effects of the profound disturbances in human affairs which have shaken the world . . . .[49]

Another exhibition was not be be held until 1936.

The early history of the Canadian Group is dominated by the figures of Arthur Lismer, A.Y. Jackson, and Lawren Harris. Lismer left the Ontario College of Art in 1927 and became supervisor of art education at The Art Gallery of Toronto,[50] a job that took up an increasing amount of his time. Yet during the early years of the decade his painting continued at a steady pace, mostly resulting from holiday sketching trips or reworkings of earlier sketches. *Baie*

Saint-Paul, Quebec (1931, cat. no. 1) was painted from a sketch done on a trip to the north shore of the Saint Lawrence in 1925. The earlier version, *Quebec Uplands* in The National Gallery,[51] is more reticent and controlled than the exuberant, later work, with its billowing clouds, rolling rhythms, and summer colours.

More characteristic of Lismer's work of the thirties are the wind-blown, Georgian Bay pines. In *Pine Wrack* (1933, cat. no. 2) the cubist-derived, planar structure of the rocks and the light shaft contrasts with the more impressionist treatment of the clouds, yet is united to it by the complex design of the twisted pines. A more successful integration of the elements is found in *Bright Morning* (1935, cat. no. 3) where the jungle-like growth covering the rocks is the primary focus, and the larger pines become subordinate elements marking the rhythm across the canvas. Lismer's work between the mid-twenties and the forties shows an increasing interest in complex structure and design. It develops logically and surely from panoramic landscapes to dramatic silhouettes, from tangled growth to still-life studies of dock-litter in the early forties.

Yet as Lismer became more involved in education he had – as Brooker had noted – less time to paint. He taught all winter at The Art Gallery of Toronto and in 1933 organized the Children's Art Centre.[52] At the same time he was writing two monthly art columns (in *Twentieth Century* and *Canadian Comment*) in which he affirmed his continuing belief in human creativity and in the necessity of art in all facets of life.[53] Familiar with world progressive educationalists and a leader in his own field, Arthur Lismer attended the New Educational Fellowship Conference in South Africa in 1934.[54] This visit resulted in an invitaton to return there to set up children's art programmes. By this time Lismer was fed up with battling Gallery administrators who weren't interested in his work[55] and was willing to leave. Financed by the Carnegie Corporation Lismer left Canada in May 1936,[56] spent a year in South Africa, and returned via Australia and New Zealand.[57]

The South African stay resulted in certain changes in Lismer's work. For the first time he started painting seriously in watercolour.[58] While his first efforts were fairly hesitant, at times they reached a marvellously expressive quality verging on caricature.[59] In oils he was painting figures and scenes of African village life which, however, lack the dramatic strength of his Canadian works.

On his return to Canada he spent one more year at The Art Gallery of Toronto; but when Carnegie funds were cut off and no support was forthcoming in Toronto for his many years of educational work, he left for New York. He taught one year at Teachers' College, Columbia University at the same time laying plans for a national children's art

2. An Artist Draws His Impressions of 'Expressionist' Art, *The Toronto Telegram*, 25 November 1933.
The works caricatured are, upper row left to right: *Sea and Rocks, Nova Scotia* by George Pepper; *Mountains in Snow* by Lawren Harris; and *Decoration* by Sarah Robertson.
Lower row left to right: *The Bather* by Prudence Heward; *Island, Georgian Bay* by Lawren Harris; and (?) *Cul-de-sac* by F. Forester.

An Artist Draws His Impressions of "Expressionist" Art!

Up at the Art Gallery they have a label on it, "Sea and Rocks." When a Telegram artist looked at it he saw gas pipes, cheese, straws and crackers. Just an impression of expressionism!

Our gastronomic Rockies! Our artist was ready to digest the mound of jelly and whipped-cream peaks—but what to do with a couple of broken chair legs!

"Flowers" they call this, but the art critic is sure they don't call them that in smart women's magazines!

Even "The Bather" made the artist hungry. He thought it was a cook watching a salad sprout with forks, spoons and all!

"Who's Afraid of the Big Bad Wolf?" Wouldn't even the three little pigs have a swell time if this impression of "Georgian Bay Islands" were really real!

Take this one seriously! It shows labor slaving for the capitalist. But our artist thinks Santa will pinch that armored car for some kid's sock!

3. A.Y. Jackson (1882 – 1974)
Grey Day, Laurentians   *c.* 1930
Oil on canvas, 25 x 32 in. (63.5 x 81.3 cm)

The Montreal Museum of Fine Arts (Purchased with the
A. Sidney Dawes and Dr F.J.Shepherd Funds, 1945)
(45.944)

centre which brought him to Ottawa in the fall of 1939. However, Eric Brown, with whom he had organized the art centre, had died in April[60] and the War cut off all funding. After a year of frustration in Ottawa, Lismer was happy to take up the educational programme at the Art Association of Montreal in January 1941.[61]

Of all the members of the Group, A.Y. Jackson typifies their popular image: robust, adventurous, a man of the soil, and a democrat. Lawren Harris was more aristocratic and intellectual, and his painting more austere and difficult of access. Arthur Lismer turned to education, and painting became secondary to his work in that field. But A.Y. remained a painter full time, making annual trips to different parts of Canada, returning each time with his quota of sketches to be painted up into canvases. His imagery remained constant and his logical stylistic developments placed little demand upon his public. The cry for an 'art of the soil' that had been a heresy fifteen years earlier had now become orthodoxy. This very consistency and reliability were both his strength and limitation.

Jackson's favorite sketching grounds remained the shores of the lower Saint Lawrence with their rolling hills, sagging barns nestling on the crest of a hillock, and curving, furrowed fields. Making annual visits, alternately to the north and south shores, he made this country his own.

The sketch for *A Quebec Farm* (1930, cat. no. 4) was probably painted around St.-Hilarion in the spring of 1930,[62] as was the sketch for *Winter, Charlevoix County* (c. 1933, cat. no. 5) two years later.[63] The lush spring earth of the earlier work contrasts with his usual predilection for the snowy expanses of late winter, just before the approach of spring. In both works he paints the landscape in rolling, linear rhythms. The meandering road, or furrows, leading from the foreground to a central motif and closed off by the hills behind is a compositional device derived from the Quebec works of James Wilson Morrice and seen in Jackson's paintings from the early twenties.[64] *Winter, Charlevoix County* is actually a reworking of *Grey Day, Laurentians* (fig. 3) painted about 1930 and now in The Montreal Museum of Fine Arts, where the broader treatment gives it a more 'Christmas card' appearance. In the later work, the more detailed rendering, complex patterns and sparkling colour create a sensuous yet solid effect.

The same impressionist colouring in pinks, yellows, and blues appears in *Iceberg* (1930, cat. no. 6) painted from a sketch[65] made on his trip to the Arctic with Lawren Harris in 1930.[66] Unlike Harris, Jackson was interested in the summer shores where the brown earth contrasts with the ice floes and the rocks and Inuit tents are set against the barren hill, or in panoramic views of the rolling Labrador mountains. Even in such a work as *Iceberg* the Inuit families contrast with the immensity of the ice. Instead of accentuating the austerity of the icebergs, as Harris did, Jackson glories in the shimmering colours and anecdotal detail. For Jackson, the forces of nature are a stimulating and demanding adversary but never overwhelming. They are reduced to the human level.

It was the changing seasons that attracted A.Y., not the bright green of summer, nor the blank whiteness of winter, but the flow of winter to spring or the blaring up of summer into autumn. In *Algoma, November* (1935, cat. no. 7) the rich oranges and blacks are highlighted by the white of the first winter snows. A dramatic burst of sunshine rises above the heavy, snow-filled clouds broadly painted in dynamic rhythms. How very different from the panoramic Algoma views of the early twenties.

In the summer of 1936, A.Y. joined his niece, Naomi Jackson, and the Lismers on a trip to Europe – visiting France for a reunion of his First World War battalion, then going on to Belgium, Germany, and England.[67] He found the political climate in Europe unpleasant and was reaffirmed in his belief that modern French art was highly overrated.[68] Jackson had for several years been fighting a rearguard battle against what he felt to be a 'diluted internationalism' and the influence of contemporary French art. In the United States, in the late twenties, American nationalists and such regionalist artists as Thomas Benton had reacted strongly against what they felt to be the swamping of the American art market by French art and art dealers and the lack of support for American artists. While A.Y. could comment ironically on the lack of 'menace' offered by modern French art to a Canadian public ignorant of contemporary developments,[69] at the same time he disapproved of anti-nationalist sentiments among the younger Toronto artists:

... there has been a lot of persistent effort to establish painting which has no reflection of the Canadian background. The international outlook is the thing and from that standpoint it is of very little importance. There has at the same time been an effort to belittle the Canadian movement by people who have no feeling for the country and it has resulted in a kind of sneer when the north country is mentioned. With all the young people here there is no longer any desire to go north. They do still life and back yards and when you try to arrange an international show it is almost impossible to find a dozen canvases of any distinction.[70]

The late thirties were a difficult time for A.Y. Jackson. His constant repetition of the need for an art created by artists with their feet in the soil was being ignored and even fought. Of the original Group of Seven, he and Carmichael were the only two left in Toronto. J.E.H. MacDonald had died, Varley was alternating between Ottawa and Vancouver, Lismer was in South Africa and New York, and Lawren Harris was in the States. At the same time Jackson recognized he was repeating himself. He tried to break out of the lethargy he felt in Toronto by exploring new areas of Canada but even when he went to the prairies in 1937[71] the same formula emerged. In *Blood Indian Reserve, Alberta* (1937, cat. no. 8), the fields might be flatter and the road straighter, but it remains the same composition derived from Morrice.

In 1938 for the first time A.Y. didn't visit Quebec in the spring. He wrote Sarah Robertson, 'It seems funny to be in town at this season. I have not missed going to Quebec since 1925 the year I taught in the art school but it had become almost too much of a habit and I want to leave the snow alone for awhile.'[72]

That autumn A.Y. went north again to visit the radium mines being developed by a friend, Gilbert Labine.[73] The barren lands, the ruggedness, and the solitude of the north were genuine stimulants for A.Y. Just as in his previous trip to Great Slave Lake in 1928, in *Northern Landscape* (1939, cat. no. 9) he turned to the silhouettes of the twisting stunted pines whose blazing colour, severity, and almost Expressionist crudeness best characterize Wyndham Lewis's view of A.Y.: 'His vision is as austere as his subject matter, which is precisely the hard puritanic land, in which he always has lived: with no frills, with all its dismal solitary grandeur and bleak beauty, its bad side deliberately selected rather than its chilly relentings . . . . There is something of Ahab in him; the long white contours of the Laurentian Mountains in mid-winter are his elusive leviathan.'[74]

While Lismer was the educator, Jackson the organizer, Lawren Harris was the enthusiast, the visionary. Even though the Group of Seven never had an official structure, Harris had often been seen as its leader, stimulating the artists into new ventures, the erection of the Studio Building, the formation of the Group of Seven and its expansion into the Canadian Group of Painters.

Like others connected with the Group of Seven, Lawren Harris was a keen student of theosophy,[75] and it was through these studies that he evolved his concepts of art and nationalism. He saw art as an initiator, 'a clarifying and objectifying process'[76] through which one could arrive at an individual experience of 'the essential order, the dynamic harmony [and] the ultimate beauty'[77] of all existence. To varying degrees art reflected this universal spirit, yet at the same time was defined by 'its own particular attitude which depends upon the interplay of its time, its place on earth and its capacity'[78] – that is, the temporal, the national, and the personal. The artist could achieve an expression of universal harmony only through concentration on these particulars.

Theosophy also taught that America was to be the principal scene of the next phase of mankind's evolution.[79] 'Europe [had] dehumanized Art by making it a thing apart from Life . . . [had] debased Religion by professionalizing it and . . . [had] perverted the idea of National Consciousness by making it stand for Political Consciousness.'[80] America was the land of optimism, faith, and spiritual growth; and the Rocky Mountains, the 'sacred and occult centres of the earth,'[81] and the North, were its spiritual centres. Harris wrote, 'We are on the fringe of the great North and its living whiteness, its loneliness and replenishment, its resignations and release, its call and answer, its cleansing rhythms. It seems that the top of the continent is a source of spiritual flow that will ever shed clarity into the growing race of America.'[82]

The necessity of the creative attitude which stressed the clarifying rôle of the arts and the rôle of the northern half of the American continent in the spiritual evolution of mankind formed the basis of Lawren Harris's art. For A.Y. Jackson, exploration was seen in terms of human adventure and geography, and more concrete national identity. But for Harris it was also a spiritual journey.

On the Arctic trip with A.Y. Jackson he was struck by the loneliness of the north, its silence, and its massive forms. Continuing the direction of the later mountain canvases, his arctic works progress from a more descriptive rendering to a generalized and symbolic representation. *Icebergs, Davis Strait* (1930, cat. no. 10), while monumental in size, appears less awesome due to the shimmering water and naturalistic sky. In *Grounded Icebergs* (c. 1931, cat. no. 11), the eerie, trapped stillness of the arctic night is magnificently portrayed while in *Icebergs and Mountains, Greenland* (c. 1932, cat. no. 12) the geometricization of the elements is carried to its extreme. The enclosed forms of the clouds reappear in his later abstractions. The blues and yellows of his arctic works, dramatically differentiated into light and shadow reflect the spiritual polarities of theosophic teachings.

While the northern voyage resulted in an impressive output of large canvases soon after his return, it soon came to a halt and for the next three years Lawren Harris painted little. Brooker commented, 'Lawren has done no painting for six months and very little for over a year. All of his things – mostly of the Arctic, I had seen at his studio often. The general impression, freely voiced seems to be that he is repeating himself and has got to the end of a

NOTES TO CHAPTER 1

phase, at least.'[83] The formation of the Canadian Group preoccupied him for a while. He would, as well, bring out old canvases and rework parts of them,[84] but, more important, it appears he was concentrating more and more on his theosophic studies,[85] recognizing he was about to make certain crucial, personal decisions. The direction of his life and studies was separating him from his wife. Finally in the summer of 1934 Lawren Harris and Bess Housser (the wife of another associate of the Group), who shared his theosophic interests, obtained divorces and were married.[86] Fred Housser married Yvonne McKague a year later;[87] however, the divorces created a great conflict of loyalties among certain intimate friends, and the Harrises felt it necessary to leave Toronto, moving to Hanover, New Hampshire.[88] The break from Toronto gave Harris the freedom to set off on his own path.

While the members of the Group of Seven dispersed, they guaranteed, through the Toronto Art Students' League and the Canadian Group of Painters, that a younger generation of followers would continue the Group tradition. Started in the fall of 1926 as an informal discussion and sketching group, the Art Students' League was formally organized in 1927 by a group of dissident students from the Ontario College of Art.[89] Stressing individual work, and outdoor sketching, they also visited artists' studios and received criticisms from Arthur Lismer, A.Y. Jackson, J.E.H. MacDonald, and Lawren Harris.

One of the artists associated with the League was Yvonne McKague. A graduate of the Ontario College of Art, she studied in the Paris academies and returned to Toronto to assist Arthur Lismer and Fred Varley at the College. Through Lismer she became interested in the teaching of the progressive educationalist Franz Cizek and spent a summer at the University of Vienna.[90]

Following the example of the Group, Yvonne McKague sketched in the Rocky Mountains and Quebec, however her favorite region remained the barren mining country of northern Ontario. The town of Cobalt had passed its peak by the early thirties, most of the mines abandoned and the houses in disrepair. In McKague's painting *Cobalt* (1931, cat. no. 13) the mining shafts accentuate the verticality of the houses as they lean this way and that.[91] The houses, the figures along the road, and the fence leading in at the left are all reminiscent of Lawren Harris's town paintings; yet the restrained, mat colouring is very much her own. Most of the Group's followers in Toronto were never able to develop beyond superficial copying; however Yvonne McKague, absorbed in the atmosphere of the Group as intimately as she was, could create works which were directly in the Group tradition and at the same time strong and individual expressions of the Canadian landscape.

1. Buffalo, The Buffalo Fine Arts Academy, 14 September – 14 October 1928, *Exhibition of Paintings by Canadian Artists*; New York, International Art Center of Roerich Museum, 5 March – 5 April 1932, *Exhibition of Paintings by Contemporary Canadian Artists.*

2. Paris, Musée du Jeu de Paume, 11 April – 11 May 1927, *Exposition d'art canadien. An Exhibition of Paintings by Contemporary Canadian Artists under the Auspices of the American Federation of Arts*; This exhibition toured opening at the Corcoran Gallery, Washington, D.C., 9 – 30 March 1930. Its organizer, Eugene Savage, was an uncle of Anne Savage. Baltimore, Baltimore Museum of Art, 15 January – 28 February 1931, *First Baltimore Pan American Exhibition of Contemporary Paintings.* College Art Association, *International 1933*, a touring exhibition which opened at the Worcester Art Museum, Worcester (Mass.), January 1933.

3. 'Canadian Art Foundations of a National School,' *Apollo*, vol. 14 (December 1931), pp. 326 – 327; Blodwen Davies, 'The Canadian Group of Seven,' *The American Magazine of Art*, vol. xxv, no. 1 (July 1932), pp. 13 – 22; Eric Brown, 'Canada's National Painters,' *The Studio*, vol. cIII (June 1932), pp. 311 – 323; Stewart Dick, 'Canadian Landscape of Today,' *Apollo*, vol. 15 (June 1932), pp. 279 – 282; 'Moderne Malerei in Kanada,' *Die Kunst für Alle*, vol. 48, no. 11 (August 1933), pp. 343 – 347.

4. 'This opposition is as natural as the native movement, and is incited into activity by the movement itself. It is part of a clarifying and stimulating process whereby any art movement is helped in its direction and evolution.' Lawren S. Harris, 'Different Idioms in Creative Art,' *Canadian Comment*, vol. II, no. 12 (December 1933), p. 5.

5. Bertram Brooker, 'The Seven Arts,' Ottawa *The Citizen* (29 December 1928).

6. Toronto, The Art Gallery of Toronto, April 1930, *An Exhibition of the Group of Seven.*

7. Bertram Brooker, 'The Seven Arts,' Ottawa *The Citizen* (19 April 1930).

8. Toronto, The Art Gallery of Toronto, December 1931, *An Exhibition By the Group of Seven.* The sixty-three works included twelve sketches by J.E.H. MacDonald.

9. T.M. [Thoreau MacDonald?], 'Decline of the Group of Seven,' *The Canadian Forum*, vol. XII, no. 136 (January 1932), p. 144.

10. Jehanne Biétry Salinger, 'Group of Seven Begins Expansion,' Toronto *Mail and Empire* (7 December 1931).

11. Bertram Brooker, Toronto, to L.L. FitzGerald, Winnipeg, 10 January 1932; private property.

12. 'The Group of Seven retains directing control – definitely invites cooperation with those painters who have been associated with them in various exhibitions.' Arthur Lismer, 'The Canadian Theme in Painting,' *Canadian Comment*, vol. I, no. 2 (February 1932), p. 25.

13. *An Exhibition of the Group of Seven* (exhibition catalogue) (Toronto: The Art Gallery of Toronto, 1930), p. 3.

14. Arthur Lismer, Toronto, to L.L. FitzGerald, Winnipeg, 24 May 1932; private property.

15. L.L. FitzGerald, Winnipeg, to Arthur Lismer, Toronto, 2 June 1932; in The McMichael Canadian Collection, Kleinburg.

16. Arthur Lismer, Toronto, to L.L. FitzGerald, Winnipeg, 24 May 1932; private property.

17. For an account of the Wembley conflict see Maude Brown, *Breaking Barriers* (Ottawa: Society for Art Publications, 1964), pp. 69 – 75; Peter Mellen, *The Group of Seven* (Toronto: McClelland and Stewart, 1970), pp. 104 – 105; and Dennis Reid, *The Group of Seven* (exhibition catalogue) (Ottawa: The National Gallery of Canada, 1970), pp. 170 – 173.

18. 'Painters Demand the Head of Art Dictator of Canada,' *Toronto Daily Star* (20 November 1926); 'Criticism of Art Director Is Effectively Disposed Of,' *Toronto Daily Star* (1 December 1926).

19. John Hammond, R.C.A. and Ernest Fosbery, R.C.A., Ottawa, to Hon. J.C. Elliott, M.P., Minister of Public Works, Ottawa, 7 March 1927; copy in The National Gallery of Canada.

20. Letters from eight Montreal artists to Dr Shepherd, Chairman of the Board of Trustees, The National Gallery of Canada, 7 March 1927; from fifteen Toronto artists and laymen, 23 March 1927; from ten Ottawa artists, 31 March 1927; all in The National Gallery of Canada.

21. Franz Johnston, A.R.C.A., O.S.A., Toronto, to Right Hon. R.B. Bennett, Ottawa, 25 January 1932; copy in The National Gallery of Canada. The letter begins, 'For generations my family has supported the Conservative party . . . .'

22. Arthur Heming, Toronto, to Right Hon. R.B. Bennett, Ottawa, 1 March 1932; copy in The National Gallery of Canada.

23. This document may have been circulating as early as spring 1931 as Louis Muhlstock signed the petition in Paris as a favour to his former teacher Edmond Dyonnet. Muhlstock returned from Paris in the summer of 1931. (Interview with Louis Muhlstock, Montreal, 15 September 1973.)

24. T.W. Mitchell, Toronto, to Right Hon. R.B. Bennett, Ottawa, 27 April 1932; copy in The National Gallery of Canada. Signatories included Wyly Grier, President of the Royal Canadian Academy, George Reid, Franz Johnston, Homer Watson, Horatio Walker, Maurice Cullen, Robert Pilot, and Edmond Dyonnet.

25. 'National Art Show Abuses Protested,' *Vancouver Sun* (31 May 1932); 'Rumored Criticism of National Gallery,' Ottawa *The Citizen* (22 June 1932).

26. 'Artists Boycott National Gallery Until Radical Reform Takes Place,' *The Ottawa Journal* (8 December 1932).

27. A.Y. Jackson, Toronto, to Edmond Dyonnet, Secretary, Royal Canadian Academy, Montreal (14 December 1932); copy in The National Gallery of Canada.

28. Telegram from H.S. Southam, Chairman, Board of Trustees, The National Gallery of Canada, Ottawa, to Emmanuel Hahn, Toronto, 27 January 1933, thanking him for the list of signatures. This document of support is in The National Gallery of Canada.

29. H.S. Southam, Ottawa, to Sir George Perley, Ottawa, 31 December 1934; copy in The National Gallery of Canada.

30. Monthly Meeting of the Ontario Society of Artists (7 March 1933). 'Ontario Society of Artists Minutes'; in the Ontario Archives, Toronto.

31. E.W. Wood, Toronto, to H.O. McCurry, Assistant Director of The National Gallery of Canada, Ottawa, 20 February 1933; in The National Gallery of Canada.

32. Lawren S. Harris, Toronto, to L.L. FitzGerald, Winnipeg, 28 November 1932; private property. This exhibition did take place. See Frank Brien, Secretary Hart House Sketch Committee, Toronto, to Arthur Lismer, Toronto, 6 February 1933; in the Art Gallery of Ontario.

33. 'J.E.H. MacDonald, Art College Head, Dies After Illness,' Toronto *Globe* (28 November 1932).

34. Lawren S. Harris, Toronto, to L.L. FitzGerald, Winnipeg, 1 January 1933; private property.

35. *Statement by the Group of Seven*. Mimeographed sheet. This was published in its entirety in 'Group of Seven Issues Statement Defending Aims,' Montreal *Gazette* (31 January 1933).

36. 'Canadian Artists Form New Group,' Montreal *Gazette* (21 February 1933). The Canadian Group of Painters was not incorporated until 1936. (*Canada Gazette*, 4 April 1936, p. 2397.) The incorporating members were A.Y. Jackson, Lawren Harris, Arthur Lismer, Frank Carmichael, A.J. Casson, Fred Varley, Edwin Holgate, and L.L. FitzGerald – all members of the Group of Seven.

37. The original members of the Canadian Group of Painters were Bertram Brooker, Frank Carmichael, Emily Carr, A.J. Casson, Charles Comfort, L.L. FitzGerald, Lawren S. Harris, Prudence Heward, Randolph Hewton, Edwin Holgate, Bess Housser, A.Y. Jackson, Arthur Lismer, Thoreau MacDonald, J.W.G. Macdonald, Yvonne McKague, Isabel McLaughlin, Mabel May, Lilias T. Newton, Will Ogilvie, George Pepper, Sarah Robertson, Albert Robinson, Anne Savage, Charles Scott, Fred Varley, W.P. Weston, and W.J. Wood.

38. Bertram Brooker, Toronto, to L.L. FitzGerald, Winnipeg, 20 March 1933; private property.

39. Lawren S. Harris, Toronto, to L.L. FitzGerald, Winnipeg, 18 March 1933; private property.

40. Bertram Brooker's employer, J.J. Gibbons Ltd., had the Heinz advertising account (Bertram Brooker, Toronto, to L.L. FitzGerald, Winnipeg, 10 January 1932; private property), and it was through this connection that the Canadian Group of Painters was invited to exhibit at Atlantic City. (Confirmed in interview with Charles Comfort, Hull [Quebec], 3 October 1973.)

41. Atlantic City, Heinz Ocean Pier, Heinz Art Salon, Annual Art Exhibition, [Summer 1933], *Paintings by the Canadian Group of Painters*.

42. The foreword to the catalogue mentions twenty-nine members, apparently including J.E.H. MacDonald as a member.

43. *Philadelphia Record* and Pittsburgh *Sun-Telegraph* quoted in Frank Bagnall, 'Canadian Artists' Show,' *Saturday Night*, vol. XLVIII, no. 50 (21 October 1933), p. 16.

44. Carlyle Burrows, 'Canadian Art at Atlantic City,' *New York Herald Tribune* (4 June 1933), quoted in 'Painting and Pickles,' *The Canadian Forum*, vol. XIII, no. 154 (July 1933), p. 366.

45. *Catalogue of an Exhibition by Canadian Group of Painters* (exhibition catalogue) (Toronto: The Art Gallery of Toronto, 1933), Foreword.

46. J.W.G. Macdonald was the only member who had no works in this exhibition.

47. 'The Artist Draws His Impressions of Expressionist Art,' *The Toronto Telegram* (25 November 1933).

48. Augustus Bridle, 'New Democracy Seen In Latest Paintings,' *Toronto Daily Star* (3 November 1933).

49. Robert Ayre, 'Canadian Group of Painters,' *The Canadian Forum*, vol. XIV, no. 159 (December 1933), pp. 98 – 99.

50. John A.B. McLeish, *September Gale* (Toronto, Vancouver: J.M. Dent & Sons [Canada] Limited, 1955), p. 120.

51. Reproduced in Robert H. Hubbard, ed., *The National Gallery of Canada. Catalogue. Paintings and Sculpture. Volume III: Canadian School* (Toronto: University of Toronto Press, 1960), p. 178.

52. Arthur Lismer, 'The Children's Art Centre,' *Canadian Comment*, vol. V, no. 7 (July 1936), pp. 28 – 29.

53. For partial listings of these articles see Dennis Reid, *A Bibliography of the Group of Seven* (Ottawa: The National Gallery of Canada, 1971), pp. 32 – 34.

54. Arthur Lismer, 'South African Impressions,' *Canadian Comment*, vol. III, no. 10 (October 1934), pp. 15 – 16. Lismer had attended a previous Fellowship Conference in Nice in 1932. See A. Lismer, 'The World of Art, The Artist Abroad,' *Canadian Comment*,

vol. I, no. 9 (September 1932), pp. 25 – 26; vol. I, no. 10 (October 1932), p. 24.

55. Arthur Lismer, McGregor Bay, to H.O. McCurry, Ottawa, [summer 1935]; in The National Gallery of Canada.

56. Arthur Lismer, Toronto, to H.O. McCurry, Ottawa, 26 May 1936; in The National Gallery of Canada.

57. Arthur Lismer, Toronto, to H.O. McCurry, Ottawa, 16 October 1937; in The National Gallery of Canada.

58. Arthur Lismer, Johannesburg, to H.O. McCurry, Ottawa, 21 October 1936; in The National Gallery of Canada.

59. Especially in *The Three Graces* (1938, watercolour on paper; 14 x 21-1/2 in., 35.6 x 54.6 cm). Present whereabouts unknown. Reproduced in Graham C. McInnes, 'Canadians versus Americans,' *Saturday Night*, vol. LV, no. 15 (10 February 1940), p. 9.

60. 'Canadian Art Loses Leader, Gallery Head,' Toronto *Telegram* (6 April 1939).

61. *Art Association of Montreal, Seventy-Ninth Annual Report 1940*, p. 9.

62. A.Y. Jackson, St.-Joachim, to Thoreau MacDonald, [Toronto?], 20 March [1930]; in The McCord Museum, McGill University.

63. A.Y. Jackson, St.-Hilarion, to Thoreau MacDonald, [Toronto?], [25 April 1932]; in The McCord Museum, McGill University.

64. One of the earlier examples of this composition in Jackson's work is *Winter Road, Quebec* (1921, oil on canvas; 21 x 25 in., 53.3 x 63.5 cm) in the collection of Mrs Charles S. Band, Toronto. Reproduced in Dennis Reid, *The Group of Seven*, p. 175.

65. The sketch is in The McMichael Canadian Collection, Kleinburg. See Paul Duval, *A Vision of Canada* (Toronto, Vancouver: Clarke, Irwin & Company Limited, 1973), p. 157 repr.

66. For an account of this voyage see A.Y. Jackson, *A Painter's Country: The Autobiography of A.Y. Jackson* (Toronto: Clarke, Irwin and Company Limited, 1967), pp. 105 – 113, and Lawren S. Harris, 'The Group of Seven in Canadian History,' *The Canadian Historical Association: Report of the Annual Meeting held at Victoria and Vancouver June 16 – 19, 1948* (Toronto: University of Toronto Press, 1948), p. 36.

67. Conversation with Naomi Jackson Groves, Ottawa, 21 January 1974. See also A.Y. Jackson, *A Painter's Country*, pp. 121 – 122.

68. A.Y. Jackson, Paris, to Sarah Robertson, Montreal, 10 June [1936]; in The National Gallery of Canada.

69. A.Y. Jackson, 'Modern Art No "Menace," ' *Saturday Night*, vol. XLVIII, no. 6 (17 December 1932), p. 3.

70. A.Y. Jackson, Toronto, to H.O. McCurry, Ottawa, 9 June [1938]; in The National Gallery of Canada.

71. A.Y. Jackson, Spring Coullee, Alberta, to Arthur Lismer, Toronto, 11 October 1937; in The McMichael Canadian Collection, Kleinburg. See also A.Y. Jackson, *A Painter's Country*, pp. 123 – 125.

72. A.Y. Jackson, Toronto, to Sarah Robertson, Montreal, 31 March 1938; in The National Gallery of Canada.

73. A.Y. Jackson, *A Painter's Country*, p. 126.

74. Wyndham Lewis, 'Canadian Nature and Its Painters,' *The Listener* (29 August 1946), reprinted in Walter Michael and C.J. Fox, eds, *Wyndham Lewis on Art. Collected Writings 1913 – 1956* (New York: Funk & Wagnalls, 1969), p. 429.

75. It was probably Roy Mitchell, member of the Arts and Letters Club and of the Toronto Theosophical Society and later stage designer for the Hart House Theatre, who originally introduced Lawren Harris to theosophy during the First World War. See William Hart, 'Theory and Practice of Abstract Art,' in *Lawren Harris Retrospective Exhibition, 1963* (exhibition catalogue) (Ottawa: The National Gallery of Canada, 1963), p. 32.

76. Lawren S. Harris, 'Revelation of Art in Canada,' *The Canadian Theosophist*, vol. VIII, no 5 (15 July 1926), p. 86.

77. Lawren S. Harris, 'Theosophy and Art,' *The Canadian Theosophist*, vol. XIV, no. 5 (15 July 1933), p. 129.

78. Lawren S. Harris, 'Creative Art and Canada,' Supplement to the *McGill News* (December 1928), p. 2. Reprinted in Bertram Brooker, ed., *Yearbook of the Arts in Canada, 1928 – 1929* (Toronto: The Macmillan Company of Canada Limited, 1929), pp. 179 – 186.

79. Fred Housser, 'Theosophy and America,' *The Canadian Theosophist*, vol. X, no. 5 (15 July 1929), p. 130.

80. Fred Housser, 'Some Thoughts on National Consciousness,' *The Canadian Theosophist*, vol. VIII, no. 5 (15 July 1927), p. 81.

81. *Ibid.*, p. 82.

82. Lawren S. Harris, 'Revelation of Art in Canada,' *The Canadian Theosophist*, vol. VII, no. 5 (15 July 1926), pp. 85–86.

83. Bertram Brooker, Toronto, to L.L. FitzGerald, Winnipeg, 10 January 1932; private property.

84. Interview with Yvonne McKague Housser, Toronto, 18 October 1973. Harris continued to rework canvases throughout his life. See Lawren S. Harris, Vancouver, to Martin Baldwin, Toronto, 3 February 1948; in the Art Gallery of Ontario.

85. A series of speeches and articles were published in *The Canadian Theosophist* and other publications. In addition to those in Dennis Reid, *A Bibliography of the Group of Seven*, p. 17, there were also Lawren S. Harris, 'Science and the Soul,' *The Canadian Theosophist*, vol. XII, no. 10 (15 December 1931), pp. 298 – 300; and Lawren S. Harris, 'Different Idioms in Creative Art,' *Canadian Comment*, vol. II, no. 12 (December 1933), pp. 5 – 6, 32.

86. Frances Loring, Toronto, to Eric Brown, Ottawa, [July 1934]; in The National Gallery of Canada.

87. Fred Housser married Yvonne McKague on 28 June 1935 and died on 28 December 1936. See 'F.B. Housser Dies Suddenly,' *Toronto Daily Star* (28 December 1936).

88. Bess Harris, Hanover (N.H.), to Doris Mills, [Toronto?], 14 November [1934]; property of Doris Spiers. Lawren Harris's uncle, with whom he had stayed in Berlin in 1904, was head of the German Department at Dartmouth College in Hanover.

89. For an account of the history of the Art Students' League, see Paul T. Breithaupt, 'History of the Art Students' League,' *Etcetera*, vol. I, no. 1 (September 1930), pp. 28 – 30; vol. I, no. 2 (October 1930), pp. 28 – 30; vol. I, no. 3 (November 1930), pp. 30 – 33. Students and associate members included Norah McCullough, Audrey Taylor, Isabel McLaughlin, and Gordon Webber.

90. Interview with Yvonne McKague Housser, Toronto, 18 October 1973.

91. An article praising this work – 'The Best Old Town I Know,' *Gold Magazine* (December 1933) – was severely criticized by a resident of Cobalt because of the painting's untruthfulness and its application of 'modern European technique' to depict the Canadian scene. See Edward Buckman, 'Cobalt and the Artists,' *Gold Magazine* (April 1934).

*1.
ARTHUR LISMER
Baie Saint-Paul, Quebec   1931

NOT IN EXHIBITION

2.
ARTHUR LISMER
Pine Wrack   1933

*3.
ARTHUR LISMER
Bright Morning   1935

4.
A.Y. JACKSON
A Quebec Farm 1930

*5.
A.Y. JACKSON
Winter, Charlevoix County   c. 1933

*6.
A.Y. JACKSON
Iceberg   1930

*5.
A.Y. JACKSON
Winter, Charlevoix County   c. 1933

*6.
A.Y. JACKSON
Iceberg   1930

7.
A.Y. JACKSON
Algoma, November   1935

*8.
A.Y. JACKSON
Blood Indian Reserve, Alberta   1937

*9.
A.Y. JACKSON
Northern Landscape   1939

*10.
LAWREN S. HARRIS
Icebergs, Davis Strait   1930

*9.
A.Y. JACKSON
Northern Landscape   1939

*10.
LAWREN S. HARRIS
Icebergs, Davis Strait   1930

2. 'The Beaver Hall Group'

The influence of the Group of Seven was not confined to Toronto. Montreal had an active group of artists who consciously allied themselves with the Ontario artists, recognizing the importance of their struggle for a contemporary, native art. In Toronto the Group had achieved a certain success in creating an interest in modern art among both collectors and the general public. Montreal, without the catalyzing influence of the Group, was a less favourable climate for new ventures.

The Art Association of Montreal was a private club of wealthy English-speaking Montrealers who still preferred the late nineteenth-century Dutch artists A.Y. Jackson had been criticizing since before the First World War. There had been an active art school at the Art Association under William Brymner and Randolph Hewton; however with the opening in 1923 of the École des Beaux-Arts, a provincial school offering free tuition, the Art Association school was closed.[1] The Royal Canadian Academy continued to offer life classes, and the Academy's influence pervaded the whole gallery.

Most of the Montreal artists associated with Toronto had originally studied under William Brymner and been involved in the Beaver Hall Group, a non-structured association of artists sharing studio space on Beaver Hall Square.[2] Formed in the fall of 1920, it survived only a year and a half though the friendships and alliances formed at this time continued throughout the next two decades.

At the time of the formation of the Beaver Hall Group, A.Y. Jackson had identified its goals as being those of the Group of Seven,[3] and over the years Jackson maintained the contact between the two cities, supporting and stimulating the Montreal artists through regular visits and correspondence. He kept them informed of events in Toronto and arranged for their works to be included in the Group exhibitions.

A.Y. Jackson was naturally closest to the landscape artists Anne Savage and Sarah Robertson. Anne Savage had been an original member of the Beaver Hall Group[4] and accompanied Pegi Nicol and Florence Wyle to the West Coast during the summer of 1927, following the example of Jackson and Edwin Holgate the previous year in connection with Marius Barbeau's documentation of the art of the native peoples of British Columbia.[5] Teaching at Baron Byng High School from 1922,[6] like many other artists, Savage had little time to devote to her painting. Her works of the thirties fall within the Group tradition with their rolling hills and panoramic views. Even in her more intimate landscapes, such as *Dark Pool, Georgian Bay* (1933, cat. no. 14), she maintains the Group's curvilinear outlines though with a greater concern

for structure and texture. Just as in Lawren Harris's *Maligne Lake, Jasper Park* in The National Gallery of Canada, the variety of projections framing the central open space create a dynamic and carefully structured interplay of angles and tensions.

Sarah Robertson's work of the late twenties had hardened into tightly controlled designs, at times stiff, and also stylistically reminiscent of Lawren Harris's work. By the mid-thirties however she had achieved a greater surety and freedom. In *Coronation* (1937, cat. no. 15) the arabesques of the branches joyfully sweep across the canvas echoing the movement of the fluttering flags. The brilliant colours are boldly applied in thick, parallel strokes. In *Village, Isle of Orleans* (1939, cat. no. 16) the colouring is much more delicate and the spatial recession more obviously determined by the curving roofs of the houses. While Sarah Robertson produced relatively few works, partly due to poor health, her oils and watercolours of the thirties have a spontaneity and brightness lacking in much of the work of the period.

While Montreal boasted several excellent landscape artists, observant art reviewers in the early thirties remarked upon the development of an independent school of artists primarily concerned with painting the human form.[7] Unlike that of the Ontario College of Art, the teaching at the Art Association school (under Randolph Hewton) and later at the École des Beaux-Arts followed a French tradition, with a greater concentration on figure work than landscape.

The key person responsible for the development of a Montreal school was Edwin Holgate, who, soon after the formation of the Beaver Hall Group, returned to Paris to study under Adolf Milman, a Russian expatriate artist. Holgate had been interested in Russian theatre and folk art since his first visit to Paris before the First World War; but what especially interested him was the Russian's concentration on draughtsmanship and strong colouring.[8]

After a year with Milman, whom Holgate says was the greatest influence in his life, he returned to Montreal and in 1928 started teaching graphics at the École des Beaux-Arts.[9] Fluently bilingual, Holgate was one of the few English-speaking Canadian artists able to cross the cultural barriers between French and English Montreal and his influence was felt in both communities. During the late twenties he was a member of an informal dining club of Quebec writers, musicians, and critics, *Les Casoars* ('The Cassawaries'), which included among its members Louis Carrier, Jean Chauvin, Albéric Morin, Adjutor Savard, and Roméo Boucher.[10] He also illustrated the works of several French-language writers.[11]

A.Y. Jackson first approached Edwin Holgate about

joining the Group of Seven in 1926 during their trip to the Skeena River,[12] though he was not actually invited to become a member until 1930. While not a reluctant member of the Group,[13] Holgate did recognize its limitations. The Group's concentration on landscape, he felt, left little room for the figurative work that interested him. Moreover, Holgate's formal interests were quite different from those of the rest of the Group. In such works as *Ludovine* (c. 1930, cat. no. 17) and *Interior* (c. 1933, cat. no. 18) he was concerned with the structure of the body and the modelling of its planes in contrast to the more linear, patterned designs of the Toronto artists. The strong colours and concentration on draughtsmanship which had attracted him to Milman are reflected in his own work.

In his later works, such as *Early Autumn* (c. 1938, cat. no. 19), while his formal concerns remain the same, the forms and colours are more gentle, lacking the psychological intensity of the earlier *Ludovine*.

Lilias Newton went to Paris in 1923 and, on the advice of Edwin Holgate, studied with another Russian artist, Alexandre Jacovleff, an associate of Milman.[14] Returning to Canada she began a successful career as a portrait-painter. Her portraits of friends and figure studies best show her ability to portray the personal characteristics of the model. Her commissioned works often have a stiffness and air of social pretension due to the demands of the commission. With friends or with models of her own choice there is a greater personal identification between sitter and artist, contributing to the intensity of the work.

In the *Portrait of Frances McCall* (c. 1931, cat. no. 20) Lilias Newton shows the same concern for solid structure derived from Cézanne as seen in Holgate's work. The unity of texture and colour successfully integrates the figure with the landscape background. In the *Portrait of Louis Muhlstock* (c. 1937, cat. no. 21) the confined space concentrates the viewer's attention on the hands and face. The restrained greens and greys of this portrait contrast with the rich blacks, reds, and beiges of *Maurice* (1939, cat. no. 22).[15] In the latter work the colour, texture, and gentle modelling create an aura of sensuous calm. In all three portraits, unlike many of her official portraits, the sitters look to the side, withdrawn into themselves, adding to the contemplative mood. In all, however, the artist concentrates on the structure and the architectonic quality of the forms.

Lilias Newton and Edwin Holgate both gave private life classes during the early thirties, and in 1934 they approached the president of the Art Association of Montreal, H.B. Walker, offering to re-open the art school with the artists bearing full financial responsibility.[16] After two years the arrangement proved to be unsatisfactory so they left. However, Dr Martin, former head of the Medical School at McGill, became president of the Art Association in 1937 and he re-opened the school the next year, inviting Lilias Newton and Edwin Holgate to direct it, with the Association bearing full responsibility for the work, space, and equipment.[17] Will Ogilvie, Charles Comfort's partner in a commercial art firm, was brought from Toronto to teach the commercial course and the school flourished for the next two years. Following the methods of his teacher Milman, Holgate was an excellent and popular teacher, but he found teaching too demanding as it left him little time for his own work. He and Lilias Newton both left the school in the spring of 1940.[18]

Figure painting was definitely the perogative of Montreal artists during the early thirties, though they did have their followers in Toronto. Bertram Brooker's *Figures in Landscape*[19] was inspired by the nudes of Edwin Holgate and Yvonne McKague's *Indian Girl*[20] by the work of Lilias Newton. Lawren Phillips Harris was also painting within a similar tradition. He spent two years, from 1931 to 1933, at the School of the Museum of Fine Arts in Boston where the teachers, graduates of the Slade in London, also concentrated on draughtsmanship and figure work.[21] But, whereas Holgate and Newton created structured forms through the interrelationship of planes, Harris, in *Decorative Nude* (1937, cat. no. 23), relies on careful modelling and silhouette, owing nothing to Cézanne.

The richness of flesh tone seen in Lawren Harris's work is also found in the paintings of Prudence Heward, the 'enfant terrible' of the Montreal figure painters. Born into a wealthy Montreal family, she received her early art training at the Art Association under William Brymner. Like Lilias Newton and Edwin Holgate, she studied in Paris after the First World War with the former Fauve artist Charles Guerin at the Académie Colarossi.[22] In 1929 she won the Willingdon Prize for her painting *Girl on a Hill* (now in The National Gallery of Canada) and returned to France.[23] She attended sketching classes at the Scandinavian Academy in Paris with Isabel McLaughlin[24] and painted at Cagnes in the south of France.

This trip to France resulted in a severe hardening of her style, especially noticeable in *Sisters of Rural Quebec* (1930, cat. no. 24) and *Girl Under a Tree* (1931, cat. no. 25). In the former work this almost sculptural treatment is uniformally applied to all the elements of the composition. In *Girl Under a Tree*, however, there are disturbing contradictions of style. John Lyman wrote an astute criticism of the work in his journal:

When an idea becomes explicit it dies . . . . She has so stiffened her will that it mutes the strings of her sensibility . . . . She [has] so concentrated on the volitional

15. SARAH ROBERTSON, *Coronation* (1937)

effort that she is numb to the lack of consistent fundamental organization – relations and rhythms . . . . [it is]
disconcerting to find with extreme analytical modulation of figures, [an] unmodulated and cloisonné-
treatment of [the] background without interrelation.
Bouguereau nude against Cézanne background.[25]
The freely-brushed vegetation in the foreground isolates
the highly finished, almost overworked, figure in the
centre, and the landscape background does have the air
of a studio backdrop; yet the work has an extremely com-
pelling quality. The staring eyes, the tension in the
muscular body, the projections and sharp angles surrounding the figure create an aura of high-strung sexuality
reminiscent of Gauguin's *La Perte du Pucelage*, in the
Walter P. Chrysler Collection, Norfolk, Virginia.

Most of Prudence Heward's works have a brooding
quality to them. She portrays strong, independent women,
women with individual lives and personalities, yet there
is always a certain tension in her work. Apart from
Ludovine (c. 1930, cat. no. 17), Edwin Holgate's women
are objects for studies in structure and form. Lilias
Newton's sitters are persons confident of their place in
society and the direction of their lives. Prudence Heward's
subjects seem disjointed and uncertain, her children
staring at the viewer, suspicious or incomprehending, as if
they were all affected by the uncertainties of her own life.

In such later works, as *Dark Girl* (1935, cat. no. 26), the
forms are softened and the surrounding landscapes more
summarily treated and more successfully coordinated with
the central figure. She also heightens the intensity of her
colours using rich, almost acidic tones. She moves from
the creation of sculptural forms on a flat surface to brilliant
rendering of colour and light.

Prudence Heward was very interested in the work of the
New Zealand artist Frances Hodgkins[26] and perhaps the
freer brushwork in her later works is partly attributable
to this interest. Frances Hodgkins's introduction of still-
life into a landscape setting also finds its reflection in
Prudence Heward's *Fruit in the Grass* (c. 1939, cat. no. 27).
However, the brilliant, acidic colours are very much her
own.

Unlike most of the other Group associates in Montreal,
Prudence Heward remained an active participant in the
newer developments in Montreal in the late thirties and
forties. A friend of John Lyman, she was one of the founding members of the Contemporary Arts Society in 1939.
Her work of the forties continued her search for newer
forms of expression and was cut short only by her death
in 1947.

1. *Art Association of Montreal, Sixty-Third Annual Report, 1924*, p. 7.
2. There are variances in the accounts of the membership of the
   Group. Norah McCullough lists Nora Collyer, Emily Coonan,
   Prudence Heward, Randolph Hewton, Edwin Holgate, Mabel
   Lockerby, Mabel May, Kathleen Morris, Lilias Torrance Newton,
   Sarah Robertson, Anne Savage, and Ethel Seath (Norah
   McCullough, *The Beaver Hall Hill Group* [Ottawa: The National
   Gallery of Canada], 1966). Edwin Holgate mentions Mabel May,
   Emily Coonan, Randolph Hewton, Adrien Hébert, Anne Savage,
   Sarah Robertson, Scoop Torrance, Lilias Torrance Newton,
   Robert Pilot, and Edwin Holgate (Interview with Edwin Holgate,
   Montreal, 20 September 1973). Lilias Newton mentions Randolph
   Hewton, Emily Coonan, Lilias Torrance Newton, Mabel May,
   Adrien Hébert, Henri Hébert, Albert Robinson, and Adam
   Sherriff Scott (Interview with Lilias Newton, Montreal, 11 Septem-
   ber 1973).
3. 'Le Groupe Beaver Hall,' Montreal *La Presse* (20 January 1921).
   Edwin Holgate, however, states that the members of the Beaver Hall
   Group were hardly aware of the activities of the Toronto artists.
   (Interview with Edwin Holgate, Montreal, 20 September 1973).
4. 'Anne Douglas Savage,' National Gallery of Canada Information
   Form, n.d. [1920s].
5. The resultant works were exhibited at Ottawa, The National
   Gallery of Canada, December 1927, *Exhibition of Canadian West
   Coast Art, Native and Modern*.
6. Leah Sherman, *Anne Savage* (exhibition catalogue) (Montreal: Sir
   George Williams University, 1968).
7. Bertram Brooker, 'The Seven Arts,' Ottawa *The Citizen* (19 April
   1930).
8. Interview with Edwin Holgate, Montreal, 20 September 1973.
9. *Idem*.
10. *Les Casoars* (Montreal: 1928).
11. Georges Bouchard, *Other Days, Other Ways* (Montreal, New York:
    Louis Carrier & Cie, 1928). Robert Choquette, *Metropolitan
    Museum* (Montreal: Herald Press, 1931). Léo-Paul Morin, *Papiers de
    Musique* (Montreal: Librairie d'action canadienne, 1930).
12. Interview with Edwin Holgate, Montreal, 20 September 1973.
13. J. Russell Harper, *Painting in Canada* (Toronto: University of
    Toronto Press, 1966), p. 315.
14. Interview with Lilias T. Newton, Montreal, 11 September 1973.
    Another Canadian portrait artist, Nan Lawson Cheney, studied
    under Alexandre Jacovleff at the School of the Museum of Fine
    Arts in Boston in 1936. ('Nan Lawson Cheney,' The National
    Gallery of Canada Information Form, n.d.)
15. Prudence Heward used a similar background with stairs ascending
    at the right in her painting *Rosaire* (1935, oil on canvas; 40 x 36 in.,
    101.6 x 91.4 cm) in The Montreal Museum of Fine Arts.
16. Interview with Lilias T. Newton, Montreal, 11 September 1973.
17. *Art Association of Montreal, Seventy-Seventh Annual Report, 1938*,
    pp. 8 – 9.
18. Will Ogilvie remained as acting director of the school and Goodridge
    Roberts was hired to take charge of the life classes. (*Art Association
    of Montreal, Seventy-Ninth Annual Report, 1940*, pp. 7 – 8). Arthur
    Lismer joined the staff as Educational supervisor in January 1941
    after Will Ogilvie left on military service (*Art Association of Montreal,
    Eightieth Annual Report, 1941*, pp. 7 – 13).
19. *Figures in Landscape* (1931, oil on canvas; 24 x 30 in., 61.0 x 76.2 cm)
    Estate of M.A. Brooker. See Dennis Reid, *Bertram Brooker* (Ottawa:
    The National Gallery of Canada, 1973), p. 53 repr.

20. *Indian Girl* (c.1936, oil on canvas; 30 x 24 in., 76.2 x 61.0 cm), The McMichael Canadian Collection, Kleinburg. See Paul Duval, *A Vision of Canada* (Toronto: Clarke, Irwin & Company Limited, 1973), p. 154 repr. This painting has also been entitled *Girl with Mulleins.*
21. Interview with Lawren P. Harris, Sackville (N.B.), 31 October 1973. The artist has destroyed most of his work from this period.
22. Prudence Heward attended the Académie Colarossi in Paris in 1925. See Clarence Gagnon, Paris, to Eric Brown, [London], 21 May 1925; in The National Gallery of Canada. See also Prudence Heward, 'Biographical Notes' (c. February 1945); in The Art Gallery of Windsor.
23. Bertram Brooker, 'The Seven Arts,' Ottawa *The Citizen* (1 February 1930).
24. Conversation with Isabel McLaughlin, Toronto, 18 February 1974.
25. John Lyman, 'Journal,' vol. II, entry for 28 April 1932; in the Bibliothèque nationale du Québec, Montreal.
26. Prudence Heward purchased a Frances Hodgkins *Still Life* from the *Exhibition of Contemporary British Painting* (Catalogue no. 31) circulated by The National Gallery of Canada in 1935.

14.
ANNE SAVAGE
Dark Pool, Georgian Bay   1933

15.
SARAH ROBERTSON
Coronation   1937

*16.
SARAH ROBERTSON
Village, Isle of Orleans   1939

*17.
EDWIN H. HOLGATE
Ludovine   c. 1930

18.
EDWIN H. HOLGATE
Interior   c. 1933

*19.
EDWIN H. HOLGATE
Early Autumn   c. 1938

*20.
LILIAS TORRANCE NEWTON
Portrait of Frances McCall   c. 1931

21.
LILIAS TORRANCE NEWTON
Portrait of Louis Muhlstock   c. 1937

22.
LILIAS TORRANCE NEWTON
Maurice 1939

*23.
LAWREN P. HARRIS
Decorative Nude 1937

*24.
PRUDENCE HEWARD
Sisters of Rural Quebec 1930

25.
PRUDENCE HEWARD
Girl Under a Tree   1931

26.
PRUDENCE HEWARD
Dark Girl   1935

*27.
PRUDENCE HEWARD
Fruit in the Grass   c. 1939

3. The Canadian Group of Painters in British Columbia

Painting in British Columbia during the thirties is dominated by the figures of Emily Carr, Fred Varley, and Jock
Macdonald. While some younger artists, such as Paul
Goranson, E.J. Hughes, and Orville Fisher turned to Social
Realism and industrial themes in prints and murals,[1] it was
the romantic, landscape tradition defined by the Group of
Seven that prevailed. Through their influence as teachers
and through their paintings, they passed on this tradition
to another generation of artists.

As has been pointed out by Maria Tippett, Emily Carr's
own story of her isolation and rejection by her community
prior to 1927 was partly exaggerated.[2] She won a second
Honourable Mention in oils at the *Ninth Annual Exhibition of the Artists of the Pacific North West* in Seattle in 1924,[3]
and she exhibited occasionally with the Island Arts and
Crafts Society in Victoria.[4] But her trips to the native
villages had ended and she had been cut off from her
emotive sources. She retained a memory of frustration,
incomprehension, and loneliness when thinking of these
years.

Emily Carr's meeting with Eric Brown, Director of The
National Gallery of Canada; her participation in the
Exhibition of Canadian West Coast Art,[5] and her introduction to the Group of Seven,[6] all in 1927, at the age of fifty-
six, marked the turning point in her career. Of all the
members of the Group it was Lawren Harris who elicited
the most sympathetic response. After her first visit to his
studio she wrote, 'Oh, God, what have I seen? Where have
I been? Something has spoken to the very soul of me,
wonderful, mighty, not of this world. Chords way down in
my being have been touched.'[7] She found in his work the
same spiritual strength that had so attracted her to totem
poles. 'It is as if a door had opened, a door into unknown
tranquil spaces.'[8]

Restimulated and reinvigorated, the following summer
Emily Carr returned to the native villages, visiting Kitwan-
cool on the Skeena River for the first time, and then
travelling up the Nass River to Grenville and across to
Skedans on the Queen Charlotte Islands.[9] The sketches
and drawings resulting from this trip as well as pre-war
sketches[10] and photographs[11] provided the sources for
most of her paintings of villages and totems during the late
twenties and early thirties.

The influence of Lawren Harris is clearly evident in
these works. The strongly modelled, simplified shapes, the
concentration on 'significant form'[12] and Vorticist light
shafts are all seen in Harris's paintings of the same period.
Moving beyond the descriptive aims of her works before
the First World War, Emily Carr achieved an intense
expression of the spirituality of the totem poles and of the
feeling of awe aroused in her by the massive coastal forests
surrounding the villages. However, the poles had deteri-
orated since her earlier visits and been badly restored,
losing their subtle beauty.

On Lawren Harris's suggestion Emily Carr turned away
from the native villages to the forests.[13] In the spring of
1933 she travelled north of Garibaldi Park to Brackendale,
Lillooet, and Pemberton,[14] though most of her sketching
was done on Vancouver Island near Victoria. In 1933 she
purchased her caravan trailer, 'The Elephant,' which provided her with greater freedom and independence.[15]

Another artist who was extremely influential in Emily
Carr's life was the American artist Mark Tobey. She first
met him in Seattle,[16] and in September 1928 he visited her
in Victoria and gave a 'short course of classes' in her
studio.[17] He stayed in her house again[18] when Emily visited
Toronto and New York in the spring of 1930,[19] and she
appears to have kept in touch with him[20] until he left for
England in 1931.[21]

As Mark Tobey told Colin Graham, 'he battled with
her to get her to accept his views of form. He had evolved
a system of volumetric analysis of forms combined with
what he called the pressure of light areas against dark, and
vice versa. The latter he had derived from the work of
El Greco, while the former . . . was a modified kind of
analytical cubism.'[22] Later he advised her to 'get off the
monotone, even exaggerate light and shade, to watch
rhythmic relations and reversals of detail, to make [her]
canvas two-thirds half-tone, one-third black and white.'[23]

Following Tobey's advice, in *Grey* (c. 1931, cat. no. 28)
Emily Carr limited her palette to a monochrome of black,
grey, and white, heightening the contrast of light and dark.
The outer trees radiate from the central cone whose sculptural form opens to reveal an inner glow at the core. She
breaks away from 'the accidentals of surface representation' to represent 'the universals of basic form.'[24]

The glowing interior fires of *Grey* contrast with the external thrust of *Tree* (c. 1931, cat. no. 29).[25] Almost surreal
representations of female and male sexual energies, they
are the most intense and concentrated expressions of Emily
Carr's vision of the dynamism of her natural surroundings. As for the creators of the totem poles, the trees have
become the embodiments of spiritual forces that are both
menacing and thrilling. Their energy radiates throughout
the forest.

Emily Carr made three trips east, in 1927,[26] 1930,[27] and
1933.[28] On each visit the most important moments were
those spent with Lawren Harris: 'The day I entered the
dreary building, climbed the cold stair, was met by Mr.
Harris and led into his tranquil studio, that day my idea of
Art wholly changed.'[29] Stimulated by the spirituality of his
work she wrote, 'I think perhaps I shall find God here, the

God I've longed and hunted for and failed to find.'[30] Harris introduced her to theosophy and advised her to read Ouspensky[31] and Madame Blavatsky. Through letters and discussions he encouraged her religious sentiments and affirmed her awareness of the spiritual search her art entailed.

While Emily Carr was influenced by her readings in theosophy,[32] she remained an ardent Christian and her journal entries up to 1934 express a deep conflict in her efforts to reconcile the two. Discussions with Fred Housser and Lawren Harris during her last visit to Toronto brought the issue to a head.[33] On her return to Victoria she attended several lectures by Raja Singh, a co-worker of Mahatma Ghandi's and decided to take her stand on Christ's side. For Emily Carr the conflict centered around a 'distant, mechanical theosophy God'[34] and a personal one. 'When I tried to see things theosophically I was looking through the glasses of cold, hard, inevitable fate, serene perhaps but cold, unjoyous and unmoving. Seeing things the Christ way, things are dipped in love. It warms and humanizes them . . . . God as love is joyous.'[35] With the robust pantheism of Walt Whitman and the love of Christ in hand, she moves from the stern psychic energies of Grey to the joyful song of A Rushing Sea of Undergrowth (c. 1932 – 1934, cat. no. 30). Her works 'swell and roll back and forth into space, pausing here and there to fill out the song, catch the rhythm, . . . go down into the deep places and pause there and . . . rise up into the high ones exalting.'[36]

To express her new sense of freedom and joy, as well as for reasons of economy, she adopted her own sketching medium, oil paints thinned with gasoline. The more fluid medium allowed her to work faster and in a more automatic manner, with a greater freedom of thought and action.[37]

In her earlier sketches, such as Tree (c. 1932–1933, cat. no. 31), she uses the thinned oils broadly, and the stalk of the tree and foliage have a certain density, similar to A Rushing Sea of Undergrowth. However, the dramatic viewpoint and the sweeping curves of the small branches, cutting across the space at different angles gives the sketch a dynamism and unity of movement not always found in the oils of the period.

Emily Carr's paintings to 1937 show a continuing effort to express the feeling of space and of movement in space. She progresses from the dense forest interiors to the sunlit clearings, to the sea shore and finally to pure skyscapes. She disassociates herself from the terrestrial spiritualism of the forest and rises to higher and higher planes – not the serene, ordered, theosophic planes of Lawren Harris, but an exultant, pantheistic freedom.

The God of Grey (cat. no. 28) is not the God of Over-

head (c. 1935, cat. no. 32). The former moves from a central core, awesome, earthy, and rich. The latter sends us spinning off into joyful songs of thanksgiving and praise for all creation. In Scorned as Timber, Beloved of the Sky (c. 1936, cat. no. 33) the glories of light and space sweep across the sky, emanating from a central tree in swirls and curves of a Van Gogh.

'I'd just begun to work into canvases what the sketches had shown me when I got ill,' Emily Carr wrote to Eric Brown.[38] She had her first heart attack in January 1937;[93] years of overwork and financial constraint finally caught up with her.

Recuperating from her illness, with temporary financial security resulting from sales in the East,[40] Emily Carr concentrated more on her writing. She returned to the totem poles, reliving their experience in both word and paint. She continued to sketch in the woods at Telegraph Bay and around Victoria, but she descended from the sky to light-filled forest interiors. There was less 'blue light painting.'[41]

The next few years saw an increase in Emily Carr's public acceptance and breakdown of her isolation. Her writing brought her into contact with the university community in Vancouver and, in the fall of 1938, she had the first of a series of annual solo exhibitions at The Vancouver Art Gallery. She had had shows and sales in the East since the rebirth of her career in 1927; however, her contacts with the East had always been plagued by uncertainty concerning the whereabouts of her works and by the lack of consistent intelligent reaction to her painting. Acceptance in the West, confirmed by actual sales, assured Emily Carr, a native Westerner, that the West had responded to her at last.

Jock Macdonald wrote of her at this time, 'In my opinion she is undoubtedly the first artist in the country and a genius without question . . . . There is a definite spiritual significance which she has given in her maturity, which is something beyond the interpretation of a Province, above the historical value of her Indian Village period, and greater than masterly technique.'[42]

While for Emily Carr, working in isolation, the thirties saw the pinnacle of her career, the Vancouver art scene was less bright. During the previous decade the art community had expanded at a rapid pace. The British Columbia Art League had been active since the early twenties striving to set up an art gallery, which finally opened in 1931.[43] The Vancouver School of Decorative & Applied Arts was formed in 1925,[44] and the following year Fred Varley arrived from Toronto and Jock Macdonald from England.[45] Around the school was a small though creative community. Harold Mortimer-Lamb, secretary of the Canadian Insti-

4. Emily Carr in Her Studio, November 1935.

5. Fred Varley, Vancouver, *c.* 1932.

tute of Mining and Metallurgy, photographer, part-time art critic, and early champion of the Group of Seven, moved to Vancouver in the early twenties. For a short period around 1927, he entered into partnership with another photographer, John Vanderpant, to run The Vanderpant Galleries.[46]

John Vanderpant first arrived in Canada in 1911 to report on the possibilities of settlement in Alberta for the Dutch government. He settled in MacLeod, Alberta, and opened a photographic studio with branches in Okotoks and Lethbridge. After the war he moved to New West-minster, British Columbia, and in 1926 to Vancouver.[47] Through Mortimer-Lamb he met Fred Varley and Jock Macdonald and became a fervent supporter of the Group of Seven. He opened up his studio to the students and staff of the art school, holding weekly musical gatherings[48] and exhibitions of their work.[49]

Varley's initial reaction to British Columbia was one of ebullient enthusiasm. He wrote back to Toronto, 'The country is full of variety . . . island forms as romantic as Wagner music or a Roerich canvas . . . then chunks of mountains, freakish stuff some of it that makes me realize why Indians are superstitious. Forests that are tropical . . . and . . . marvellous canyons.'[50] He became a 'constant worshipper of moving waters and mists, jack-pines . . . [and] rocky promontories, rushing torrents, glaciers and snow peaks, silver rain, and an atmosphere so changing with forms playing hide and seek and again stark and hard seen through an air so translucent that colours appear as if seen through still waters or crystallized in ice.'[51]

The beauty of the landscape stimulated Varley's studies of Chinese painting, for he found in it 'more of the spirit of British Columbia than any painting I have ever seen.'[52] As well, he renewed his interest in Oriental philosophy and occultism, having had personal experiences of sym-pathetic symptoms and perceptions of auras.[53]

Varley's reputation rests primarily on his work as a portrait-painter, yet during his first three years in Van-couver he confined himself almost totally to landscapes. Commissions were almost non-existent;[54] however, he did return to figure work through his relationship with a stu-dent, Vera Weatherbie. From 1929 to 1932 he did numer-ous drawings, watercolours, and oils of Vera, mostly iso-lated bust or head studies in heightened, non-naturalistic colouring. Varley believed in colour coordinates of spiritual states (blue and green, for example, suggested the highest states of spirituality, red more terrestrial and base ones),[55] and at the Vancouver School he taught the Munsell colour theory, based on the use of complementary tones, to create a colour sphere reflecting the aura of the sitter.[56] In *Dhârâna* (c. 1932, cat. no. 34),[57] Vera's aura of blue and

green permeates the mountain landscape and sky. The rails and post of the cottage porch and the bare trees accentuate the tension of her posture, contrasting with the solid curve and flow of the hills and mountain stream.

The contemplative character of *Dhârâna* is also found in *Open Window* (c. 1932, cat. no. 35) where the cool greens and blues flow across the open water to the snow-crested peaks beyond. The serenity of the work recalls the Zen Buddhist 'sound of one hand clapping.' Varley's numerous watercolours and oils of the British Columbia landscape painted during the thirties, with their mist-covered moun-tains and tiny figures meandering along the paths have a Taoist quality like the Chinese landscapes he so admired.

Jovial, lyrical, and a great sensualist, Fred Varley was an attractive and influential figure for both students and fellow artists alike. One artist closely involved with Varley was Philip Surrey. Born in Calgary, at the age of sixteen Surrey was employed with Brigden's in Winnipeg. While there, he took night classes in sketching at the Winnipeg School of Art under LeMoine FitzGerald. In the fall of 1929 he moved to Vancouver to work with the Cleland-Kent Engraving Company,[58] and the following year met Fred Varley and became a close friend of Fred's oldest son, John. While Surrey attended only a few life classes given by Varley, the expansive areas of cool, sensuous colour, glowing light, and mist-bathed peaks in *Going to Work* (1935, cat. no. 36,) are strongly reminiscent of the senior artist's work at this time. Working long hours, Surrey quickly developed a preference for evening, or early morning, ur-ban scenes when the lights reflect on the wet streets and the mood is more sombre.

Jock Macdonald joined the staff of the Vancouver School of Decorative & Applied Arts in 1926 as Head of Design and Instructor of Commercial Advertising.[59] En-couraged by Fred Varley and by Barbara, his wife (a gradu-ate in painting of the Edinburgh College of Art), for the first time, Jock seriously started to paint, going on sketching trips to the Fraser Canyon near Lytton, Garibaldi Park,[60] and the Gulf Islands.[61] An early work, *The Black Tusk, Garibaldi Park, B.C.* (1932, cat. no. 37) bears a close rela-tion to Varley's landscapes of the late twenties, such as *Mountain Landscape, Garibaldi Park*.[62] In the latter work the paint is rich and luminous and the snow flows like lava. In *The Black Tusk* the paint is drier and stiffer, and the fore-ground rocks more linear; however, the thrust of the rock silhouetted against the turbulent, richly painted sky creates a dynamic expression of the mountain's natural forms.

While the decade opened full of hope and with a bur-geoning art community, the Depression soon intervened. Varley, supporting a family of five, had continual financial difficulties. Purchases declined, and he had to have a forc-

6. Graduation ceremonies at the British Columbia College
of Arts, *c.* 1934 – 1935. On the platform: standing, J.W.G.
Macdonald; seated, second from right, Fred Varley.

ed sale of his sketches in Toronto.[63] The final blow was a threatened closing of the School by the Vancouver Board of Education in the winter of 1933. Charles Scott, the principal, managed to get the Board to agree to let them run the School on the revenue from fees, the provincial government grant – plus premises and janitorial services. New salaries were based on three and a half days' teaching time for Varley, Macdonald, and Grace Melvin,[64] and full time for Scott. This meant about a sixty per cent reduction in income for the three teachers and only a thirty per cent reduction for the principal.[65] Varley and Macdonald found this 'grossly unfair' and left to organize their own school, the British Columbia College of Arts.[66]

They were joined in this venture by a Viennese stage designer, Harry Taüber, former pupil of Franz Cizek and gold medallist in the Theatre Arts Exhibition at the 1925 *International Exhibition of Decorative Art* in Paris.[67] Taüber arrived in Vancouver in 1931 via Havana and Toronto, possibly seeking entry to the United States to work in Hollywood. He offered private classes in German Expressionism and stage design,[68] and organized a group of marionette players who presented productions of *Petroushka* and *The Witch Doctor* at The Vancouver Art Gallery in February 1932.[69] Taüber met Fred Varley and Jock Macdonald soon after his arrival, and the three of them joined forces to set up the new school.

The British Columbia College of Arts attempted to unite under one roof all the arts in an anthroposophic 'Goetheanum,' modelled on the teachings of Rudolf Steiner.[70] Varley taught drawing and painting, colour and composition, mural decoration, and book illustration. Jock Macdonald was in charge of industrial design, commercial advertising, colour theory, wood carving, and children's classes, while Harry Taüber taught architecture, theatre arts, film scenario, staging, costume design, art and metaphysics, and eurythmics. They were assisted by Beatrice Lennie in sculpture and modelling, Vera Weatherbie in drawing and painting, and Margaret Williams in design.[71] At the same time the school aimed to create an environment uniting the best qualities of the Pacific Rim cultures, 'drawing together from the east and the west the powerful forces of the art world, welding them together on the B.C. Coast.'[72] Contacts were initiated with the Japanese consulate and efforts made to attract Oriental students.[73]

A garage was rented near the art gallery and large curtains hung to divide the working spaces. Sponsors were found and the school opened in September 1933 with sixty-six students in the day classes, mostly former senior students from the Vancouver School of Art. Directed by three strong and magnetic personalities, the school generated a great deal of enthusiasm during its two years of ex-

istence. Courses in painting, theatre, dance, music, and eurythmics were supplemented by theatre productions, puppet shows, and exhibitions of student work.

However, the College was competing with a subsidized school in the middle of an economic depression. Few students had money; the teachers less. The scheme was over-ambitious, and after two years Jock Macdonald was forced to call in the Directors and organize the closure of the school.[74] Soon the artists left Vancouver.

The Macdonalds, with Harry Taüber and his lover, Les Planta, moved to Nootka on the west coast of Vancouver Island, squatting on land a few miles from Friendly Cove.[75] Jock stayed at Nootka for eighteen months, sketching a great deal. A show of his sketches in Vancouver was well received.[76] Life was hard but exciting and he gathered a great deal of material for later work. However, during the summer of 1936 he dislocated his spine getting out of a boat in a stormy sea.[77] Unable to do hard physical labour, he had to leave Nootka and took a part-time teaching job in Vancouver at the Canadian Institute of Associated Arts.[78]

The stay at Nootka had been a great stimulant to Jock Macdonald. Living in an environment so determined by the natural elements, and near a people so in tune with these forces, he became more and more interested in a spiritual expression beyond mere external representation. His first canvases completed in Vancouver depicted native life at Friendly Cove. *Indian Burial, Nootka* (1937, cat. no. 38) shows a great advance in the use of colour and paint from his earlier landscapes.

More important to Jock were his experiments which he called 'modalities.' He defined his intent in a letter to Harry McCurry: 'It means "Expressions of thought in relation to nature" and was considered by Kant to relate to creative expressions which could not be said to relate to nature (objectively) nor relate to abstract thoughts (subjectively) about nature, but rather included both expressions.'[79] As early as 1934 Jock had painted *Formative Colour Activity*,[80] which he later referred to as an 'automatic' painting.[81] While perhaps painted without a subject consciously intended, the work itself remains entirely representational. The representational element is also present in the modalities which bear such titles as *Rain, Winter, Daybreak*, and *Edge of the Sea*, all subjects taken from nature. While more descriptive than some of his modalities, *Pilgrimage* (1937, cat. no. 39) contains many of their qualities, including strong patterning, stylization of natural forms, and heightened colour. As in *Indian Burial, Nootka* (cat. no. 38), a natural Gothic arch reaches over the central funereal motif.

Overwork, lack of funds, undernourishment, and depression finally took their toll on Jock Macdonald. His right lung collapsed in the spring of 1937.[82] Confined to his bed, worrying about his family, fed up with Vancouver, Jock was at his wits' end. The Vancouver Art Gallery purchased his painting, *Indian Burial, Nootka*, giving him time to recover.[83] In September he visited California, possibly to explore job possibilities in Hollywood,[84] and was restimulated by visits to art galleries and by interest expressed in his 'modalities.'[85] Returning to Vancouver, he wrote, 'B.C. has that vapour quality which seems to me to be much more clairvoyant in its inspiration than that blazing and relentless sunshine down south. I am more certain now that Canada is the land where artists can find the environment for true creative activity.'[86]

Jock continued working on his modalities. When first exhibited, they were well-received by the Vancouver public, and he was encouraged to continue.[87] In the fall of 1938 he obtained a new post at Templeton Junior High[88] and a contract to do a mural for the reopening of the Hotel Vancouver.[89] The following autumn, after a second trip to California, he transferred to the Vancouver Technical High School.[90] He was still plagued by financial difficulties and hated teaching uninterested students; however, with the outbreak of war in September, he still could write, '[I] realized that expressions of beauty and truth are the most essential qualities of life, and this endeavour of study must not be smothered under any condition.'[91]

After the closing of the British Columbia College of Arts, Fred Varley, 'forced into the life of a hermit,'[92] moved to Lynn Valley. He still loved the country and rhapsodized in word and paint about its mystery and beauty. But desperately poor, he dreamed of returning to England and 'of arousing the populace into ecstasy over the prophetic utterances of my work in paint. Such profound utterances though have not been given expression because of the failure to procure materials and "the tubes are twisted and dried." Since hearing of the Group show I have been stricken with the lonesomeness of the West.'[93] A purchase by The National Gallery enabled him to go east.

In Ottawa he obtained a portrait commission, sold some sketches, and continued work on a painting of the resurrection of Christ, aptly entitled *Liberation*, which he planned to send to the Royal Academy in England. But all the time he longed to return to Lynn Valley and finally did go west[94] – only to return to teach at the Ottawa Art Association in October.[95]

Philip Surrey had moved to Montreal in the spring of 1937, and Fred visited him during the Easter holidays. 'His visit resulted in "108 hours of enthusiasm" and a 34 x 40 canvas,'[96] – the latter, *Night Ferry, Vancouver* (1937, cat. no. 40). Compositionally close to *Open Window* (cat.

no. 35), what a difference there is between the cool, serene, open spaces of the earlier work and the impassioned expression of his separation from Vancouver.

Varley had an exhibition in Montreal in May[97] and spent some time with Philip Surrey.[98] He returned to Vancouver in August and wrote back, 'The country here is more entrancing than ever but Vancouver is a drear drab place for an artist to be imprisoned in. I have seen several old students of mine who have great promise but it hurts terribly to find them so numbed by adversity. As for myself I am marking time, making drawings until I solve the problem of procuring more paints.'[99]

Once more he left for the East to teach in Ottawa,[100] and the next summer he accompanied the Federal Government arctic expedition on the *Nascopie*.[101] The splendour of the colours and the Inuit people entranced him. The lushness of his British Columbian landscapes reappears in *Summer in the Arctic* (c. 1939, cat. no. 41), in the rich, flowing colour and freely-brushed rocky ground.

When war broke out in 1939, the Ottawa Art Association classes were cancelled. After a year of terrible loneliness and dire poverty, he moved to Montreal where, with the help of friends, he began to work again.

NOTES TO CHAPTER 3

1. Graham C. McInnes, 'Contemporary Canadian Artists No. 12 – Orville Fisher,' *The Canadian Forum*, vol. XVII, no. 204 (January 1938), pp. 350 – 351. 'Three Young Artists Paint Vancouver for the World,' *Vancouver Daily Province* (24 March 1939). (re murals for the B.C. Government pavilion, San Francisco Golden Gate International Exposition, 1939).

2. Maria Tippett, ' "A Paste Solitaire in a Steel Claw Setting": Emily Carr and her Public,' *B.C. Studies*, no. 20 (Winter 1973 – 1974), pp. 3 – 14.

3. Seattle, Seattle Fine Arts Society, 4 – 30 April 1924, *Ninth Annual Exhibition of the Artists of the Pacific Northwest*, no. 10 (*Macaulay Point*).

4. Emily Carr exhibited with the Victoria Island Arts and Crafts Society from 1924 to 1926.

5. Ottawa, The National Gallery of Canada, December 1927, *Exhibition of Canadian West Coast Art Native and Modern*. Exhibited with a partially illustrated catalogue at The Art Gallery of Toronto, January 1928.

6. Emily Carr met Fred Varley in Vancouver on 10 November 1927 and A.Y. Jackson, Arthur Lismer, and Lawren Harris in Toronto between 14 November and 14 December 1927. See Emily Carr, *Hundreds and Thousands* (Toronto: Clarke, Irwin & Company Limited, 1966), pp. 3 – 18.

7. Emily Carr, *op. cit.*, p. 6.

8. *Ibid*, p. 19.

9. 'I tried to [visit Kitwancool] fifteen years ago but the white people would not let me.' Emily Carr, South Bay, Queen Charlotte Islands, to Mr and Mrs Eric Brown, Ottawa, 11 August 1928; in The National Gallery of Canada.

10. *Big Raven* in The Vancouver Art Gallery was painted from a 1912 watercolour, *Cumshewa* in The National Gallery of Canada. See Doris Shadbolt, *Emily Carr* (exhibition catalogue) (Vancouver: The Vancouver Art Gallery, 1971), nos 45 and 62.

11. *Blunden Harbour* in The National Gallery of Canada was painted from a photograph, presently in the Provincial Archives, Victoria, inscribed, '*This enlargement from a 4 x 5 negative was loaned Miss Emily Carr about 1930 by W.A. Newcombe. Miss Carr painted "Blunden Harbour" now in the National Gallery, Ottawa, from it, never having had an opportunity of visiting this village personally*,' and signed *W.A. Newcombe*. Edith Hembroff-Schleicher notes, 'She quite often worked from Mr Newcombe's photographs, particularly . . . after her first illness in 1937.' See E. Hembroff-Schleicher, Victoria, to Charles Hill, Ottawa, 9 April 1974; in The National Gallery of Canada.

12. Clive Bell's book, *Art* (London: Chatto & Windus, 1914) in which he formulated the concept of 'significant form,' was one of the books Lawren Harris recommended to Emily Carr. (Emily Carr, *op. cit.*, p. 18.)

13. Emily Carr, *Growing Pains* (Toronto: Oxford University Press, 1946), p. 343.

14. Emily Carr, *Hundreds and Thousands*, pp. 34 – 40.

15. *Ibid.*, p. 49.

16. Mark Tobey, Seattle, to Donald Buchanan, Ottawa (received 15 April 1957); in The National Gallery of Canada. Mark Tobey erroneously dates this meeting between 1922 and 1925.

17. Emily Carr, Victoria, to Eric Brown, Ottawa, 1 October [1928]; in The National Gallery of Canada. A painting by Mark Tobey, *Emily Carr's Studio*, is dated 1928. See *Mark Tobey, A Retrospective Exhibition from Northwest Collections* (exhibition catalogue) (Seattle: Seattle Art Museum, 1959), repr.

18. Mark Tobey, Seattle, to Donald Buchanan, Ottawa (received 15 April 1957); in The National Gallery of Canada. Tobey remarks, 'Also I stayed in her studio when she went East the second time.'

19. Emily Carr left Victoria late March ('On Way East to Attend Exhibitions of Her Work,' Victoria *Daily Colonist* [1 April 1930]) and was in New York sometime in May (Lawren Harris, Toronto, to Katherine Dreier, 18 June 1930; in the Dreier Archive, Yale Collection of American Literature, Beinecke Rare Book and Manuscript Library, Yale University, New Haven). For an account of her trip to New York see Emily Carr, *Growing Pains*, pp. 241 – 250.

20. Emily Carr, *Hundreds and Thousands*, p. 21. Entry dated 24 November 1930.

21. William C. Seitz states Tobey left for England in 1930. See *Mark Tobey* (exhibition catalogue) (New York: Museum of Modern Art, 1962), p. 49. However, Edward Weston notes a visit from Mark Tobey on 30 August 1931. See *The Daybooks of Edward Weston* (Rochester [N.Y.]): George Eastman House, 1966), vol. II, p. 223.

22. Colin Graham, Victoria, to Donald Buchanan, Ottawa, 19 July 1957; in The National Gallery of Canada.

23. Emily Carr, *Hundreds and Thousands*, p. 21.

24. *Ibid.*, p. 25.

25. Georgia O'Keeffe was painting similar organic natural forms at this time. Emily Carr met Georgia O'Keeffe in New York in 1930. (Emily Carr, *Growing Pains*, p. 250.)

26. Emily Carr, *Hundreds and Thousands*, pp. 3 – 19.

27. *Ibid.*, p. 21.

28. *Ibid.*, pp. 68 – 83.

29. Emily Carr, *Growing Pains*, p. 340.

30. Emily Carr, *Hundreds and Thousands*, p. 7.

31. *Ibid.*, p. 18.

32. Much of her writing has a theosophic character to it. See, for example, Emily Carr, *Hundreds and Thousands*, p. 33.

33. *Ibid.*, pp. 79 – 80.

34. *Ibid.*, p. 93.

35. *Ibid.*, p. 149.

36. *Ibid.*, p. 138.

37. The first dated oil sketch is *Forest Interior* (1932), Collection of Mr John McDonald, Vancouver. See Doris Shadbolt, *Emily Carr*, no. 77 repr. Emily Carr first wrote about her new medium in her journal entry for 27 January 1933. See Emily Carr, *Hundreds and Thousands*, p. 33.

38. Emily Carr, Victoria, to Eric Brown, Ottawa, 4 March 1937; in The National Gallery of Canada.

39. Emily Carr, *Hundreds and Thousands*, p. 274.

40. *Ibid.*, pp. 285 – 289.

41. Emily Carr, Victoria, to Nan Cheney, Vancouver, [postmarked 30 November 1937]; in The University of British Columbia, Vancouver.

42. J.W.G. Macdonald, Vancouver, to H.O. McCurry, Ottawa, 24 October 1938; in The National Gallery of Canada.

43. Charles H. Scott, 'A Short Art History of British Columbia.' in *Behind the Palette 1946 – 1947* (Vancouver: Vancouver School of Art, 1947).

44. *Idem.*

45. While Jock Macdonald, an Edinburgh College of Art graduate, was Scottish, he had been teaching the previous year at the Lincoln School of Art in England. (*British Columbia College of Arts Limited, Illustrated Prospectus, 1934 – 1935*, hereafter referred to as *Prospectus*.)

46. The firm's letterhead at this time lists John Vanderpant and Harold Mortimer-Lamb as 'Associates.'

47. Conversation with Mrs Anna Vanderpant Ackroyd, Vancouver, 20 November 1973.

48. Ada F. Currie, 'The Vanderpant Musicales,' in *The Paintbox* (Vancouver: Vancouver School of Decorative & Applied Arts, 1928), p. 48.

49. A large exhibition was held at the time of the opening of The Vancouver Art Gallery to encourage the purchasing committee to buy contemporary works by British Columbia artists. See Reta Myers, 'In the Domain of Art,' *Vancouver Daily Province*, 12 April 1931.

50. Fred Varley, Vancouver, to Arthur Lismer, Toronto, [c. February 1928]; in The McMichael Canadian Collection, Kleinburg.

51. Fred Varley, Vancouver, to L.L. FitzGerald, Winnipeg, 25 September 1934; private property.

52. Fred Varley, Vancouver, to Eric Brown, Ottawa, 18 February 1928; in The National Gallery of Canada.

53. Conversation with Peter Varley and Mrs Maude Varley, Toronto, 17 October 1973. John Varley, the oldest son, was extremely interested in astrology as well as oriental and Rosicrucian teachings. (Interview with Philip Surrey, Montreal, 14 September 1973.)

54. During the summer of 1930 he taught at the Art Institute of Seattle ('Famous Artist is Added to Institute,' *Seattle Times*, 6 July 1930) and completed a portrait of Dr C.W. Sharples for the Seattle General Hospital (Fred Varley, Seattle, to H.O. McCurry, Ottawa [July 1930]; in The National Gallery of Canada).

55. These theories were common in theosophic and Oriental mystical teachings. See discussion of Lawren Harris's abstracts below, pp. 76 – 77.

56. Telephone conversation with John Aveson, Vancouver, 18 November 1973.

57. Donald Buchanan defines *dhârâna* as a 'Buddhist term signifying the power to project oneself into one's surroundings.' See Donald Buchanan, 'The Paintings and Drawings of F.H. Varley,' *Canadian Art*, vol. VII, no. 1 (Autumn 1949), p. 3. *The Oxford English Dictionary* defines 'dharna' as a 'Hindi term for the act of sitting in restraint' and 'sitting dharna' as 'a mode of extorting payment or compliance with a demand, effected by the complainant or creditor sitting at the debtor's door without tasting food till his demand shall be complied with.'

58. Interview with Philip Surrey, Montreal, 14 September 1973.

59. *Prospectus.*

60. J.W.G. Macdonald, Vancouver, to H.O. McCurry, Ottawa, 9 April 1932; in The National Gallery of Canada.

61. Reta Myers, 'In the Domain of Art,' *Vancouver Daily Province* (5 July 1931).

62. *Mountain Landscape, Garibaldi Park* (c. 1928, oil on canvas; 34 x 40 in., 86.4 x 101.6 cm) Power Corporation of Canada, Limited, Montreal. See Dennis Reid, *The Group of Seven*, p. 225 repr. This work was formerly in the collection of John Vanderpant.

63. Bertram Brooker, Toronto, to L.L. FitzGerald, Winnipeg, 10 January 1932; private property.

64. Grace Melvin, Charles Scott's sister-in-law, had joined the staff in 1927, teaching design and crafts. ('Grace Melvin,' The National Gallery of Canada Information Form, 27 May 1933.)

65. Charles Scott, Vancouver, to Arthur Lismer, Toronto, 10 October 1933; in the Art Gallery of Ontario.

66. Fred Varley, Vancouver, to Eric Brown, Ottawa, 5 April 1933; in The National Gallery of Canada. The name originally considered for the new school was 'National Art School of British Columbia.'

67. *Prospectus.* Taüber also studied under a professor 'Hoffman,' probably Josef Hoffmann (1870 – 1955), the noted Viennese Art Nouveau architect.

68. Interview with Isabel Wintemute, Vancouver, 17 November 1973.

69. Reta Myers, 'In the Domain of Art,' *Vancouver Daily Province* (24 January 1932).

70. Harry Taüber was a student of anthroposophy, an outgrowth of theosophy developed by Rudolf Steiner when he broke away from the Theosophical Society directed by Annie Besant.

71. *Prospectus.*

72. Fred Varley, Vancouver, to H.O. McCurry, Ottawa, 16 April 1934; in The National Gallery of Canada.

73. H.E. Torey, 'Where East Meets West,' *Saturday Night*, vol. XLIX, no. 24 (21 April 1934), p. 10.

74. J.W.G. Macdonald, Vancouver, to H.O. McCurry, Ottawa, 29 December 1936; in The National Gallery of Canada. The school closed during the summer of 1935.

75. Conversation with Barbara Macdonald, Toronto, 16 October 1973. Harry Taüber and Les Planta later moved to Duncan, B.C. See J.W.G. Macdonald, Vancouver, to John Varley, [Nootka?], 8 December 1936; copy in the Burnaby Art Gallery.

76. 'Recent Nootka Sketches at Art Emporium,' *Vancouver Daily Province*, 1 February 1936.

77. J.W.G. Macdonald, Nootka, to A.Y. Jackson, Toronto, 28 August 1936; in The National Gallery of Canada.

78. J.W.G. Macdonald, Vancouver, to H.O. McCurry, Ottawa, 29 December 1936; in The National Gallery of Canada.

79. J.W.G. Macdonald, Vancouver, to H.O. McCurry, Ottawa, 22 July 1938; in The National Gallery of Canada.

80. *Formative Colour Activity* (1934, oil on canvas; 30-3/8 x 26-1/8 in., 77.1 x 66.4 cm) The National Gallery of Canada, Ottawa. See R. Ann Pollock and Dennis Reid, *Jock Macdonald* (exhibition catalogue) (Ottawa: The National Gallery of Canada, 1969), p. 36 repr.

81. J.W.G. Macdonald, Toronto, to Maxwell Bates, [Calgary?], 30 July 1956; in The McCord Museum, McGill University.

82. William Firth MacGregor, Vancouver, to H.O. McCurry, Ottawa, 21 April 1937; in The National Gallery of Canada.

83. A.S. Grigsby, Secretary, The Vancouver Art Gallery, Vancouver, to H.O. McCurry, Ottawa, 4 May 1937; in The National Gallery of Canada.

84. 'Things are exceedingly difficult – so difficult in fact that it appears likely that I will leave Canada for further south,' J.W.G. Macdonald, Vancouver, to H.O. McCurry, Ottawa, 12 August 1937; in The National Gallery of Canada.

85. J.W.G. Macdonald, Vancouver, to H.O. McCurry, Ottawa, 23 October 1937; in The National Gallery of Canada.

86. *Idem.*

87. J.W.G. Macdonald, Vancouver, to H.O. McCurry, Ottawa, 16 June 1938; in The National Gallery of Canada.

88. J.W.G. Macdonald, Vancouver, to H.O. McCurry, Ottawa, 7 September 1938; in The National Gallery of Canada.

89. Nan Cheney, Vancouver, to Eric Brown, Ottawa, 23 January 1939; in The National Gallery of Canada. The hotel, a victim of the Depression, had been left uncompleted and closed for seven years. For reproductions of the decorations in the hotel, see Robert Ayre, 'Murals in Our Public Buildings,' *Saturday Night*, vol. LV, no. 30 (25 May 1940), p. 2.

90. J.W.G. Macdonald, Vancouver, to John Varley, Ottawa, 9 September 1939; copy in The Burnaby Art Gallery.

91. J.W.G. Macdonald, Vancouver, to H.O. McCurry, Ottawa, 2 December 1939; in The National Gallery of Canada.

92. Fred Varley, Upper Lynn (B.C.), to Eric Brown, Ottawa, 7 December 1935; in The National Gallery of Canada.

93. Fred Varley, Upper Lynn (B.C.), to H.O. McCurry, Ottawa, 23 February 1936; in The National Gallery of Canada.
94. A.Y. Jackson, Montreal, to H.O. McCurry, Ottawa, 22 August 1936; in The National Gallery of Canada.
95. Telegram, Fred Varley, Field (B.C.), to H.O. McCurry, Ottawa, 10 October 1936; in The National Gallery of Canada.
96. Philip Surrey, Montreal, to John Vanderpant, Vancouver, 23 April 1937; private property.
97. Montreal, W. Scott & Sons, from 26 May 1937, *Frederick H. Varley, A.R.C.A.*
98. Interview with Philip Surrey, Montreal, 14 September 1973.
99. Fred Varley, Upper Lynn (B.C.), to Eric Brown, Ottawa, 30 August 1937; in The National Gallery of Canada.
100. Fred Varley, Ottawa, to John Vanderpant, Vancouver, 5 November 1937; private property.
101. Charles Camsell, Deputy Minister of Mines and Resources, Ottawa, to Eric Brown, Ottawa, 1 July 1938; in The National Gallery of Canada.

*28.
EMILY CARR
Grey   c. 1931

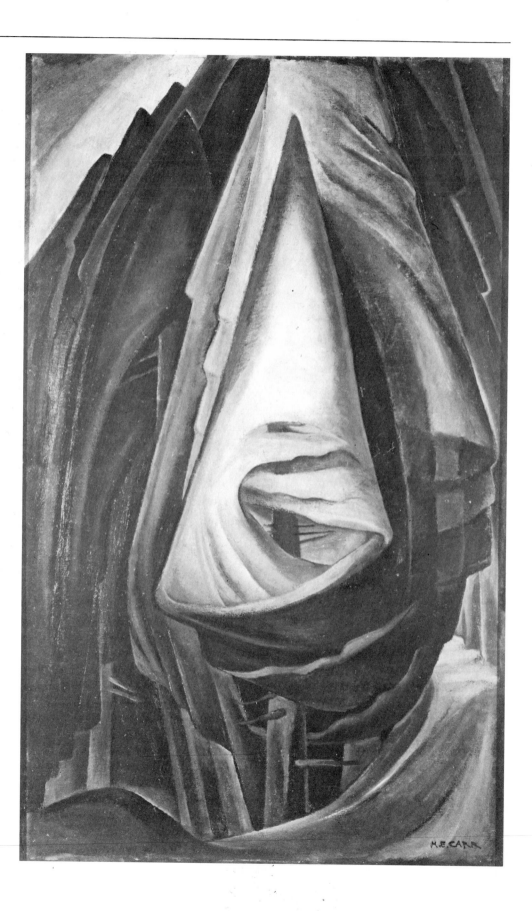

29.
EMILY CARR
Tree   c. 1931

30.
EMILY CARR
A Rushing Sea of Undergrowth   c. 1932 – 1934

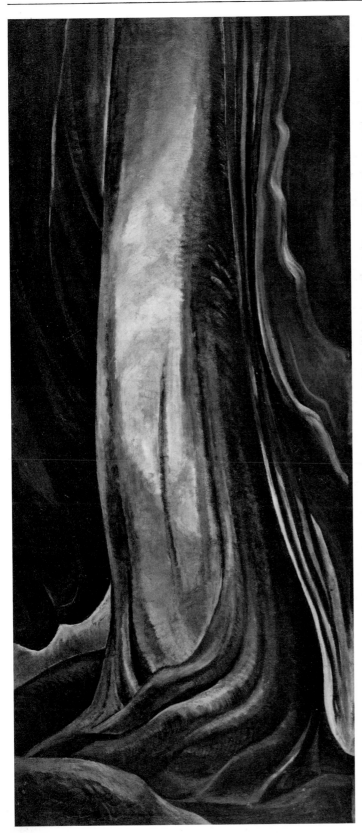

*31.
EMILY CARR
Tree   c. 1932 – 1933

*32.
EMILY CARR
Overhead   c. 1935

*31.
EMILY CARR
Tree   c. 1932 – 1933

*32.
EMILY CARR
Overhead   c. 1935

33.
EMILY CARR
Scorned as Timber, Beloved of the Sky   *c. 1936*

34.
F.H. VARLEY
Dhârâna   *c. 1932*

35.
F.H. VARLEY
Open Window   *c.* 1932

*36.
PHILIP SURREY
Going to Work   1935

*37.
J.W.G. MACDONALD
The Black Tusk, Garibaldi Park, B.C.   1932

38.
J.W.G. MACDONALD
Indian Burial, Nootka   1937

39.
J.W.G. MACDONALD
Pilgrimage   1937

*40.
 F.H. VARLEY
 Night Ferry, Vancouver   1937

*41.
F.H. VARLEY
Summer in the Arctic   c. 1939

4. The Independents

Most Canadian artists during the thirties concentrated in the large urban centres – like Toronto, Montreal, and Vancouver – where they could associate with other artists, see exhibitions, and participate in current events. However, there were some, such as LeMoine FitzGerald and David Milne, who consciously maintained or sought out isolation from the mainstream to allow themselves to develop along more integrally personal lines. After leaving for the United States, Lawren Harris's painting also evolved in directions quite distinct from anything in Canada.

After five months at the Art Students League in New York under Boardman Robinson and Kenneth Hayes Miller, LeMoine FitzGerald returned to Winnipeg and in the fall of 1924 joined the staff of the Winnipeg School of Art, becoming its principal five years later.[1] Sometime during the late twenties FitzGerald came into contact with the Group of Seven,[2] a relationship strengthened by Bertram Brooker, a native Winnipegger and close friend of the Group. An exhibition of FitzGerald's drawings at Dent's Publishing House in Toronto was greatly admired by Lawren Harris who purchased one of the drawings[3] – a purchase that resulted in an invitation to exhibit in the Group show in 1930. That same year FitzGerald went east and for the first time met several of the Toronto artists.[4] In March 1932 Arthur Lismer visited FitzGerald in Winnipeg during his cross-country lecture tour, and Lismer was made aware of the provincialism of the Group's concept of a Canadian identity.[5] The quality and direction of Fitz-Gerald's work, as well as the need to broaden the geographic base of the Group, were the deciding factors in inviting FitzGerald to become a member of the Group of Seven. While, as a member, he exhibited with them only in one private show,[6] he was 'pleased to feel a definite connection'[7] with the Eastern artists.

FitzGerald remained an isolated figure in Winnipeg all during the thirties, making only two trips outside Manitoba, both in connection with his work at the School. His tour of the United States and Central Canada in 1930 was made to report on art-education facilities in the different centres.[8] In 1938 he went east again to locate a new assistant.[9] FitzGerald, however, recognized certain advantages to his separation: 'It seems impossible for the artist to attain any height without sacrificing at least a little of the ordinary necessities, not to mention the loss of ordinary social contact, that are so essential to others. The desire to create something . . . fills the artist's mind, and to do this requires time for active work and quiet thought.'[10]

At the same time FitzGerald's teaching duties left him little time to paint; *Doc Snider's House* (1931, cat. no. 42), completed in 1931, the result of two winters' work,[11] was the last large canvas he painted for many years. While

occasionally he resented the lack of time, he wrote, 'It is necessary to earn a living, but much better to find some other forms of activity to cover that than to sacrifice the real joy of having given full rein to the power that has been given you. I think the person born with a real art sense usually manages to scramble through the material side and keep a certain healthy attitude to the real thing.'[12]

FitzGerald's concern for qualities of light, colour, and texture, seen in his Impressionist canvases of the early twenties, continues in his later work. He slowly breaks away from atmospheric rendering, and the light, instead of blending the compositional elements, isolates them, stressing their formal relationships. In *Doc Snider's House* the trees become plastic units revolving in an elliptical motion within the blue-white space of the yard. The contrasting straight and curved lines and closed and open spaces are unified by the muted colouring, limited to browns and blues – with a touch of pale green in the house at the right.

While the texture of the snow in *Doc Snider's House* still owes something to Lawren Harris, the careful brushwork of *Farm Yard* (1931; cat. no. 43) is very much FitzGerald's own. Applied thinly, layer over layer, the dry paint has almost the quality of a bas relief, intensifying the internal structure of each of the forms. The compositional elements interrelate in a complex schema of vertical, diagonal, and horizontal lines. While most of the canvas is painted in bleached tones of similar values, a subtle richness is added by the green on the boards at the left and faint purples in the shadows on the barn.

In *Broken Tree in Landscape* (1931, cat. no. 44), the rich greens and blues of the shadows seem to vibrate in intensity – in contrast to his usual delicate colouring, seen in the clearing and trees. While FitzGerald still creates a complex spatial arrangement of line and form, the shapes are softer, the stylized foliage almost like air-filled cotton, and the splintered tree smoothly honed.

FitzGerald's approach to his art demanded 'a greater emphasis on study than on picture-making alone.'[13] In countless studies in pencil and oil he would work out each detail of the picture, building up the form and studying the relation of the elements to each other before uniting them in the finished work.

These formal concerns owe a great deal to his interest in the work of the Pointillist Seurat. Visiting the Chicago Art Institute in 1930, FitzGerald commented on the 'great feeling of reality' he found in Seurat's *A Sunday Afternoon on the Island of La Grande Jatte* and the beauty and 'alive' quality of his drawings.[14] Another artist who interested FitzGerald was the American Precisionist Charles Sheeler.[15] Sheeler's tonal colouring and careful rendering of simpli-

7. L. L. FitzGerald, *Lake Winnipeg*, c. 1929.

fied form studied under strong sunlight find their parallel in FitzGerald's work. However, whereas Sheeler's themes are mechanical and functional objects, FitzGerald confines himself to more natural surroundings. Less concerned with the final result than with the study itself, FitzGerald produced few completed paintings – thereby occasioning plaintive letters from the East requesting works for exhibition. He replied, 'I find it very difficult to keep up with the shows. I seem to require so much time to do even a small drawing that I only get through a very few things during the year even though I am working all the spare time I have.'[16] To an expressed preference for oils over drawings, he answered, 'For the time being the drawings seem to satisfy my desire to create and I am egotist enough to think that some of them are darn fine things with just as much in them as any painting I have done.'[17]

Concentrating his studies resulted in periods when he preferred to work in only one medium, almost to the exclusion of any other. The oils of the early thirties were replaced by drawings as he became more and more interested in drawing in increasingly subtle relationships. Oil became almost too rich a medium for him: 'Recently I have had a peculiar feeling . . . . It has almost amounted to a physical nausea at the thought of looking at paintings by the wholesale.'[18]

In *The Pool* (1934, cat. no. 45), one of the few oils of the mid-thirties, the linear interaction of verticals, parabolas, and ellipses reflect his predominant interest in drawing. The paint is applied in thin, short strokes and flecked at the edges – creating a series of concentric lines echoing the curves of the reeds. The linear quality of the paint is so strong the reeds appear almost as if incised. At the same time, the texture, gently curving horizontals, and subtle colouring of the trees and clouds reflected in the water give the work a richness and complexity beyond two-dimensional pattern.

FitzGerald's increasing interest in geometric relationships is seen also in *Jar* (1938, cat. no. 46). As usual in his still-lifes, he confines himself to one or two objects chosen for their elementary contours and formally juxtaposed with each other and within the whole environment. The abrupt perspective flattens the jar, accentuating the smooth curves to the mouth, contrasting with the enclosing diagonals. The intersecting lines in the upper left are almost Constructivist in the subtlety of their minimal forms. The flecked stroke gives a solidity to the individual elements and an overall surface unity.

It is evident that these formal studies would eventually lead to pure abstraction. However, several years earlier FitzGerald had discarded that possibility. After talking with a friend, FitzGerald wrote in his journal, '[We] agreed

on the feeling that [the] purely abstract has a tendency to lose contact with the living thing . . . and that the move today is rather a swing towards . . . an eternal contact with humanity and nature and a greater sense of unity.'[19] The Realism of Courbet held more attraction for him at this time, and it was only much later, in the early fifties, that he would make the break.

FitzGerald's art is a steady progress in the study of formal relationships. While choosing places and objects familiar to him, he was, unlike the rest of the Group of Seven, convinced that subject-matter was essentially unimportant. For him it was more important to make 'the picture a living thing, one great thought made up of many details but all subordinated to the whole.'[20]

FitzGerald's interests find their parallel in an artist quite similar yet at the same time quite different in expression, David Milne. After having lived in New York State for twenty-five years, Milne returned to Canada in the spring of 1929, first settling at Temagami[21] and in the fall moved to Weston, just outside Toronto.[22] The following spring he moved to Palgrave, Ontario,[23] where he was to remain for three years.

During his first two years in Canada, Milne re-established contact with The National Gallery, sized up the Canadian art scene, and sought exhibition outlets. He only made his first sale in Canada in 1931 when Vincent Massey purchased his painting, Window.[24]

As it was for FitzGerald, 'for David Milne the process of art, not the content of it, was paramount.'[25] Milne wrote, 'Do you like flowers? So do I, but I never paint them. I didn't even see the hepaticas. I saw, instead, an arrangement of the lines, spaces, hues, values and relations that I habitually use. That is, I saw one of my own pictures, a little different from ones done before, changed slightly, very slightly, by what I saw before me.'[26]

Milne used words as a part of the process to concentrate his vision.[27] First there were notes on the pictures as they were painted, 'a half-way technical analysis of each sketch, with some extensions into the theory of painting in general, and occasional notings of weather, incidents and thoughts outside the strictly painting thing,'[28] – points of reference for future work. The other method Milne called 'the inventory method,' a verbal inventory of his immediate environment: 'The point of it is in the everything. Not merely things you would usually see but things so simple that you wouldn't ordinarily think of them.'[29]

His actual painting method is admirably described in his letter to his friend James Clarke in New York: the choice of elements, the arrangement, at first 'purely observation and reason,' the first drawing with his brush, something catches, his interest heightens, then the brushing in of

colour and values, the adding and subtracting, all at a feverish pitch.[30]

David Milne's Palgrave landscapes are studies in line and separation of value and hue. 'All line is put in detail first – though the rest is planned at the same time – then is made readable, simplified by emphasis and reduction with values and hues or by simplifying the arrangement of the line itself.'[31] In Blind Road (1930, cat. no. 47) the lines create a complex of open and shut spaces relieved by the blank space above. In Splendour Touches Hiram's Farm (1932, cat. no. 48) the hues are higher in intensity, there are fewer open spaces, demanding a larger rest area above. The contrast of values, with a limited number of hues, gives the 'kick.'

In Palgrave (I) (1931, cat. no. 49) he reverses the motifs, from a serene, empty sky and detailed landscape to a concentration on the upper part of the picture, with the earth becoming a 'foil for the sky.'[32] However, unlike the other Palgrave pictures, it is the contrast of hues, and not blank spaces, that plays against the sky. 'The thing that "makes" a picture,' he remarked, 'is the thing that "makes" dynamite – compression. It isn't a fire in the grass, it is an explosion.'[33]

From a painting point-of-view, David Milne's time at Palgrave was extremely productive; however, economically it was difficult. Tensions at home, aggravated by financial constraints, resulted in his separating from his wife and moving to Six Mile Lake near Severn Falls, Ontario, in May 1933.[34]

Having no contacts with other Canadian artists at this time, David Milne was unable to exhibit with the Canadian Group of Painters, the main outlet for 'modern' work in oil.[35] Hampered by lack of funds, he could not risk shipping paintings to exhibitions where they might be rejected by juries.[36] Without exhibitions, there were no sales. He began to consider the possibility of selling all the pictures he had ever painted – '$5,000 for a lifetime's work'[37] – and finally approached the Vincent Masseys, the only Canadian collectors he knew. The arrangement as finally agreed upon was the purchase by the Masseys of all his work painted in the last five years, with a few earlier works he had brought to Canada with him.[38] The Masseys also arranged for an exhibition of Milne's work at Mellors Galleries in Toronto,[39] the first one to be followed by annual exhibitions during the next three years.[40] Through the Masseys and the Mellors exhibitions Milne soon came in contact with several people who were to be extremely important in his life.

Milne decided to live in the country, isolated from other artists, partly for economic reasons but, more importantly, to allow himself the time to concentrate on the thing that interested him most, his painting. Like FitzGerald, Milne's art depended on the formulation and solution of certain formal, artistic problems and the consistent development and concentration of his inner self. For this, time and space were needed, not social contacts or change of scene. However, the few personal connections he did have, and especially his correspondence with these people, were important to him. They allowed him to share his observations about Canadian art and theorize about art with persons on an equal level in a creative dialogue. Over the next few years his correspondence with his American associate, James Clarke, diminished as he developed new contacts and friends in Canada.

Donald Buchanan first saw Milne's work at the Masseys' house in Port Hope and in October 1934 visited Milne at Six Mile Lake.[41] Articulate about art and aware of contemporary developments seen through the writings of the aestheticians Clive Bell and Roger Fry, Buchanan struck up a close friendship with David Milne, as witnessed by their correspondence over the next few years. Donald Buchanan wrote the introduction to the catalogue of the first Mellors exhibition[42] and several excellent articles which at last brought Milne to public attention.[43]

Douglas Duncan and Alan Jarvis first saw Milne's work at Mellors Galleries in 1934, and the next summer visited him at Six Mile Lake.[44] Douglas Duncan was completely captivated by both Milne and his work, and over the years did more than any one else to establish his reputation. At first, he arranged private sales of Milne's works, and after that an exhibition of his drypoints,[45] as these were not covered by the contract with Mellors Galleries.

The arrangement between Mellors Galleries and David Milne had originally been made by Mrs Massey for the sale of works from the 1934 purchase, with any profit going to buy works by contemporary Canadian artists. The contract was renewed after the Masseys left for England, with Milne sending more recent works to be included in the exhibitions. However, when he finally asked for an accounting of the costs and profits he found that he had *lost* money on the arrangement.[46] He then left Mellors and joined the Picture Loan Society.

Through Douglas Duncan, David Milne met some of the younger Toronto artists, including Will Ogilvie and Carl Schaefer. He also met Alan Plaunt, a collector of contemporary Canadian art and one of the persons instrumental in the creation of the Canadian Broadcasting Corporation.[47] Douglas also interested J.S. McLean, President of Canada Packers and a noted collector, in Milne's work and resultant sales finally guaranteed Milne some economic security.

When Milne first moved to Six Mile Lake in 1933 there was a period of adaption from the 'open skies of Palgrave to the closed in material of the bush.'[48] New material stimulated new methods. Instead of concentrating on line, value, and hue, he would now use a colour where before he would use a value. He would work up a painting in his shack rather than completing it at one sitting at the site. He no longer painted several versions of one motif, but sought out a variety of subjects around his camp. In *Young Poplars Among Driftwood* (1937, cat. no. 50) he still uses the blank space as a resting area to contrast with the cluttered space below. However, the brushwork is freer and broader, building up the forms from the inside in an almost painterly manner. The few hues are all of a similar intensity.

The still-lifes of the mid-thirties, starting with *Raspberry Jam* (1936, cat. no. 51) were, as Milne called them, studies in progression, across the canvas in a measured beat, in this case from black to light blue by way of red, grey, and green.[49] A similar progression is seen in *Red Nasturtiums* (1937, cat. no. 52), from areas of brilliant colour to black-white areas, with black unifying the whole. He still confines himself to a few hues at maximum intensity, swiftly laid on against the white paper, which is itself incorporated as a hue.

Milne started painting in watercolour again during the summer of 1937, attracted by the decisiveness and immediacy of the medium and he confined himself almost totally to watercolour for the next few years.[50] In 1939 he moved from Six Mile Lake to Toronto and then to Uxbridge. As usual, a change in place resulted in a change in colour, form, and theme in his work of the forties.

Lawren Harris arrived in Hanover, New Hampshire, in November 1934, originally intending to stay only a few months;[51] however, the sympathetic atmosphere of Dartmouth College, the White Mountains nearby, and the accessibility of New York City convinced him to remain. Freed from a difficult personal situation in Toronto, newly married, and in a congenial environment, he began to paint again.

Drawings made on sketching trips to the White Mountains were reworked in his studio through successive stages of abstraction[52] and then transferred to canvas. In studies of wood-grain patterns, rock formations, and mountain landscapes, he sought a form of abstract expression derived from natural elements.

Both *Riven Earth I* (c. 1936, cat. no. 53) and *Resolution* (c. 1937, cat. no. 54) retain definite landscape references. *Riven Earth I* relates compositionally to certain Lake Superior canvases as well as to a symbolic, though representational, landscape of 1935 entitled *Winter Comes from the Arctic to the Temperate Zone*.[53] *Resolution's* vertical format

45. L.L. FITZGERALD, *The Pool* (1934)

and conical peaks refer to the later Rocky Mountain paintings.[54] However, Lawren Harris was not merely attempting to create geometricized landscapes.

In his 1948 statement on abstraction he defined two categories: 'One kind is derived from the accumulated experience of nature over many years. In these the endeavor is to embody and concentrate this accumulated experience in organization of line, mass and colour in such a way that they express the motivating spirit in nature . . . .The second kind of abstractions aim at statements of ideas and intimations of a philosophic kind in plastic, aesthetic and emotive terms.'[55] Both *Riven Earth I* and *Resolution* fall somewhere between the two categories. They express not only the experience of nature, be it open arctic spaces or soaring mountains heights, but Lawren Harris's theosophic interpretation of these places and experiences.

The similarities between *Riven Earth I* and *Winter Comes from the Arctic to the Temperate Zone*[56] naturally suggest his belief in the 'spiritual flow' from the North 'that will ever shed clarity into the growing race of America.'[57] The mountains were also seen as spiritual centres in theosophic teachings; and the waves emanating from the base of the 'peak' possibly refer to these energies, in a depiction curiously similar to Bertram Brooker's early abstractions. However, the inscription on the back of the stretcher implies a more complex symbolism: *RESOLUTION/ INTERLOCKING FORMS – SYMBOL OF STEAD-FASTNESS, COURAGE.*[58]

Without further research, it is difficult to determine to what extent Lawren Harris had formulated a system of symbolic form and colour. He was familiar with the work of Wassily Kandinsky and Piet Mondrian,[59] both of whom had developed their abstractions with the aid of theosophy.[60] One of the sources of Kandinsky's analysis of form and colour, *Thought Forms* by Annie Besant and C.W. Leadbeater,[61] had been reviewed in *The Canadian Theosophist* at the time of the book's second printing. The anonymous critic wrote, 'It is difficult to suppose that the shapes and images of either psychic or artistic imagination shall always be standard conceptions by which we might recognize these aspects of the karmic nature which they are intended to represent . . . though the colours may more nearly represent the reality.'[62]

It is possible that Lawren Harris had already in his arctic landscapes adopted certain aspects of the theosophic colour symbolism as interpreted by Kandinsky:[63] blue expressing the desire for purity and transcendence, the call to the infinite; yellow, a more typically earthly colour; and white, purity and stillness pregnant with potentialities. In *Riven Earth I* the spiritual blues and whites rise above the browns and yellows of the foreground elements. In *Resolution* the green-grey in the background and black of the 'shadow' crowning the triangular 'peak' are both colours of rest, immobility, and death – silence with no potentialities.[64]

Lawren Harris first exhibited his abstracts in the Canadian Group of Painters exhibition in 1937,[65] and again in 1939.[66] The general reaction had been anticipated in an article by Arthur Lismer: 'the artist turns from the world of other men's making and goes to the vast unexplored world of abstract thought, psychological and metaphysical, where the emotional and scientific union of intellect and speculation releases the spirit into lands less forlorn, into a world of order and mathematical divination but which takes from him all contact with his fellow men into a stratosphere of rarified purity of design and colour.'[67] Other reviewers echoed this criticism of Harris's apparent rejection of humanity,[68] to which Harris replied, 'many folks have the idea that so-called abstract art is *not* in terms of Humanity. This, because most folks don't know its language and therefore mistake their limitations for infallible criteria.'[69] Not surprisingly his abstractions were not included in any of the Canadian representations in international art exhibitions, not even in the Canadian art section of the San Francisco Golden Gate International Exposition (1939) which Harris himself organized.[70]

During the spring and summer of 1938, Lawren and Bess Harris had made a motor trip to New Mexico to explore the possibilities of settling there,[71] returning to Maine in July.[72] While in Santa Fe, they met Raymond Jonson who was in the process of organizing a group of abstract artists and Lawren Harris was invited to join them.[73] Harris moved to New Mexico in September.[74]

The Transcendental Painting Group was organized during the summer of 1938 while Lawren Harris was still in Maine.[75] Recognizing its roots in the art of Kandinsky, the new group sought to promote an art that expressed 'the immaterial by means of material substances,'[76] and 'to carry painting beyond the appearance of the physical world . . . to imaginative realms that are idealistic and spiritual.'[77] The seal of the group was a stylized butterfly symbolizing metamorphosis, 'the constant renewal of forms toward a higher, freer, always transcendant life.'[78] The painter's group, primarily an exhibiting organization, had an educational adjunct in the American Foundation for Transcendental Painting. With Lawren Harris as the first president, its aims were to protect, preserve, and promote transcendental painting.[79] Exhibitions were organized in Santa Fe and Albuquerque and paintings by members were included in the state representations at the New York World's Fair [80] and the San Francisco Golden Gate International Exposi-

NOTES TO CHAPTER 4

tion. Works sent to the Gruggenheim Museum in New York [81] were included in two exhibitions of 'Non-Objective Painters.' [82]

Lawren Harris's Santa Fe works show an increasing maturity and familiarity with 'non-representational' painting. In *White Triangle* (c. 1939, cat. no. 55) he avoids all representational references. The complex interaction of directional lines and overlapping forms gives the central motif a solid feeling of three-dimensionality and weight floating in a glowing atmosphere of white and blue. The theosophic triangle, painted in white, the colour of joy, purity, and silence, symbolizes the three principles of spirit, force, and matter.

It is probable that Lawren Harris was experimenting with dynamic symmetry at this time. Dynamic symmetry, 'a mathematical system of composition . . . based on the relationship of the diagonal to the sides of a rectangle,' [83] was derived by its author, Jay Hambidge, [84] from a study of ancient Egyptian painting and Greek vases. [85] This system purported to be a compositional aid in the solution of space problems and was popular in the United States during the twenties, being used by such artists as George Bellows, Robert Henri, and Leon Kroll. [86] Franz Johnston, one of the original Group of Seven, used it from the mid-twenties [87] and it was taught at the Roerich art school in New York. [88] Emil Bisttram, one of the members of the Transcendental Painting Group, was an authority on dynamic symmetry, [89] and Bess Harris studied it with Bisttram while in New Mexico. [90] Certain aspects of the system, such as the concept of a mathematical 'law' derived from ancient sources, would appeal to Lawren Harris's theosophic interests.

Lawren Harris enjoyed New Mexico, the purity of its air, the altitude, and the convivial surroundings, as well as his involvement with the Transcendental painters. He had no plans to return to Canada. However, with the outbreak of the Second World War, the Canadian government blocked the export of funds from Canada, and he had to leave. [91] He visited Vancouver in October 1940 [92] and decided to stay the winter. [93] He was to remain there for the next thirty years.

1. L.L. FitzGerald, Chronology (dated 1953), in his 'Journal'; private property. He attended classes at the Art Students League from November 1921 to March 1922.
2. The earliest extant correspondence between FitzGerald and any member of the Group is a letter from J.E.H. MacDonald dated 10 February 1928; private property.
3. Bertram Brooker, Toronto, to L.L. FitzGerald, Winnipeg, 28 December 1929; private property.
4. FitzGerald kept a diary of this trip which, however, does not include the period of his visit to Montreal, Ottawa, and Toronto. In the 1953 chronology he notes these stops. Lawren Harris later wrote FitzGerald regretting having missed him during his visit to Toronto. (Lawren Harris, Toronto, to L.L. FitzGerald, Winnipeg, 23 November 1930; private property.)
5. Arthur Lismer, Toronto, to Eric Brown, Ottawa, 21 April 1932; in The National Gallery of Canada.
6. An exhibition of works by the Group of Seven was held in Hart House at the University of Toronto in December 1932. See Chap. I, n. 32.
7. L.L. FitzGerald, Winnipeg, to H.O. McCurry, Ottawa, 6 July 1932; in The National Gallery of Canada.
8. L.L. FitzGerald, Chronology, in his 'Journal'; private property. On this trip he visited Minneapolis, Chicago, Pittsburgh, Washington, Philadelphia, New York, Montreal, Ottawa, and Toronto.
9. *Idem*. On this trip he visited Ottawa and Toronto.
10. From unpublished notes quoted in Ferdinand Eckhardt, *L.L. FitzGerald 1890 – 1956. A Memorial Exhibition* (exhibition catalogue) (Winnipeg: The Winnipeg Art Gallery, 1958).
11. L.L. FitzGerald, Winnipeg, to H.O. McCurry, Ottawa, 18 March 1937; in The National Gallery of Canada.
12. From unpublished notes quoted in Ferdinand Eckhardt, *op. cit.*
13. *Idem.*
14. L.L. FitzGerald, 'Journal,' entry for 7 June 1930; private property.
15. *Idem.*
16. L.L. FitzGerald, Winnipeg, to Eric Brown, Ottawa, 22 April 1936; in The National Gallery of Canada.
17. L.L. FitzGerald, Winnipeg, to H.O. McCurry, Ottawa, 18 March 1937; in The National Gallery of Canada.
18. L.L. FitzGerald, Winnipeg, to Bertram Brooker, [Toronto], 17 June 1935; property Estate of M.A. Brooker.
19. L.L. FitzGerald, 'Journal,' entry for 29 June 1930; private property.
20. *Idem.*
21. David Milne, Weston, to H.O. McCurry, Ottawa, [October 1929]; in The National Gallery of Canada.
22. *Idem.*
23. David Milne, Palgrave, to James Clarke, [Yonkers, N.Y.], 27 May 1930; in the Public Archives of Canada.
24. David Milne, Palgrave, to H.O. McCurry, Ottawa, 23 February 1931; in The National Gallery of Canada. See also Vincent Massey, *What's Past is Prologue* (Toronto: Macmillan Company of Canada, 1963), p. 88.
25. David Silcox, 'Introduction,' *David Milne 1882 – 1953* (exhibition catalogue) (Kingston: Agnes Etherington Art Centre, Queen's University, 1967).
26. *Exhibition of Little Pictures by David B. Milne* (exhibition catalogue) (Toronto: Mellors Galleries, 1936).
27. Emily Carr used words in a similar way. 'It seems to me it helps to write things and thoughts down. It makes the unworthy ones look more shamefaced and helps to place the better ones for sure in our minds. It sorts out jumbled up thoughts and helps to clarify them,

and I want my thoughts clear and straight for my work.' (Emily Carr, *Hundreds & Thousands* [Toronto: Clarke, Irwin & Company Limited, 1966], p. 20.)

28. David Milne, Big Moose (N.Y.), to James Clarke, Yonkers (N.Y.), 13 November 1927; in the Public Archives of Canada.

29. *Idem.*

30. David Milne, Temagami, to James Clarke, Yonkers (N.Y.), 21 June 1929; in the Public Archives of Canada, published in David Silcox, *David Milne (1882 – 1953) A Survey Exhibition* (exhibition catalogue) (Montreal: Galerie Godard Lefort, 1971).

31. David Milne, Palgrave, to H.O. McCurry, Ottawa, 17 March 1931; in The National Gallery of Canada.

32. David Milne, Palgrave, to James Clarke, Yonkers (N.Y.), 10 April 1932; in the Public Archives of Canada.

33. David Milne to Donald Buchanan, quoted in Donald W. Buchanan, 'David Milne as I Knew Him,' *Canadian Art,* vol. xi, no. 3 (Spring 1954), p. 90.

34. David Milne, Severn Park, to H.O. McCurry, Ottawa, 15 February 1934; in The National Gallery of Canada.

35. As with the Group of Seven, artists could exhibit with the Canadian Group of Painters by invitation only.

36. David Milne, Severn Park, to H.O. McCurry, Ottawa, 15 February 1934; in The National Gallery of Canada.

37. David Milne, Severn Park, to James Clarke, Yonkers (N.Y.), 14 June [1934] (continued 28 June); in the Public Archives of Canada.

38. David Milne, Severn Park, to James Clarke, Yonkers (N.Y.), 22 November 1934; in the Public Archives of Canada.

39. Toronto, Mellors Galleries, 27 November – 8 December 1934, *Exhibition of Paintings by David B. Milne.* This exhibition was also sent to James Wilson & Company in Ottawa and W. Scott & Sons in Montreal.

40. Toronto, Mellors Galleries, through November [1935], *Exhibition of Paintings by David B. Milne;* Toronto, Mellors Galleries, 24 October – 7 November 1936, *Exhibition of Little Pictures by David B. Milne;* Toronto, Mellors Galleries, 15 – 29 January 1938, *Exhibition of Recent Pictures by David B. Milne.*

41. H.O. McCurry, Ottawa, to Mrs Vincent Massey, Port Hope, 25 October 1934; copy in The National Gallery of Canada.

42. Donald W. Buchanan, Ottawa, to David B. Milne, Severn Park, 30 October 1934; property of David Milne, Jr, Toronto.

43. Donald W. Buchanan, 'Milne – An Artist In a Forest Hut,' *Lethbridge Herald* (2 November 1934); Donald W. Buchanan, 'An Artist Who Lives In The Woods,' *Saturday Night,* vol. L, no. 4 (1 December 1934), p. 2; Donald W. Buchanan, 'David Milne,' *The Canadian Forum,* vol. xv, no. 173 (February 1935), pp. 191 – 193.

44. Alan Jarvis, 'Douglas Duncan,' in Pierre Théberge, *Gift from the Douglas M. Duncan Collection and the Milne-Duncan Bequest* (exhibition catalogue) (Ottawa: The National Gallery of Canada, 1971), p. 28. Reprinted in Alan Jarvis, ed., *Douglas Duncan A Memorial Portrait* (Buffalo, Toronto: University of Toronto Press, 1974), p. 10.

45. Toronto, Picture Loan Society, 10 – 24 December [1938], *Exhibition of Colour Drypoints by David B. Milne.*

46. David Milne, Severn Park, to Mr and Mrs Massey, London, 1 September 1938; in the Public Archives of Canada.

47. Alan Plaunt and his wife, now Mrs Dyde, were important collectors and supporters of contemporary Canadian art in the late thirties, before his early death in 1941. See J.F.B. Livesay, 'Alan Plaunt, An Appreciation,' *The Ottawa Journal* (15 September 1941).

48. David Milne, Severn Park, to James Clarke, Yonkers (N.Y.), 11 June 1933; in the Public Archives of Canada.

49. David Milne, Severn Park, to Graham C. McInnes, Toronto, 16 February 1938; in the Public Archives of Canada.

50. David Milne, Toronto, to Donald Buchanan, [Ottawa?], 14 January 1940; in The National Gallery of Canada.

51. Bess Harris, Hanover, to Doris Spiers, [Toronto?], 14 November 1934; property of Doris Spiers, Pickering (Ontario).

52. A number of these New Hampshire drawings are in the collection of the artist's son, Howard Harris, Vancouver.

53. Bess Harris and R.G.P. Colgrove, *Lawren Harris* (Toronto: The Macmillan Company of Canada Limited, 1969), p. 97 repr.

54. An abstraction by Lawren Harris of about the same date and similar composition is entitled *Mountain Experience* (Collection of the University of Manitoba Library, Winnipeg). See 'Art on the Campus, '*The Alumni Journal / University of Manitoba,* vol. 23, no. 4. (Summer 1963), p. 8 repr. (cropped).

55. Quoted in Sydney Key, 'The Paintings,' *Lawren Harris Paintings 1910 – 1948* (exhibition catalogue) (Toronto: The Art Gallery of Toronto, October 1948), p. 32. In later essays Lawren Harris expanded these categories to three and then four. However, as this was his earliest statement and apparently referred to his own summation of his development to that date, I shall only refer to these two categories.

56. The arctic reference of *Riven Earth I* is confirmed by hanging icicles in *Riven Earth II* in the collection of Mrs Charles S. Band, Toronto. (Bess Harris and R.G.P. Colgrove, *op. cit.,* p. 108 repr.)

57. Lawren S. Harris, 'Revelation of Art in Canada,' *The Canadian Theosophist,* vol. vii, no. 5 (15 July 1926), p. 86.

58. My thanks to Peter Larisey for informing me of this inscription.

59. Both artists had works included in the *International Exhibition of Modern Art,* assembled by the Société Anonyme and brought to Toronto by Lawren Harris and exhibited at The Art Gallery of Toronto, 1 – 24 April 1927. Kandinsky had three works: *Whimsical Line, Gaiety* (repr. cat.), and *Rote Tiefe.* Mondrian had two works: *Clarification I* and *Clarification II.*

60. Sixten Ringbom, 'Art in "The Epoch of the Great Spiritual." Occult Elements in the Early Theory of Abstract Painting,' *Journal of the Warburg and Courtauld Institute,* vol. 29 (1966), pp. 386 – 418. Robert P. Welsh, 'Mondrian and Theosophy,' in *Piet Mondrian 1872 – 1944* (exhibition catalogue) (New York: The Solomon R. Guggenheim Museum, 1971), pp. 35 – 51.

61. Annie Besant and C.W. Leadbeater, *Thought Forms* (Adyar, India: The Theosophical Publishing House, 1925). One of the artists who illustrated the original 1901 edition of this book was John Varley, a follower of Madame Blavatsky, and probably a relative of Fred Varley.

62. 'Thought Forms,' *The Canadian Theosophist,* vol. vii, no. 4 (15 June 1926), p. 77. My thanks to Dennis Reid for bringing this and the article by Sixten Ringbom to my attention.

63. In the artist's library, presently the property of his children, is a book by Oskar Rainer, *Musikalische Graphik. Studien und Versuche über die Wechselbeziehungen Zwischen Ton und Farbharmonien* (Musical Art. Studies and Experiments in the Interlations Between Tone and Colour Harmonies) (Vienna, Leipzig, New York: Deutscher Verlag für Jungen und Volk Gessellschaft, 1925).

64. Wassily Kandinsky, trans. Michael Sadleir, adapt. Francis Golffing and others, *Concerning the Spiritual in Art* (New York: George Wittenborn, Inc., 1947), p. 58 – 61.

65. Toronto, The Art Gallery of Toronto, November 1937, *Canadian Group of Painters.* Exhibited at the Art Association of Montreal, January 1938.

66. Toronto, The Art Gallery of Toronto, November 1939, *Canadian Group of Painters*. Exhibited at the Art Association of Montreal, January 1940.

67. Arthur Lismer, 'Art in a Changing World,' *Canadian Comment*, vol. IV, no. 2 (February 1935), p. 23.

68. Graham McInnes, 'Upstart Crows,' *The Canadian Forum*, vol. XVI, no. 184 (May 1936), p. 16.

69. Quoted in Fred Housser, Toronto, to Arthur Lismer, South Africa, 20 July 1936; in The McMichael Canadian Collection.

70. San Francisco Golden Gate International Exposition (1939), *Contemporary Art*. Lawren Harris did exhibit an abstract in the United States section of the exhibition (no. 169, *Composition*).

71. A.Y. Jackson, Toronto, to H.O. McCurry, Ottawa, 14 February [1938]; in The National Gallery of Canada.

72. Lawren Harris, Prout's Neck (Maine), to Eric Brown, Ottawa, 28 July 1938; in The National Gallery of Canada.

73. Raymond Jonson, Albuquerque (N.M.), to Peter Larisey, Ottawa, 14 November 1973; property of Peter Larisey, Ottawa. My thanks to Peter Larisey for making this letter available to me and for his extensive assistance with my research into Lawren Harris's work in the United States.

74. Lawren Harris, St. Catharines (Ont.), to Eric Brown, Ottawa, 23 September 1938; in The National Gallery of Canada. Lawren Harris returned to Santa Fe via Montreal where he had his portrait painted by Lilias Newton (A.Y. Jackson, Toronto, to H.O. McCurry, Ottawa, 3 August 1938; in The National Gallery of Canada.)

75. Alfred Morang, 'The Transcendental Painting Group,' Santa Fe *The New Mexico Daily Examiner* (21 August 1938), Magazine Section, p. 3. The Group was founded on 10 June 1938. Lawren Harris is not listed as a member in this article.

76. *Idem.* This article, written by a supporter of the Group, is interesting for its rejection of theosophy and its linking of mystical cultures with the rise of fascism.

77. *Transcendental Painting Group,* pamphlet, n.d. Members listed include Raymond Jonson (Chairman), Bill Lumpkins (Secretary Treasurer), and Lawren Harris from Santa Fe, Emil Bisttram, Robert Gribbrock, Florence Miller, and H. Towner Pierce from Taos, Agnes Pelton from Cathedral City, California, and Stuart Walker from Albuquerque, New Mexico.

78. 'The Transcendental Movement Opens a New Period in the American Arts,' Santa Fe *The New Mexico Daily Examiner* (21 August 1938), Magazine Section, p. 3.

79. Alfred Morang, *Transcendental Painting* (Santa Fe: American Foundation for Transcendental Painting, Inc., August 1940).

80. New York, World's Fair, 1939, *American Art Today* (exhibition catalogue). Lawren Harris exhibited *Composition No. 10* (no. 211, repr. p. 92).

81. Alfred Morang, 'Transcendental Painting Group Invited to Send Examples to Guggenheim,' Santa Fe *New Mexican* (11 April 1940).

82. New York, Museum of Non-Objective Painting, 14 May – 27 June 1940, *Twelve American Non-Objective Painters*; New York, Museum of Non-Objective Painting, 6 August – 30 September 1940, *Six American Non-Objective Painters*.

83. Milton W. Brown, *American Painting from the Armory Show to the Depression* (Princeton: Princeton University Press, 1955), p. 164.

84. Jay Hambidge was born in Canada and was a close friend of C.W. Jefferys ('Hambidge Dead, But Left A Great Legacy,' *Toronto Daily Star,* 1 February 1924).

85. Jay Hambidge wrote several books on dynamic symmetry, the first being *Dynamic Symmetry* (Boston: n.p., 1919).

86. Milton W. Brown, *op. cit.*, p. 164.

87. 'Johnston Never Member of the Group of Seven Is Exponent of Dynamic Symmetry,' Toronto *The Star Weekly* (11 October 1924).

88. L.L. FitzGerald, 'Journal', entry for 19 June 1930; private property.

89. Raymond Jonson, Albuquerque (N.M.), to Peter Larisey, Ottawa, 14 November 1973; property of Peter Larisey, Ottawa.

90. Bess Harris, Santa Fe, to Doris Spiers, [Toronto?], 19 February 1939; property of Doris Spiers, Pickering.

91. A.Y. Jackson, Toronto, to L.L. FitzGerald, Winnipeg, 19 November [1940]; private property.

92. Emily Carr, Victoria, to Nan Cheney, Vancouver, 13 October [1940]; in The University of British Columbia, Vancouver.

93. Lawren S. Harris, Toronto, to Raymond Jonson, Santa Fe, 28 November 1940; in the Jonson Archives, Jonson Gallery, The University of New Mexico, Albuquerque, N.M. This correspondence is also on microfilm in the Archives of American Art, Smithsonian Institution, Washington. My thanks to Jean-René Ostiguy for making typescripts of this correspondence available to me.

*42.
L.L. FITZGERALD
Doc Snider's House   1931

43.
L.L. FITZGERALD
Farm Yard 1931

*44.
L.L. FITZGERALD
Broken Tree in Landscape 1931

43.
L.L. FITZGERALD
Farm Yard 1931

*44.
L.L. FITZGERALD
Broken Tree in Landscape 1931

45.
L.L. FITZGERALD
The Pool   1934

46.
L.L. FITZGERALD
Jar   1938

*47.
DAVID MILNE
Blind Road   1930

*48.
DAVID MILNE
Splendour Touches Hiram's Farm   1932

49.
DAVID MILNE
Palgrave (I)   1931

50.
DAVID MILNE
Young Poplars Among Driftwood   1937

51.
DAVID MILNE
Raspberry Jam   1936

*52.
DAVID MILNE
Red Nasturtiums   1937

*53.
LAWREN S. HARRIS
Riven Earth I *c.* 1936

*54.
LAWREN S. HARRIS
Resolution *c.* 1937

*53.
LAWREN S. HARRIS
Riven Earth I *c.* 1936

*54.
LAWREN S. HARRIS
Resolution *c.* 1937

55.
LAWREN S. HARRIS
White Triangle   c. 1939

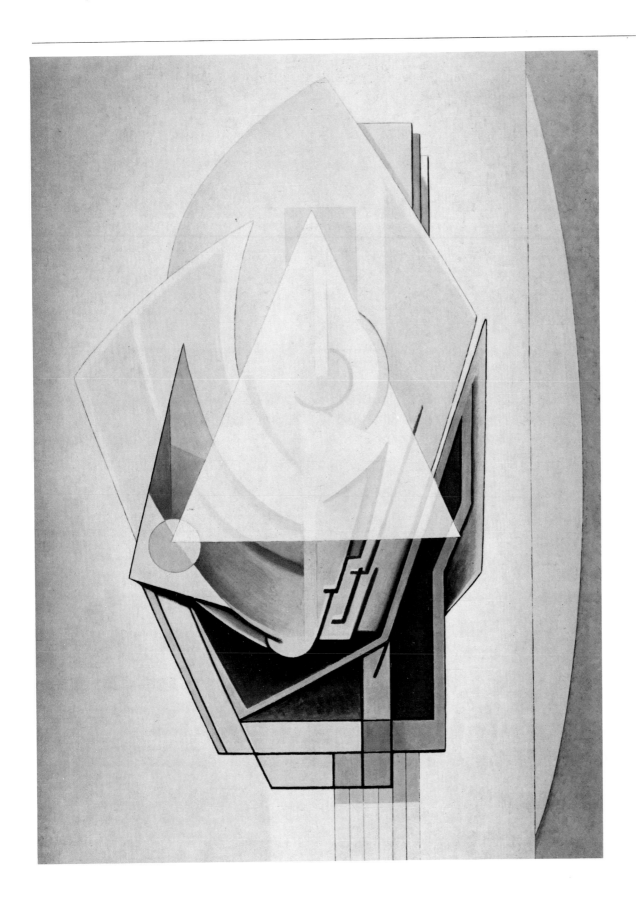

5. New Developments in the Canadian Group of Painters

While the Canadian Group of Painters was a national body and did offer young artists from across the country the opportunity to exhibit, it remained, during the thirties, a Toronto-dominated group. All organizational meetings and opening exhibitions were held in Toronto, the group's originators were Torontonians, and the Canadian Group was consciously identified as an expansion of the Toronto-based Group of Seven. This image survived the second Canadian exhibition in January 1936 with the addition of only one new member, André Biéler, to replace Thoreau MacDonald.[1] Tom Thomson's *West Wind*, according to Arthur Lismer, remained the symbol of the Group.[2]

Lawren Harris's departure from Toronto was a great blow to the Toronto art community.[3] He had been a great stimulator and enthusiast and there was no one to replace him. Personal animosities within the Canadian Group, resulting from his divorce, aggravated the situation.[4] Moreover, his departure occurred at the same time as many artists were having severe financial difficulties, and it seemed doubly difficult to pick up again and go on. There was even hesitation to hold a meeting while the president, Lawren Harris, was in the States.[5]

However, with the incorporation of the Canadian Group and the election of a new president, A.Y. Jackson, in 1936,[6] spirits began to revive. The Canadian Group finally fell into the hands of younger artists when Isabel McLaughlin was elected president in 1939. Anne Savage, Carl Schaefer, Charles Comfort, and George Pepper were elected to the executive.[7] Seven new artists were brought into the group in 1936,[8] and by 1942 the membership had expanded to forty-three.[9]

The strongest Toronto artist to develop the Group tradition into an individual expression was Carl Schaefer. Born on a farm near Hanover, Ontario, of German ancestry, he was raised by his father and maternal grandparents. He entered the Ontario College of Art in 1921 during the early days of the Group of Seven, studying under Arthur Lismer and J.E.H. MacDonald. He later worked with MacDonald on the decorations for Saint Anne's Church, the Claridge Apartments, and the Concourse Building in Toronto – and was staff designer with the T. Eaton Company for about a year until he was let off with sixteen others (out of a staff of eighteen) in 1930, the first year of the Depression.[10] He then worked freelance doing lettering and layout for Brigden's Limited, Eaton's, and occasionally for J.E.H. MacDonald. In the fall of 1930 Peter Haworth, head of the art department at Central Technical High School in Toronto offered him half a day a week teaching printing. This was increased to a full day two years later.[11]

While freelance commercial work was available in Toronto during the early thirties, pay was low. Schaefer was earning next to nothing teaching, and income from the sale of his art was pitifully low. With a family to support, he was unable to remain in Toronto the entire year, so from 1932 until he left for Vermont in 1940, he spent all his summers and Christmas holidays with his grandparents in Hanover.[12]

From an early age, Schaefer had been imbued with a feeling for the land around Hanover and with a love of history. Through J.E.H. MacDonald he encountered the writings of Walt Whitman and Thoreau whose robust love of democracy and nature held a great appeal for him. Returning to Hanover year after year, Carl Schaefer interpreted the landscape in all its many moods and facets, becoming a 'regionalist' artist in the truest sense of the term.

Schaefer's early paintings retain strong elements of design derived from his decorating work and from his admiration for Lawren Harris. In *Ontario Farmhouse* (1934, cat. no. 56) the foreground wheat field leading the viewer's vision into the picture, and the light shafts, are reminiscent of Lawren Harris's work, even to his interest in early Ontario architecture. However, unlike Harris's more picturesque rundown urban homes, Schaefer's house becomes a symbol of survival in the face of adversity. The dead tree, a recurring image in Schaefer's work, symbolizes both destruction and regeneration affirmed by the glowing gold of the wheat.

Carl Schaefer's sensitivity to the regenerative qualities of nature is also apparent in *Storm Over the Fields* (1937, cat. no. 57). The heavy stormclouds, derived from J.E.H. MacDonald's work of the early twenties, menace the countryside, casting dark shadows over the earth; yet in its midst glows a golden field. From the potential destruction of the storm comes rain and growth. The same work shows Schaefer's increasing freedom with the painting medium, the greater fluidity stressing the rhythms and modulations of the land.

However, by 1937 Carl Schaefer was becoming increasingly interested in watercolour and was painting few oils. His first efforts in this medium, resulting from a trip with Frank Carmichael and Joe Gauthier to Haliburton in 1932, were primarily stimulated by his interest in drawing,[13] though the medium had the added advantages of speed, immediacy, and low cost.

Fields with Stubble (1937, cat. no. 58) retains a certain linear quality, reflecting Schaefer's interest in the work of the Englishman Paul Nash.[14] There is a similar interweaving of rhythms and geometric organization of trees and clouds. However, most characteristic of his watercolours is the colouring. He applies them very dry in rust browns, brown-greens, and blacks, often creating a sense of unease, sterility, or death.[15]

8. Carl Schaefer, Hanover, Ontario, July 1936.

Shaefer's financial and professional situation improved during the late thirties. As well as teaching part-time at Central Technical High School, he taught at Hart House and at Trinity College School in Port Hope.[16] With the opening of the Picture Loan Society[17] and the interest of the collector J. S. McLean in his work, sales increased. Recognition of his work was growing.

In spite of this, an increasing sentiment of violence and death appears in Schaefer's painting of the late thirties. From his earliest works he had shown a great receptivity to the more awesome elements of nature, reflected in his interest in Northern European painters like Bruegel, Altdorfer, and Ruysdael. The Depression had affected him personally and accentuated this brooding, Gothic side of his personality. Being of German ancestry, with relatives still in Germany, he was increasingly conscious of the approach of war. Much of his work of 1939 and 1940 is painted in deathly greens and blacks, with sharp, angular projections, similar to the work of Charles Burchfield during the same period.[18] Others, like *Yellow Apples on a Fall Landscape* (1939, cat. no. 59) more subtly express this sentiment of impending menace. While the apples still hold out the possibility of abundance and regeneration, the storm clouds, dead trees, and autumn colours bespell decay. This aspect of Schaefer's work carried over into his Vermont paintings[19] and eventually into his war work.

A close friend and associate of Carl Schaefer during the thirties, was Charles Comfort. Born in Edinburgh, Comfort was brought to Winnipeg by his family in 1912. Two years later at the age of fourteen, he was employed by Brigden's of Winnipeg Limited.[20] In 1920, on a visit to Toronto, he saw the first Group of Seven exhibition. Overwhelmed by the strength and colour of the work, he determined to make his career in art.[21]

Charles Comfort spent the winter of 1922–1923 at the Art Students League, studying with Robert Henri and Euphrasius Allan Tucker[22] who introduced him to the work of contemporary American artists. Comfort returned to Winnipeg and married, and in April 1925 moved permanently to Toronto, still employed by Brigden's.[23]

The International Exhibition of Modern Art assembled by the Société Anonyme and shown in Toronto in 1927 had a great impact on Charles Comfort's commercial work and he furthered a successful career in this field. In 1929 he signed a two-year contract with Rapid-Grip to work on Canadian National Railway publicity. However, with the Crash in October of that year, all railway work was cancelled, and two years later Comfort found himself unemployed. He then opened a commercial studio with Harold Ayres and Will Ogilvie which was successful though profits lean.[24]

Charles Comfort's most striking works of the late twenties and early thirties are large full-length portraits in oil and watercolour. The *Portrait of John Creighton* (1931–1933, cat. no. 60), originally full-length though later cut down by the artist,[25] shows Comfort's strength in expressive characterization of his sitters, achieved through the use of dramatic lighting and concentration on the hands.

In *Young Canadian* (1932, cat. no. 61), a portrait of Carl Schaefer, the hands are again used to dramatize the sitter. The rock and barn, framing the horizontal clouds, focus attention on the staring eyes. With its sombre tones and expectant pose, it truly does characterize the mood and situation of many Canadians at the time.

Charles Comfort's reputation as a 'virtuoso'[26] was well merited, yet, at the same time, it was one of his greatest dangers. His commercial work demanded instantaneous, eye-catching effects. Incorporated into his paintings these same effects occasionally caused inner strength to be sacrificed for immediacy.

While visiting a former Winnipeg friend, Robert Fawcett, in Ridgefield, Connecticut, in 1933, Charles Comfort met the American Precisionist, Charles Sheeler.[27] Comfort's work already showed a certain affinity with that of the Precisionists, as seen in his painting *Lumber Town* of 1932.[28] However, in *Tadoussac* (1935, cat. no. 62), commissioned by Vincent Massey before Massey left for England,[29] the artist carried this simplification of form to the extreme. The smooth curve of the peninsula, the wood-block houses, and the lovely expanse of blue water blending into the sky create a feeling of great serenity, so different from his usually more concentrated and dynamic portrayals.

Charles Comfort was the only Canadian artist during the thirties to have the opportunity to work on a number of mural projects. Few post offices in Canada – unlike those in the United States – bore decorations by native artists; there was no system of government patronage. The Toronto architect Ferdinand Marani[30] commissioned Comfort's first mural in 1932 for the North American Life Building.[31] In 1936, taking its cue from the San Francisco Exchange,[32] the Toronto Stock Exchange invited Charles Comfort to paint eight large panels for their new building. Painted on canvas sixteen feet high and four feet wide (4.87 x 1.21 m) they represent the main industries of the Exchange: transportation and communication, mining, smelting, pulp and paper, refining, agriculture, oil, and construction (fig. 9).[33] In the Luncheon Club of the San Francisco Exchange, the Mexican Communist artist Diego Rivera had combined such industries as mining, forestry, and oil in one organic whole dominated by the massive figure of the goddess of nature.[34] Charles

9. Charles F. Comfort, Sketches for the murals in The
Toronto Stock Exchange, 1936.
Left to right: Construction, Smelting, Agriculture.

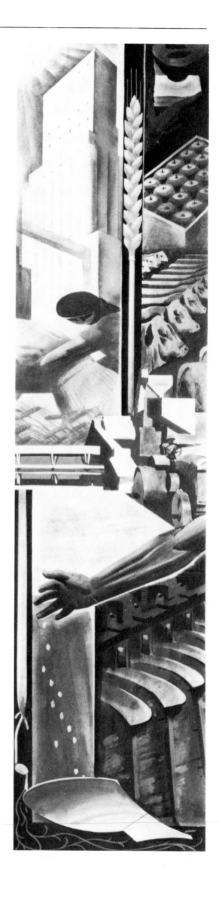

Comfort breaks up the different components of each industry with arbitrary geometric divisions, and abrupt changes in perspective and proportion derived from Thomas Benton's murals in the New School for Social Research in New York.[35] In the panel devoted to construction this is used with great effectiveness. However, where Rivera's and Benton's figures have a naturalism and individuality stressing the humanity of the persons depicted, Charles Comfort's workers become mechanical units arranged in anonymous rows and swamped by the dynamism of industry. Even in the panel of Agriculture, the most 'organic' industry, the cows are aligned in docile rows for slaughter and the kernels of wheat become gold coins of profit for the shareholders. Interpreted as a statement of faith in the recuperative powers of industry, or as a paean of praise for the Capitalist system, these murals are a curious, if not naïve, expression in the midst of the Depression.

In the spring of 1937, while he was completing these panels, Charles Comfort was commissioned by the International Nickel Company to do a large mural, *The Romance of Nickel*, for the Paris International Exposition. In this he used a similar dramatic perspective and geometricization of elements dominated by the large figure of a miner drilling.[36] In 1939, he painted the mural of *Captain George Vancouver* for the Hotel Vancouver.[37]

Charles Comfort won the first prize in the Great Lakes Exhibition of 'regional paintings' in Buffalo (1938) for his painting, *Lake Superior Village*,[38] and during the last years of the decade he became involved in art education. He started teaching mural-painting at the Ontario College of Art in 1935, and in 1938 joined the staff at the University of Toronto as a lecturer in the history of art.[39] His interest in fresco-painting and art history took him to Italy during the following summer.[40]

At the time of the formation of the Canadian Group of Painters, Charles Comfort and Bertram Brooker opposed the strong nationalist bias adopted by the new group.[41] Both these artists, during the late twenties were part of an active and outward-looking community in Toronto,[42] aware of international developments in art and literature.

Bertram Brooker had moved to Toronto from Winnipeg in 1921, and by 1926 was working as a freelance journalist to allow him more time for his own creative ventures.[43] His first abstractions, perhaps stimulated by his relationship with Lawren Harris and, through Harris, with the Société Anonyme,[44] as well as by his interest in music, were exhibited at the Arts & Letters Club in January 1927.[45]

Few of Brooker's works of the late twenties are pure abstractions: they combine abstracted concepts of spiritual awakening and natural phenomena with representational elements. While the earlier works are more flowing, employing naturalistic modelling and relying on the expressive qualities of colour, the later abstractions are more Cubist, perhaps influenced by the work of his friend Kathleen Munn. Munn, a former student at the Summer School of the New York Art Students League in Woodstock, New York, and a great admirer of the work of El Greco and Cézanne,[46] as early as 1923 was exhibiting Cubist paintings similar to those of Franz Marc.[47]

During the next few years, as well as painting, Bertram Brooker wrote a weekly art and literary column, 'The Seven Arts,' for the Southam Publishing Company,[48] illustrated an edition of *Elijah*,[49] wrote a book on advertising layout and another on copy writing,[50] and edited the *Yearbook of the Arts in Canada*.[51]

Visiting Winnipeg in the summer of 1929, Bertram Brooker met LeMoine FitzGerald[52] and, as a result, his painting took a sudden turn away from abstraction. On his return to Toronto, he wrote FitzGerald, 'Your attitude toward your work and your companionship in the few days I had with you have had a very considerable effect on me. . . . So far its effect has been that I have become perhaps too realistic . . . but I hope to grow out of that to a bigger appreciation of form – particularly. To boil it down to one word – form is the thing that obsesses me. Colour is no longer a thing that interests me for its own sake, as it did.'[53] This new concern for form and structure was reflected in his admiration for Edwin Holgate's nudes and the figure work of Prudence Heward.[54] Brooker himself, following the example of LeMoine FitzGerald,[55] began doing life studies. He had earlier commented on the resistance to nude figure painting in Canada,[56] but it was brought home to him more directly when The Art Gallery of Toronto refused to hang his own work, *Figures in Landscape*, after it had been accepted by the jury.[57]

Another object of the attacks of Toronto's Methodist puritans was Morley Callaghan, whose novel *It's Never Over*, had been criticized for its sexual content.[58] The winter following the controversy at the Art Gallery, Brooker painted Morley Callaghan's portrait (1932, cat. no. 63).[59] He was still primarily concerned with the construction of form through naturalistic modelling, especially noticeable in the face where certain areas appear almost overworked. However, the intersecting angles of the folds of the coat add a greater solidity to the body.

Bertram Brooker's concern for form naturally turned him to still-lifes. His first works followed a traditional format of objects arranged on a surface against a drapery backdrop. However, perhaps his most original contributions to this genre were combinations of interior scenes

10. Paraskeva Clark, Toronto, *c.* 1936.

and still-lifes, such as *Ski Poles* (1936, cat. no. 64). The
arbitrary perspective projects the objects forward, creating
a vertical as well as horizontal progression. The objects
are clearer and sharper and more carefully structured than
in the earlier still-lifes. In arrangement, concern for texture, and choice of typically Canadian subject matter, the
work parallels Charles Sheeler's classic American interiors
of the thirties.

Despite Toronto's proprietory forces, Bertram Brooker
continued to paint and exhibit female nudes. The 'Leda
and the swan' pose in *Torso* (1937, cat. no. 65) accentuates
the interrelationship of the different volumes and intersecting lines, as well as the eroticism of the subject. The
rough texture of the brush stroke, like that in FitzGerald's
Jar (cat. no. 46) creates an overall surface tension, contributing to the solidity of the forms.

David Milne, Charles Comfort, Bertram Brooker, and
even LeMoine FitzGerald turned away from the traditional
theme of contemporary Canadian art: landscape. The
concern for the 'formal' or 'aesthetic' qualities of painting
began to replace the stress on subject-matter. All these
artists received their stimulus from Cézanne, the Cubists,
or the Fauves through the United States, continuing an
American derivation of European Post-Impressionism.

Paraskeva Clark was the exception in this group of
artists, having arrived in Canada directly from Europe,
already a mature artist. Born in Leningrad, she received
her first art education in night courses at the Petrograd
Academy of Fine Arts, while working days in a shoe fac-
tory.[60] After the Revolution of 1917, the Academy became
'Free Studios' open to all persons interested in art. Paraskeva Clark spent three years, from 1918 to 1921, at the
Free Studios studying under Kuzma Petrov-Vodkin, a follower of Cézanne,[61] then worked in theatre decoration at
the Mali Theatre in Leningrad where she met her first
husband, Oreste Allegre. After the birth of a son, they
were preparing to leave for Paris when her husband
was drowned. Nonetheless, in the fall of 1923, Paraskeva
joined her father-in-law in Paris. Employed in an art-glass
store, she met Harry Adaskin, then studying in Paris, and
his friend Philip Clark. In June 1931 Paraskeva married
Philip Clark in London and moved to Toronto.[62]

Paraskeva Clark had had little opportunity to paint in
France; however, she soon met several artists in Toronto
and, motivated by the activity around her, began to paint
again. She was not overly impressed by the work of the
Toronto artists,[63] dominated as it was by landscape
painting in what she felt to be decorative patterns. She felt
more kinship with the Montreal artists who placed more
emphasis on structure.

One of the first works Paraskeva Clark exhibited in

Canada was her *Self-Portrait* (1933, cat. no. 66) in which she portrayed herself pregnant with her second child. The boldly structured figure shows her debt to Cézanne and, perhaps, to Picasso's classic heads. The roughly applied paint, the sharply receding background, and complex structure create a work of vigorous strength.

One of Paraskeva Clark's first Canadian landscapes was *Wheatfield* (1936, cat. no. 67), formerly in the collection of Douglas Duncan. In format and viewpoint it is similar to Carl Schaefer's Hanover works; yet where Schaefer creates a feeling of depth and solidity in the fields through flowing rhythm and fluid paint, Paraskeva uses a Cubist-derived pattern of intersecting straight lines. Her trees are more angular and the paint texture more coarse.

Having received her art training through the 'Free Studios' created by the Soviet government, Paraskeva Clark was naturally sympathetic to Leftist causes. Pegi Nicol introduced Paraskeva to Norman Bethune when he came to Toronto to set up the Medical Aid Committee[64] for Spain and she became active in the Committee to Aid Spanish Democracy.[65] From Spain, Norman Bethune sent her a page from a mediaeval missal and a scarf and cap of the International Brigade – all three of which she incorporated into a still-life, *Presents From Madrid*.[66]

Norman Bethune returned from Spain in June 1937, at the same time that Paraskeva Clark was working on *Petroushka* (1937, cat. no. 68). Instigated by a newspaper account of the murder of five strikers by Chicago police,[67] the painting depicts a puppet show in which a puppet policeman, egged on by the 'Capitalist,' beats a fallen worker while the audience naïvely laughs. The foreground worker raises the clenched fist of the Popular Front. The Futurist arrangement of the apartment houses, like a theatre backdrop, heightens the drama of oppression and resistance.

During the late thirties, Paraskeva Clark made several trips north of Toronto and to the Gatineau and turned increasingly to landscape and still-life painting. In *Trout* (1940, cat. no. 69), she combines a few ordinary objects in a carefully studied formal arrangement, projected forward by the arbitrary perspective. The paint texture and contrast of angles and curves create a dynamic construction.

Pegi Nicol, born near Ottawa,[68] studied for three years with Franklin Brownell, followed by a year at the École des Beaux-Arts in Montreal.[69] In 1928 she painted in the Skeena River area in British Columbia with Marius Barbeau[70] and in 1931 won the Willingdon Prize for her landscape, *The Log Run*.[71] She moved to Montreal about this time, rented a studio, and had an exhibition of her works;[72] however, her studio burned down in the fall of 1932 and she was forced to return to Ottawa.[73]

Pegi Nicol's figure work of the late twenties is very close to that of Edwin Holgate in composition, concern for structure, and concern for the plastic qualities of paint; however, her landscapes and studies of children (working in the school garden across the street from her parent's Ottawa house)[74] are more flowing, with graceful interweavings of arabesques. She first prepared watercolour sketches and occasionally worked them up in oil; the largest of these is *School in a Garden* (c. 1934, cat. no. 70). By the repeated curves of the bending figures and contours of the garden plots, and bright summer colours she expresses the joy of the children's work. She retained this interest in group activity and concern for humanity throughout her career.

After moving to Toronto in the fall of 1934,[75] Pegi Nicol became involved in theatre work and found employment preparing window displays for the T. Eaton Company under René Cera. Cera had come to Canada about 1929 to work in the new College Street store as head of design, and during the mid-thirties he offered work and much needed money to several of the younger artists, including Charles Comfort, Carl Schaefer, Paraskeva Clark, and Caven Atkins.[76] Pegi Nicol completed several projects for Cera, including the decoration of one of the Eaton's restaurants.[77]

In Pegi Nicol's works there is often a conflict between her innate spontaneity and the necessity of restraint to give some structure to her work. As she wrote herself, 'Spontaneity should be in the fingers. In me it was spontaneity in the mind.'[78] In *Descent of Lilies* (1935, cat. no. 71) the freedom of her fantasy is expressed with great control and direction. She creates a swirling vision of floating lilies, wildly kicking horses, and sensuous women, the whole 'integrated through the decorative arrangement of shapes, and color relationships.'[79]

Yet it is in her watercolours of Toronto street scenes that Pegi Nicol achieved the most direct expression of her love of life. In *Jarvis Street Sidewalk* (c. 1936, cat. no. 72), the costumed children parade along the sidewalk, the shadows and trees echoing their joy. The masked child on the bicycle is swiftly brushed in with a minimum of line expressive of the intensity of her need to paint and of her spontaneous fantasy.

Pegi Nicol was an active and popular member of the Toronto art community, contributing art criticism, drawings, and even an anti-fascist Christmas card to *The Canadian Forum*.[80] Through Norman Bethune she became involved in the Committee to Aid Spanish Democracy,[81] and, with Douglas Duncan and Gordon Webber, was one of the founders of the Picture Loan Society. Early in 1936 Pegi met Norman MacLeod, an engineer from Fredericton,

11. At the Kingston Conference, June 1941.
Left to right: Pegi Nicol MacLeod, A.Y. Jackson, André
Biéler, unidentified.

and married him in December. [82] Soon after they moved to New York and in the fall she gave birth to a daughter, Jane. [83]

Pegi Nicol MacLeod was overwhelmed by the New York art scene and found it difficult to find a niche in such a highly competitive environment. [84] She obtained work illustrating children's books, [85] but disliked commercial work. Feeling confined by her marriage and by Belleville, New Jersey, [86] she transferred her energies and affection into an almost obsessive relationship with her daughter, painting endless studies in watercolour and oil of Jane asleep, playing, reading, or painting. In *Children in Pliofilm* (1939, cat. no. 73), Jane flies across the streets of Belleville, over the heads of the other children, encased in the transparent pliofilm. The colours are brighter and more joyful than the sophisticated tones of *Descent of Lilies* (cat. no. 71).

The MacLeods moved back to Greenwich Village in New York in the fall of 1939, [87] and the following year, Pegi spent the first of many summers at the University of New Brunswick in Fredericton. [88]

The Maritimes were fallow ground for the visual arts during the early thirties. Efforts had been made during the previous decade to stimulate interest in the arts through the efforts of Elizabeth Nutt in Halifax, the art department at Mount Allison University, and Walter Abell at Acadia University in Wolfville, Nova Scotia. Exhibitions organized by The National Gallery, the College Art Association, and the American Federation of Arts toured the major centres and local art societies provided outlets for artists to exhibit their work. Commercial galleries were non-existent and public taste was extremely conservative.

Walter Abell received his appointment at Acadia University in 1928 [89] through a grant from the Carnegie Corporation. Recognizing the difficult situation of the arts in the Maritimes, he was instrumental in organizing the Maritime Art Association, a cooperative effort of art societies, clubs, and women's organizations in Nova Scotia, New Brunswick, and Prince Edward Island. Formed in the spring of 1935, [90] the new association toured exhibitions and lecturers, arranged distribution of educational material, promoted greater communication between the different centres and, most important, organized annual exhibitions of Maritime art to tour the provinces. In 1940 the association began the publication of *Maritime Art,* the first periodical in Canada, beyond art gallery bulletins, to be entirely devoted to art and providing national information about Canadian art and artists. [91]

One artist aware of the lack of support for artists was Jack Humphrey. Born in Saint John, he spent three years, from 1920 to 1923, at the School of the Museum of Fine Arts in Boston and then transferred to the National Academy of Design in New York [92] where he met Charles Hawthorne. An extremely popular teacher with his own art school at Provincetown, Hawthorne's teaching concentrated on the relationship of colours, the importance of silhouette, and the creation of form through colour. [93] Jack spent five summers at Provincetown studying with Hawthorne and retained a life-long admiration for his teacher. [94]

While Jack Humphrey planned to stay at Provincetown for the winter of 1929, relatives offered to send him to Europe [95] and in October he sailed for France. In Paris he visited museums and galleries, being especially interested in contemporary work, [96] and sketched in the open studios of the Academies. [97] On the recommendation of fellow Hawthorne students [98] he went to Munich studying three months with Hans Hofmann. [99] He then spent several months travelling in Italy, France, and Holland returning to Saint John in the summer of 1930.

The most immediate result of Jack Humphrey's European trip was a greater appreciation of the work of Cézanne as is seen in *Studio Chair and Still-Life* (1932, cat. no. 74). The selection of objects follows Hawthorne's dictates to find beauty in commonplace things. However, whereas Hawthorne emphasized careful modulation of form, Humphrey concerns himself with the more plastic qualities of form in earthy, almost sombre, colours, stressing the structure of the component units and their interrelationship.

This same concern for formal organization is seen in *Untitled (Houses)* (1931, cat. no. 75), the watercolour being quickly washed over the charcoal drawing in a Cubist arrangement similar to the work of the American artist John Marin. The sparse laying-on of colour and line in faceted planes creates a feeling of great dynamism and terseness, yet is ordered in a careful harmony.

Having studied in the United States for nine years, he naturally considered moving there when he returned from Europe. His father's wholesale firm had closed and the Depression had paralyzed the province. Jack wrote to Eric Brown, 'When the economic depression relaxes, unless more favourable opportunity offers itself, I have the exceedingly unpleasant prospect of returning to some form of unskilled and ill paid labor at night in New York City in order to attempt to support the thus impoverished efforts of contributing to art and civilization by day.' [100]

Determined to continue with his art, he sought teaching jobs in the States and in Toronto, but without success. As Arthur Lismer wrote him, 'There are dozens at present who are teaching to earn a living.' [101]

During the summer of 1933, Jack Humphrey visited relatives in Vancouver, working as a guard for immigration prisoners being transferred across Canada,[102] returning that fall via Ottawa[103] and Montreal. Through his cousin John Humphrey, he met John Lyman, Jori Smith, and her husband Jean Palardy, and he stayed with the Palardys for a few months[104] before returning to Saint John.[105]

On the recommendation of Arthur Lismer, Jack Humphrey started children's classes in his studio;[106] however, students were few. The paucity of sales and indifference to his work accentuated the bitterness of his love-hate relationship with Saint John.[107] Wanting to leave, with nowhere to go, he was at the same time wedded to an environment he knew: the streets and people of Saint John. As Walter Abell, his main support at this time, wrote him, 'You have cast your lot for the first factor [to be able to work] choosing to pursue your creative work above all else, and unfortunately sacrificing a living to it.'[108]

Walter Abell managed to sell Jack's watercolours in the Maritimes; however, it was only when his work was brought to the attention of Toronto critics that his situation began to improve. An article by Walter Abell in *The Canadian Forum*,[109] a show of his work at Macdonald Galleries,[110] the interest of Graham McInnes, and an exhibition of watercolours at the Picture Loan Society[111] finally brought his work to public attention.

Early in 1938, a bequest from a friend[112] enabled Jack Humphrey to visit Mexico for a few months,[113] resulting in over a hundred watercolours and drawings[114] which were exhibited at the Picture Loan Society the following spring.[115] In the fall of 1938 John Lyman invited Jack to join the newly founded Eastern Group in Montreal,[116] and soon after he became one of the charter members of the Contemporary Arts Society.[117]

Perhaps for reasons of economy, Jack Humphrey concentrated predominantly on watercolour during the mid-thirties. With increasing sales he returned to oil and, perhaps stimulated by the work of Miller Brittain,[118] began to experiment with new techniques. *Charlotte* (1939, cat. no. 76), painted in oil over tempera, reverts to the work of Hawthorne in its concentration on silhouette and painterly brush-stroke. There is no longer the concern for structural relationships seen in the earlier works, but a greater concentration on mood and character.

Miller Brittain rented a studio next door to Jack Humphrey in the fall of 1938. He had studied at the Art Students League in New York, intending to work as a commercial illustrator; however, his teacher, Harry Wickey, introduced him to the work of Rembrandt, Hogarth, and Goya and he 'was completely lost when [he] tried to turn out the tricky slap-dash demanded by art

directors.'[119] He returned to Saint John in 1932 after two years at the League and worked at various construction and office jobs.[120]

Sometime during the thirties, Frank Buchman, founder of the Oxford Group, lectured in Saint John, and Miller Brittain, swept up by the talk, for a short period became an active worker for the Group.[121] A Christian movement, the Oxford Group stressed 'moral rearmament' and a Christian solution to social issues and took a great interest in the problems of workers and unions.

Miller Brittain expressed his social commitment in large charcoal drawings, in which he documented and satirized the contemporary scene. B.K. Sandwell became interested in his drawings and reproduced them in the magazine he edited, *Saturday Night*, bringing Miller's work to public attention for the first time.[122] As Graham McInnes noted, Miller Brittain's drawings are the sole example of social satire in Canadian art of the thirties.[123]

The proximity of their studios resulted in certain parallels between the work of Miller Brittain and Jack Humphrey around 1940. *Edith White* (1939, cat. no. 77) by Humphrey and *Master McCullough* (1939, cat. no. 78) by Brittain both follow a fifteenth-century Italian portrait composition adopted by Reginald Marsh and other artists of the New York Fourteenth Street School. However, Humphrey's work is more painterly, the surface mat, and its psychological concentration less intense. Brittain's work verges on caricature, its linear treatment accentuated by the use of egg tempera and glazes.[124] The portraits of the young newspaper boy and girl, prematurely old and sombre, are expressive documents of the Depression years.

From single figures, Miller Brittain moved to larger, social themes. In *Longshoremen* (1940, cat. no. 79) he uses a German Renaissance composition, linking the men by telling gestures and glances. The massive figures are crowded into a confined space, accentuating the intensity of the scene. In his paintings of the next few years, Miller Brittain depicted his human environment in all its political and social aspects. He wrote, 'I have no patience with those individuals who think of pictures merely as embellishments to a decorative scheme . . . . A picture ought to emerge from the midst of life and be in no sense divorced from it . . . . And I think artists should be rooted in their native heath . . . . And they will be so if their life and work are one and the same.'[125]

12. At the Kingston Peninsula, New Brunswick, *c.* 1937. Left to right: Miller Brittain, Kjeld Deichmann, Jack Humphrey.

NOTES TO CHAPTER 5

1. 'Members "Canadian Group of Painters,"' *Catalogue of an Exhibition of Paintings by the 'Canadian Group of Painters'* (Toronto: The Art Gallery of Toronto, 1936).
2. A.L. [Arthur Lismer], 'Foreword,' *Ibid.*
3. A.Y. Jackson, Toronto, to Sarah Robertson, Montreal, [late November 1934]; in The National Gallery of Canada. A. Y. Jackson, Toronto, to L.L. FitzGerald, Winnipeg, 28 September [1935]; private property. Emily Carr, Victoria, to Nan Cheney, [Montreal?], 25 October [1935]; in The University of British Columbia, Vancouver.
4. Arthur Lismer, Toronto, to L.L. FitzGerald, Winnipeg, 12 February [1936]; private property.
5. Bertram Brooker, Toronto, to Mrs. L.L. FitzGerald, Winnipeg, 5 February 1935; copy property Estate of M.A. Brooker.
6. Arthur Lismer, Toronto, to L.L. FitzGerald, Winnipeg, 12 February 1936; private property. Fred Housser remained secretary of the Canadian Group of Painters.
7. Pearl McCarthy, 'Art and Artists,' Toronto *Globe and Mail* (29 July 1939).
8. A.Y. Jackson, Toronto, to H.O. McCurry, Ottawa, [received 13 January 1936]; in The National Gallery of Canada. New members included Carl Schaefer, Rody Courtice, Paraskeva Clark, Gordon Webber, Pegi Nicol, Kay Daly, and John Alfsen.
9. *Canadian Group of Painters* (Toronto: The Art Gallery of Toronto, 1942). New members included Mabel Lockerby, Kathleen Morris, Jack Humphrey, Ethel Seath, Louis Muhlstock, Caven Atkins, Henri Masson, David Milne, Lawren P. Harris, and Peter Haworth.
10. Carl Fellman Schaefer, 'Personal Reminiscences,' in J. Russell Harper, *Carl Schaefer Retrospective Exhibition / Paintings from 1926 to 1969* (exhibition catalogue) (Montreal: Sir George Williams University, 1969), pp. 4 – 6.
11. Interview with Carl Schaefer, Toronto, 11 October 1973.
12. *Ibid.*
13. *Ibid.*
14. Carl Fellman Schaefer, *op. cit.*, p. 8.
15. Similar colours appear in David Milne's watercolours painted during the war.
16. Carl Fellman Schaefer, *op. cit.*, p. 8.
17. The first solo exhibition at the Picture Loan Society was *Exhibition by Carl Schaefer*, 9 – 22 January 1937.
18. Carl Schaefer visited Charles Burchfield in Buffalo around 1937 and admired his work greatly. (Interview with Carl Schaefer, Toronto, 11 October 1973).
19. Carl Schaefer was the recipient of the J.S. Guggenheim Fellowship for Creative Painting in 1940, the first year it was offered to Canadian artists. He spent the year in Vermont. See Robert Ayre, 'Carl Schaefer The Industrious,' Montreal *Standard* (13 April 1940).
20. H.M. Jackson, *Charles Comfort, The Man and the Artist,* n.p. (Christmas 1935, New Year 1936).
21. Interview with Charles Comfort, Hull (Quebec), 3 October 1973.
22. Patricia E. Glover, *Charles Fraser Comfort / Fifty Years* (exhibition catalogue) (Winnipeg: The Winnipeg Art Gallery, 1973).
23. Interview with Charles Comfort, Hull (Quebec), 3 October 1973.
24. *Idem.*
25. Conversation with John Creighton, Vancouver, 21 November 1973.
26. Patricia E. Glover, *op. cit.*
27. Interview with Charles Comfort, Hull (Quebec), 3 October 1973.
28. *Lumber Town*, exhibited at the Canadian National Exhibition, Toronto, 1932 (no. 95) and reproduced in the catalogue. *Lumber Town, Unpainted Barn,* and *The Brothers* were left in storage at Hart

House during the war and could not be located when Charles Comfort returned to Toronto. (Interview with Charles Comfort, Hull (Quebec), 3 October 1973.)

29. Charles Comfort, Toronto, to H.O. McCurry, Ottawa, 15 November 1935; in The National Gallery of Canada.

30. Ferdinand Marani (Canadian, 1893 – 1971) was the architect of the Bank of Canada Building in Ottawa for which he commissioned Jacobine Jones to do the sculptural decoration.

31. Interview with Charles Comfort, Hull (Quebec), 3 October 1973.

32. John Lyman, 'Art,' The Montrealer (April 1937).

33. Robert Ayre, 'Toronto Stock Exchange Murals Greatly Stimulate Canadian Art,' Montreal Gazette (24 April 1937). Charles Comfort also designed the frieze across the front of the new building.

34. Hans F. Secker, Diego Rivera (Dresden: Verlag der Kunst, 1957), p. 177 repr. Rivera's mural was painted in 1930.

35. Interview with Charles Comfort, Hull (Quebec), 3 October 1973. See Lloyd Goodrich, 'The Murals of the New School,' The Arts, vol. XVII, no. 6 (March 1931), pp. 399 – 403, 422.

36. Graham C. McInnes, 'Mural – "Romance of Nickel,"' Saturday Night, vol. LII, no. 36 (10 July 1937), p. 6.

37. Robert Ayre, 'Murals in Our Public Buildings,' Saturday Night, vol. LV, no. 30 (25 May 1940), p. 2. This mural is presently in the Confederation Art Gallery and Museum, Charlottetown.

38. 'Artist's Work Wins Acclaim,' Toronto Globe and Mail (29 October 1938). Lake Superior Village (1937, oil on canvas; 42-1/2 x 70 in., 108.0 x 177.8 cm) is in the collection of the Art Gallery of Ontario. See Helen Bradfield, Art Gallery of Ontario: The Canadian Collection (Toronto: McGraw-Hill Company of Canada, 1970), p. 77 repr.

39. Interview with Charles Comfort, Hull (Quebec), 3 October 1973.

40. 'Toronto Artist Impressed by Art of Modern Italy,' The Toronto Telegram (19 August 1939).

41. Bertram Brooker, Toronto, to L.L. FitzGerald, Winnipeg, 20 March 1933; private property.

42. This community consisted of, among others, Lawren Harris and Dr Harold M. Tovell, chairman of The Art Gallery of Toronto's Exhibition Committee which brought the Société Anonyme exhibition to Toronto in 1927, and owner of Marcel Duchamp's Chess Players, now in the Louise and Walter Arensberg Collection, Philadelphia Museum of Art. See Anne D'Harnancourt and Kynaston McShine, Marcel Duchamp (exhibition catalogue) (New York: Museum of Modern Art, 1973), repr. p. 247. Others in this community were the writers Merrill Denison and Morley Callaghan, and Harry Adaskin of the Hart House Quartette.

43. Dennis Reid, Bertram Brooker 1888 – 1955 (Ottawa: The National Gallery of Canada, 1973), p. 10.

44. Lawren Harris was already in contact with Katherine Dreier by the summer of 1926 and two of his works were included in the International Exhibition of Modern Art (assembled by the Société Anonyme) at the Brooklyn Museum, 19 November 1926 to 1 January 1927.

45. 'New Young Toronto Artist Paints Subjective Group,' Toronto Daily Star (5 February 1927).

46. Conversation with Kathleen Munn, Toronto, 18 February 1974. It is uncertain when Bertram Brooker first met Kathleen Munn. The first reference to her by Brooker is in a letter to FitzGerald, 28 December 1929; private property.

47. The Dance (Collection of the Artist) was exhibited at Toronto, The Art Gallery of Toronto, 22 November 1923 – 2 January 1924, The Forty-Fifth Exhibition of The Royal Canadian Academy of Arts, no. 127.

48. Bertram Brooker wrote the column 'The Seven Arts' from October 1928 to November 1930.

49. Bertram Brooker, Elijah (New York: William Edwin Rudge, 1929).

50. Richard Surrey (pseudonym), Layout Technique in Advertising (New York: McGraw Hill, 1929) and Copy Technique in Advertising (New York: McGraw Hill, 1930).

51. Bertram Brooker, ed., Yearbook of the Arts in Canada, 1928 – 1929 (Toronto: The Macmillan Company of Canada Limited, 1929).

52. Bertram Brooker, Toronto, to Lawren Harris, [?] , 19 August 1929; copy property Estate of M.A. Brooker.

53. Bertram Brooker, Toronto, to L.L. FitzGerald, Winnipeg, 28 December 1929; private property.

54. Bertram Brooker, 'The Seven Arts,' Ottawa The Citizen (1 March 1930).

55. L.L. FitzGerald, Winnipeg, to Bertam Brooker, Toronto, 11 January [1930]; property Estate of M.A. Brooker.

56. Bertram Brooker, 'The Seven Arts,' Ottawa The Citizen (1 March 1930).

57. 'Nudes in Landscape Causes Art Dispute,' Toronto Daily Star (7 March 1931).

58. Bertram Brooker, 'Nudes and Prudes,' in William A. Deacon and Wilfred Reeves, eds, Open House (Ottawa: Graphic Publishers Limited, 1931), p. 97.

59. Bertram Brooker, Toronto, to L.L. FitzGerald, Winnipeg, 10 January [1932]; private property.

60. Conversation with Paraskeva Clark, Toronto, 30 January 1974.

61. Paraskeva Clark, Toronto, to H.O. McCurry, Ottawa, 3 June 1944; in The National Gallery of Canada.

62. Conversation with Paraskeva Clark, Toronto, 30 January 1974.

63. A.Y. Jackson, A Painter's Country (Toronto: Clarke, Irwin & Company Ltd., 1958), p. 119.

64. Pegi Nicol, Toronto, to Marian Scott, Montreal, [October 1936]; property of Marian Scott, Montreal. See also, Roderick Stewart, Bethune (Toronto: New Press, 1973), p. 90.

65. Paraskeva Clark, Toronto, to H.O. McCurry, Ottawa, 16 August 1939; in The National Gallery of Canada. At this time the Committee was attempting to bring Picasso's Guernica to Toronto to raise funds for Loyalist refugees.

66. Presents From Madrid (1937, watercolour on paper; 19 x 21 in., 48.3 x 53.4; private collection).

67. 'Five Steel Strikers Killed In Clash With Chicago Police,' Toronto Daily Star (1 June 1937).

68. She was born Margaret Nichol at Listowel, Ontario, 17 January 1904. ('Pegi Nichol MacLeod,' The National Gallery of Canada Information Form, 15 July 1942.)

69. Pegi Nicol attended the École des Beaux-Arts at the same time as Marian Scott, i.e., 1925 – 1926. (Interview with Marian Scott, Montreal, 15 September 1973.)

70. Eric Brown, Ottawa, to Emily Carr, Victoria, 8 October 1928; copy in The National Gallery of Canada.

71. The Willingdon Prize was offered by the Governor General of Canada, Lord Willingdon, from 1929 to 1931 when he left for India.

72. Montreal, The T. Eaton Co. Ltd., [February 1932], Pegi Nicol.

73. Interview with Marian Scott, Montreal, 15 September 1973.

74. Donald W. Buchanan, 'Pegi Nicol MacLeod 1904 – 1949,' Canadian Art, vol. VI, no. 4 (Summer 1949), p. 158.

75. Pegi Nicol spent the summer of 1934 with the Masseys in Port Hope (Pegi Nicol, Toronto, to Marian Scott, Montreal, [c. December 1934]; property of Marian Scott, Montreal) and prepared sets for a Hart House Theatre Production of 'The Piper' in December. See 'Vivacious Artist,' Saturday Night, vol. L, no. 14 (9 February 1935), p. 16.

76. Walter Abell, Toronto, to Jack Humphrey, Saint John, 15 July 1936; property of Mrs J.W. Humphrey, Saint John.

77. 'Causerie,' *The Canadian Forum*, vol. xv, no. 177 (August 1935), p. 323.

78. Pegi Nicol MacLeod, Belleville (N.J.), to Marian Scott, Montreal, [October 1938]; property of Marian Scott, Montreal.

79. Graham C. McInnes, 'Contemporary Canadian Artists No. 8 – Pegi Nicol,' *The Canadian Forum*, vol. xvii, no. 200 (September 1937), p. 202.

80. Pegi Nicol, 'Merry Christmas,' *The Canadian Forum*, vol. xvi, no. 191 (December 1936), p. 3.

81. Conversation with Paraskeva Clark, Toronto, 30 January 1974.

82. Pegi Nicol, Toronto, to Marian Scott, Montreal, [postmarked 17 December 1936]; property of Marian Scott, Montreal.

83. Pegi Nicol, New York City, to Marian Scott, Montreal, [autumn 1937]; property of Marian Scott, Montreal.

84. Interview with Marian Scott, Montreal, 15 September 1973.

85. Pegi Nicol MacLeod, Belleville (N.J.), to H.O. McCurry, Ottawa, [received 17 October 1938]; in The National Gallery of Canada.

86. Pegi Nicol MacLeod, Belleville (N.J.), to Marian Scott, Montreal, [autumn 1938]; property of Marian Scott, Montreal.

87. Pegi Nicol MacLeod, New York City, to Marian Scott, Montreal, [postmarked 19 September 1939]; property of Marian Scott, Montreal.

88. 'Association News: Fredericton Art Club,' *Maritime Art*, vol. i, no. 1 (October 1940), p. 27.

89. Conversation with Mrs Walter Abell, Ottawa, 12 June 1974.

90. Walter Abell, 'Co-operative Art in the Maritimes,' *Saturday Night*, vol. lii, no. 32 (12 June 1937), p. 7.

91. The first issue of *Maritime Art* is dated October 1940. *Maritime Art* was superceded by *Canadian Art* in 1943.

92. J. Russell Harper, 'A Painter in the Maritimes,' in *Jack Humphrey, A Retrospective Exhibition* (exhibition catalogue) (Fredericton: Beaverbrook Art Gallery, 1966), p. 7.

93. *Hawthorne on Painting From Students' Notes Collected by Mrs. Charles W. Hawthorne* (New York, Chicago: Pitman Publishing Corporation, 1938).

94. Jack Humphrey, Saint John, to Eric Brown, Ottawa, 7 May 1931; in The National Gallery of Canada. It is possible Jack Humphrey spent some time at the Art Students League in New York as among his papers is a student card in his name for the League for the year ending 1 October 1930. However, Humphrey left for Europe in October 1929.

95. Jack Humphrey, Provincetown, to Ruth Humphrey, [Victoria?], 10 June 1929; property of Ruth Humphrey, Vancouver.

96. Jack Humphrey, Paris, to Ruth Humphrey, [Victoria?], 8 November 1929; property of Ruth Humphrey, Vancouver.

97. Jack Humphrey, Paris, to Ruth Humphrey, [Victoria?], 16 December 1929; property of Ruth Humphrey, Vancouver.

98. J. Russell Harper, *op. cit.*, p. 8.

99. 'Jack Weldon Humphrey,' The National Gallery of Canada Information Form, [May 1931].

100. Jack Humphrey, Saint John, to Eric Brown, Ottawa, 7 May 1931; in The National Gallery of Canada.

101. Arthur Lismer, Toronto, to Jack Humphrey, Saint John, 3 July 1932; property of Mrs J.W. Humphrey, Saint John.

102. J. Russell Harper, *op. cit.*, p. 10.

103. Marius Barbeau, Ottawa, to Arthur Lismer, Toronto, 30 October 1933; in the Art Gallery of Ontario.

104. Interview with John Humphrey, Montreal, 18 September 1973.

105. Jack Humphrey, Saint John, to Arthur Lismer, Toronto, 26 January 1934; in the Art Gallery of Ontario.

106. 'St. John Artist to Hold Exhibition of Works May 10 to 12,' *Saint John Times-Globe* (4 May 1934).

107. Jack Humphrey, Saint John, to H.O. McCurry, Ottawa, 26 October 1935; in The National Gallery of Canada. 'I spent a few days in Grand Manan recently. Was a great relief after this preposterous hole of a city.'

108. Walter Abell, Wolfville (N.S.), to Jack Humphrey, Saint John, 19 June 1935; property of Mrs J.W. Humphrey, Saint John.

109. Walter Abell, 'Jack Humphrey – Painter,' *The Canadian Forum*, vol. xvi, no. 185 (June 1936), pp. 16 – 18.

110. Graham C. McInnes, 'World of Art,' *Saturday Night*, vol. lii, no. 14 (6 February 1937), p. 16. There was not a single sale from this exhibition. See A.A. Macdonald, Toronto, to Jack Humphrey, Saint John, 17 February 1937; property of Mrs J.W. Humphrey, Saint John.

111. Graham C. McInnes, 'World of Art,' *Saturday Night*, vol. liii, no. 14 (5 February 1938), p. 7.

112. Jack Humphrey, Saint John, to H.O. McCurry, Ottawa, 28 September 1937; in The National Gallery of Canada.

113. A.Y. Jackson, Toronto, to H.O. McCurry, Ottawa, 2 May [1938]; in The National Gallery of Canada.

114. Douglas Duncan, Toronto, to H.O. McCurry, Ottawa, 17 May 1938; in The National Gallery of Canada.

115. Graham C. McInnes, 'World of Art,' *Saturday Night*, vol. liv, no. 22 (1 April 1939), p. 20.

116. John Lyman, Montreal, to Jack Humphrey, Saint John, 23 September 1938; property of Mrs J.W. Humphrey, Saint John.

117. 'Contemporary Arts Society List of Artist Members,' Montreal, 16 May 1939; in The Montreal Museum of Fine Arts.

118. Pegi Nicol, 'Miller Brittain,' *Maritime Art*, vol i, no. 4 (April 1941), p. 17. Experimentation with new techniques became very popular in the United States during the late twenties and thirties, first at the Art Students League and later, at the Fogg Museum in Cambridge (Mass.), a research programme was conducted under the Works Progress Administration Federal Art Project. Participants in this project gave demonstrations at the Kingston Conference in 1941.

119. Artist's statement in Pegi Nicol, 'Miller Brittain,' *Maritime Art*, vol. i, no. 4 (April 1941), p. 17.

120. *Ibid.*, p. 16.

121. Interview with Ted Campbell, Saint John, 29 October 1973. The Oxford Group later developed into the Moral Rearmament movement.

122. Pegi Nicol, *op. cit.*, p. 15.

123. Graham C. McInnes, 'Contemporary Canadian Artists No. 11 – Miller Brittain,' *The Canadian Forum*, vol. xvii, no. 203 (December 1937), p. 312.

124. 'When in 1938 I began to paint seriously, I sought an approach that would enable me to give full expression to plastic surfaces, and finally found it in an egg-tempera medium combined with oil and varnish glazes in various ways.' See artist's statement in Pegi Nicol, *op. cit.*, p. 17.

125. Artist's statement in Pegi Nicol, *op. cit.*, pp. 17 – 18.

56.
CARL SCHAEFER
Ontario Farmhouse   1934

57.
CARL SCHAEFER
Storm Over the Fields   1937

*58.
CARL SCHAEFER
Fields with Stubble   1937

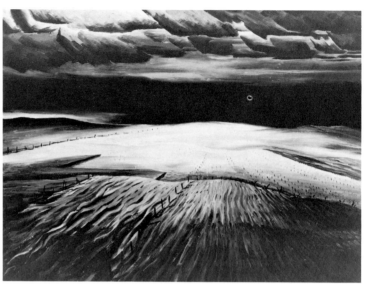

*59.
CARL SCHAEFER
Yellow Apples on a Fall Landscape   1939

*60.
CHARLES COMFORT
Portrait of John Creighton   1931 – 1933

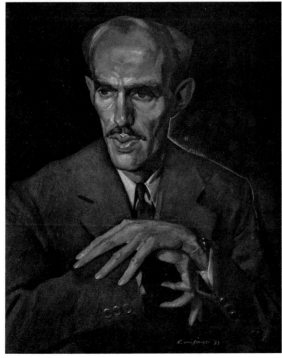

*61.
CHARLES COMFORT
Young Canadian   1932

62.
CHARLES COMFORT
Tadoussac 1935

*63.
BERTRAM BROOKER
Portrait of Morley Callaghan 1932

64.
BERTRAM BROOKER
Ski Poles   1936

65.
BERTRAM BROOKER
Torso   1937

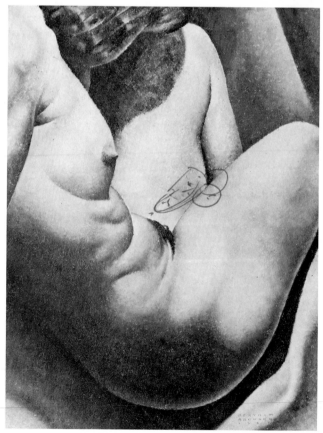

64.
BERTRAM BROOKER
Ski Poles   1936

65.
BERTRAM BROOKER
Torso   1937

66.
PARASKEVA CLARK
Self-Portrait   1933

***67.**
PARASKEVA CLARK
Wheat Field   1936

66.
PARASKEVA CLARK
Self-Portrait   1933

***67.**
PARASKEVA CLARK
Wheat Field   1936

68.
PARASKEVA CLARK
Petroushka   1937

*69.
PARASKEVA CLARK
Trout 1940

70.
PEGI NICOL MACLEOD
School in a Garden c. 1934

*71.
PEGI NICOL MACLEOD
Descent of Lilies 1935

*72.
PEGI NICOL MACLEOD
Jarvis Street Sidewalk   c. 1936

73.
PEGI NICOL MACLEOD
Children in Pliofilm   1939

*74.
JACK HUMPHREY
Studio Chair and Still-Life   1932

*75.
JACK HUMPHREY
Untitled (Houses)   1931

76.
JACK HUMPHREY
Charlotte   1939

77.
JACK HUMPHREY
Edith White   1939

***78.**
MILLER BRITTAIN
Master McCullough   1939

79.
MILLER BRITTAIN
Longshoremen 1940

6. Regionalist Manifestations in Quebec

As was English-speaking Montreal, the French-speaking art community was dominated by senior Royal Canadian Academicians. The painters Suzor-Coté and Edmond Dyonnet and the sculptors Alfred Laliberté and Henri Hébert were the most publicized artists in Quebec. Of the leading painters of the twenties, Clarence Gagnon was in Paris preparing illustrations for *Maria Chapdelaine*,[1] and Adrien Hébert was painting reticent urban scenes of the port of Montreal. The Quebec tradition of religious art, revived by the teachings of the French Symbolist Maurice Denis, was continued by Ozias Leduc and the younger artists Rodolphe Duguay and Paul-Émile Borduas.

One of the more popular contemporary Quebec artists at this time was Marc-Aurèle Fortin. Born in Sainte-Rose in 1888 he first studied under Ludger Larose and Edmond Dyonnet and then in Chicago, New York, and Boston. He returned to Canada about 1914; however, it was only in the mid-twenties that he began actively to pursue a painting career. His favourite themes were the large elms in small Quebec villages, hay wagons on country roads, and the flowing curves of Quebec farmhouses. Like that of the Group of Seven in Toronto, Fortin's style derived from the Art Nouveau decorative art of the turn of the century, specifically the work of Frank Brangwyn.[2]

Around 1930 he painted a series of views of Montreal seen from the area around his Notre Dame Street East apartment. *Landscape at Hochelaga* (c. 1931, cat. no. 80) breaks from the more delicate, earlier landscapes; the paint is applied with more firmness, the composition is more complex, and the contrast of colours is more striking. In its interplay of vibrating lines of colour and rolling rhythm it is close to J.E.H. MacDonald's *Gleams on the Hills*,[3] though lacking the more sombre moods of the latter's work.

In 1935 Marc-Aurèle Fortin spent some time in France and upon his return moved to Sainte-Rose. For a period in the mid-thirties he painted over a black undercoat[4] giving his work of this period an almost brutal quality. In the late thirties and all through the forties he painted in the lower Saint Lawrence area and in the Gaspé around Saint-Simon.[5]

Marc-Aurèle Fortin was a regionalist artist in the same sense as the Group of Seven. While less vocal or self-conscious than the members of the Group, exploring and interpreting different areas of the province, he transformed the landscape into an expression of a national identity.

The traditional way of life of the rural inhabitants of Quebec played an important rôle in the concept of a French-Canadian identity, historians and writers having equated its preservation with the struggle against assimilation of the French in North America. Quebec artists also continually returned to the themes of rural life. Horatio Walker, in the manner of Jean-François Millet, idealized the farmers and their Christian faith. James Wilson Morrice, A.Y. Jackson, and Marc-Aurèle Fortin concentrated on its more picturesque qualities while Clarence Gagnon, in his illustrations for *Maria Chapdelaine*, explored is human drama. Now a younger generation of artists, continuing and transforming this tradition, looked at it with new eyes.

Born in Switzerland, André Biéler was brought to Canada by his family in 1908 at the age of twelve. He fought with the Princess Patricia's Light Infantry during the First World War, was gassed at Passchendaele, and returned to Montreal very ill. He spent the next year in the southern United States recuperating and painting, and during the summers of 1920 and 1921 he studied with Charles Rosen and George Bellows at the Summer School of the New York Art Students League in Woodstock, New York.[6] The teaching there was greatly influenced by Cézanne, with a concentration on figure work. Working with Bellows, a member of the American 'Ash Can School,' also predisposed Biéler to a greater consciousness of his social environment.[7]

André Biéler left for Europe in October 1921 and the following spring worked with his uncle, Ernest Biéler, in Switzerland.[8] The art of Ernest Biéler shows many similarities with that of Alexandre Jacovleff and Adolf Milman, the teachers of Lilias Newton and Edwin Holgate, employing similar compositional devices and concentrating on careful drawing and structure.[9] Also of great interest to André was his uncle's work in fresco.

After returning to Canada, inspired by the regionalist literature that had developed in France during the twenties, Biéler sought a region of Quebec where he could live and paint.[10] His first choice was the Gaspé; however, finding the winter too severe, in the fall of 1927 he moved to the Île d'Orléans, Horatio Walker's terrain, where he remained for three years.[11]

This period on the Île d'Orléans determined the themes and character of André Biéler's work for the next decade. Fascinated by the traditional way of life of the farmers, he completed numerous sketches of women baking, religious processions, and people at church. Some of the single figures are close to Holgate's work both in colouring and composition;[12] however, Biéler was more concerned with the depiction of groups of people and their interrelationships.

In 1930 Biéler left the Île d'Orléans,[13] and rented a studio in Montreal. Recognizing the importance of the Studio Building to the Toronto artists, Biéler, with Edwin Holgate and Lilias Newton, found a sponsor to fund a similar effort in Montreal; however, the project fell through. He soon met John Lyman, recently returned from France, and the plans for a studio building turned into a school, the Atelier.[14]

The staff of the Atelier consisted of John Lyman, André Biéler, Elizabeth Frost, George Holt,[15] and Kenneth Crowe – with Hazen Sise as chairman.[16] The first year classes were held in Elizabeth Frost's apartment with about a dozen pupils,[17] and the following autumn quarters were found in the building occupied by the Montreal Repertory Theatre.[18] Efforts were made to plan joint activities with the theatre, and a production of André Obey's *Noé* included sets and costumes by André Biéler in traditional Quebec materials and designs.[19] However, the school had few students, finances were difficult, and it closed in the spring of 1933.[20]

For the next few years André and his wife Jeannette Meunier designed furniture and interiors utilizing Quebec handicrafts.[21] Wanting to have more time to devote to his painting, André Biéler moved to Sainte-Adèle in the fall of 1935 and the following year obtained a position as artist in residence at Queen's University. Coming from a family of teachers he fitted into his new job with ease and was to remain there until his retirement in 1963.[22]

Stimulated by the work of his brother, Jacques Biéler, one of the founders of the League for Social Reconstruction, André Biéler became concerned about the rôle of the arts in society. Looking to the United States and Mexico he saw artists involved with their communities and with contemporary political and social issues, even offering direction to the people through their art. He found Canadian artists obsessed by geography with no reflection of social concerns or idealism.[23]

In his own art André Biéler increasingly concentrated on his human environment. In *Corpus Christi Procession, Sainte-Adèle* (1936, cat. no. 81) the figures, integrated with the landscape, are still subordinated to its rhythms. In *Before the Auction* (1936, cat. no. 82) the figures are more individualized and become the dominant theme of the work. He leaves behind the decorative rhythms of the Group of Seven for a greater concern for the structure and reality of the people.

Just as Horatio Walker, inspired by the work of Millet and in the spirit of nineteenth-century Christian socialism, ennobled the labourers of the Île d'Orlèans, André Biéler, following the model of Diego Rivera and the Marxist art of the w.p.a., sanctifies the rural family in *Gatineau Madonna* (1940, cat. no. 83). With this increasing idealization, Biéler attains a greater surety of expression, combining the fluidity and the structure of the earlier works in a unified whole.

André Biéler's interest in the rural life and folk arts of Quebec was shared by a group of artists and historians working in the lower Saint Lawrence region. Marius Barbeau, the noted ethnologist, had been studying the art and social customs of Quebec since the mid-twenties, organizing annual folk festivals at the Château Frontenac in Quebec City where traditional songs and dances were revived and crafts displayed. Gérard Morisset, at the Musée de la Province de Québec, was preparing important studies on the history of art in Quebec and in 1934 began the massive inventory of Quebec arts.[24] Working with Barbeau and Morisset were the artists Jean Paul Lemieux, Jean Palardy, Jori Smith, and Stanley Cosgrove.

This interest in the traditional folk arts was paralleled by the appearance of the Murray Bay Primitives – chief among whom were the Bouchard sisters. In the United States the cult of primitive or naïve artists had been initiated by 'progressive' artists interested in the work of the Douanier Rousseau and the eccentric Louis Elsheimius, the untrained artist being seen as an expression of pure creativity unhampered by academic restraints. During the thirties, with the popularity of the American Regionalists, the primitive artists reached a wider public as examples of a regionalist, native art unsullied by foreign influences. It is not surprising, therefore, that the first sponsor of the Charlevoix or Murray Bay Primitives was an American, Patrick Morgan,[25] who organized an exhibition of their work in New York in 1937.[26]

Jean Paul Lemieux's interest in the folk arts of Quebec began at a fairly early age. Born in Quebec City, he first visited the Charlevoix area in 1921[27] and while a student at the École des Beaux-Arts in Montreal illustrated several novels based on regionalist and historical themes.[28] In 1929 he visited France, travelling in Brittany and the Basque area, and in Paris met Clarence Gagnon.[29] Returning to Montreal, he formed, with Jean Palardy and Jori Smith (fellow students at the École des Beaux-Arts), a commercial art studio that survived six months before disbanding.[30] After spending some time travelling in the United States he returned to the École des Beaux-Arts in Montreal where he studied wood engraving under Edwin Holgate and took life classes at Holgate's studio in the evenings. Lemieux's landscapes from this early date show a strong influence of Holgate – with their smoothly flowing, though solidly structured forms.[31]

After teaching at the École des Beaux-Arts for two years, in 1935 he secured a new post at the École du Meuble. The Quebec government had organized this school the previous year[32] to improve the quality of the crafts made and sold in Quebec, with one eye on tourism, as well as to provide a solution to rural poverty. While conservative in its reliance on traditional crafts and values, the École du Meuble under its director, Jean-Marie Gauvreau, was to become the most progressive art school in Montreal.

At the École du Meuble, Jean Paul Lemieux worked with Marcel Parizeau, professor of architecture, through whom he discovered the artists of the School of Paris.[33] He broke from his earlier style to develop a more personal expression, a greater freedom of colour and paint and a slightly brittle, linear brushstroke seen in *Landscape in the Eastern Townships* (1936, cat. no. 84).

From 1935 Lemieux spent most of his summers in Charlevoix county with Jori Smith and her husband, Jean Palardy, especially after 1937 when he started teaching at the École des Beaux-Arts in Quebec City.[34] With Marius Barbeau they collected furniture, pottery, and carvings and spent a great deal of time with the Bouchard family and the other artists at Baie Saint-Paul. Lemieux became extremely interested in folk arts and by consequence such fifteenth-century Sienese artists as Giovanni di Paolo. The stylistic simplifications as well as the sincerity and simplicity of expression appealed to his modernist interests. He also saw in the folk arts a truly native and proletarian production, a breaking away from the Fine Arts. Just as the Mexican artists had incorporated native art forms into their politicized art, Jean Paul Lemieux wanted to relate his art to the social and political life of the people around him.

In an article he wrote for *Le Jour* Jean Paul Lemieux denounced the isolationism and conservatism of art teaching in Quebec and the decadence of church decoration. He praised the mural work of the Mexicans and w.p.a. projects in the United States for their social and educative rôle and for their employment of younger, more modern artists.[35] In his own work he turned away from landscape to anecdotal and satirical depictions of country life, the most successful of which is *Lazarus* (1941, cat. no. 85). In composition and theme this work has many parallels with Jock Macdonald's *Indian Burial, Nootka* (cat. no. 38); however, Jock Macdonald creates a more naturalistic depiction with a greater concentration on landscape. Jean Paul Lemieux allegorizes by the combination of multiple events in one composition, as in the Sienese works he so admired. The slightly comical parishioners patiently listen to the sermon while in the graveyard, the Lazarus of the priest's sermon rises from the dead symbolizing the ressurection of the family shot down on the country road by the parachutists. In this work Jean Paul Lemieux raises the anecdotal genre of social realism to the level of religious symbolism. It is unfortunate it was never incorporated in a church decoration.

Jean Paul Lemieux's attitude to rural life was very

different from André Biéler's. Both were city-born and city-based, viewing the country from a distance; both artists were socially and politically committed; however, where Biéler idealizes, Jean Paul Lemieux satirizes. Perhaps Lemieux's more intimate contact with the reality of rural poverty in Quebec at the height of the Depression made it less easy to romanticize the farmer's life.

Jori Smith and Stanley Cosgrove also were attracted to the Charlevoix area, the former by its inhabitants, the latter by the country life and people. Jori Smith first studied at the École des Beaux-Arts in Montreal though she left in 1929, rejecting its academic training. After the commercial studio with Jean Paul Lemieux proved unsuccessful, she studied for awhile with Edwin Holgate. All during the thirties, she and Jean Palardy spent the summers at Baie Saint-Paul, painting and collecting crafts and furniture, and from November to April, in Montreal surviving on a few dollars a week and the generosity of friends.[36]

Like Pegi Nicol MacLeod, Jori's passionate nature and deep humanitarian concern got her involved in the work of the League for Social Reconstruction and she avidly followed events in Spain during the Civil War. Jori's essential humanism also attracted her to the children of Charlevoix County. They were poor and often ill with tuberculosis, and their sad faces fascinated her. *Mlle Rose* (1936, cat. no. 86) still shows the influence of Holgate's emphasis on structure and form, yet the freer quality of the brushwork presages the almost violent Expressionism of her later work. However, it was only after Pellan's arrival from France that she broke away from the muted tones of her Beaux-Arts training and was able to purify her colour.[37]

Stanley Cosgrove also joined the Palardys and Lemieux at Charlevoix in the summers during the late thirties. Born of an Irish father and French-Canadian mother, Cosgrove spent four years studying drawing at the École des Beaux-Arts in Montreal and one year with Edwin Holgate at the Art Association.[38] Like his other pupils, Cosgrove praises the seriousness of Holgate's teaching and his concern for the formal qualities of his art.

During the summer of 1936, with money given him by Huntley Drummond,[39] he spent four months painting in the Gaspé. The following three summers he joined the Palardys and Lemieux at Baie Saint-Paul collecting furniture and painting the farms and people of the area. Much of his work parallels the American genre painting of the period; however, in *Madeleine with Short Hair* (1939, cat.no. 87) he stresses the plastic qualities of the figure with an almost crude strength of brushwork. The muted colours and coarse texture however impose a restraint

NOTES TO CHAPTER 6

that creates an expression of serenity belying the actual boldness of the work.

Like Jean Paul Lemieux, Cosgrove was interested in the American and Mexican revival of mural painting. In 1938 he decorated the church of Saint-Henri in Montreal with Maurice Raymond, and the following year assisted Edwin Holgate with the murals for the Canadian pavilion at the New York World's Fair.[40] Though the David Scholarship[41] that Cosgrove received in August 1939 was for studies in France, the war intervened. In December, he went to New York; however, finding that city too expensive, he travelled to Mexico where he was to remain for four years.[42]

1. Louis Hémon, *Maria Chapdelaine* (Paris: Éditions Mornay, 1933). Illustrations by Clarence Gagnon.
2. Jean-René Ostiguy, *Marc-Aurèle Fortin* (exhibition catalogue) (Ottawa: The National Gallery of Canada, [1964]).
3. *Gleams on the Hills* (1920, oil on canvas; 32 x 34 in., 81.3 x 86.4 cm) in The National Gallery of Canada. See R.H. Hubbard, ed., *The National Gallery of Canada. Catalogue. Paintings and Sculpture. Volume III: Canadian School* (Toronto: University of Toronto Press, 1960), p. 191 repr.
4. 'Marc-Aurèle Fortin,' *La Presse* (14 November 1936).
5. Jean-René Ostiguy, *op. cit.*
6. Frances K. Smith, 'The Chronology,' in *André Biéler 50 Years: A Retrospective Exhibition 1920 – 1970* (exhibition catalogue) (Kingston: Agnes Etherington Art Centre, Queen's University, 1970).
7. Interview with André Biéler, Glenburnie (Ontario), 18 December 1973.
8. Frances K. Smith, *op. cit.*
9. See J.B. Manson, *Ernest Biéler / Peintre Suisse* (Lausanne: Éditions la Concorde, 1936).
10. Interview with André Biéler, Glenburnie (Ontario), 18 December 1973.
11. Frances K. Smith, *op. cit.*
12. See André Biéler, *Le Gars au Cormoran, Gaspé* (1930, oil on canvas; 26 x 20 in., 66.1 x 50.1 cm, collection Dr and Mrs Albert Fell, Kingston; repr. in Francis K. Smith, *op cit.*, fig. 16) and Edwin Holgate, *The Lumberjack* (1926, oil on canvas; 25-3/4 x 21-1/2 in., 65.4 x 54.7 cm, Sarnia Public Library and Art Gallery; repr. in Peter Mellen, *The Group of Seven* [Toronto: McClelland and Stewart Limited, 1970], p. 166).
13. Frances K. Smith, *op. cit.*
14. Interview with André Biéler, Glenburnie (Ontario), 18 December 1973.
15. George Holt later worked on the w.p.a. artists' techniques research project at the Fogg Museum where he specialized in mosaics. He was also a member of the Boston 'Painter's Workshop' which lectured on painting techniques at the 1941 Kingston Conference.
16. *The Atelier: A School of Drawing Painting Sculpture,* n.d. [November 1931]. Prudence Heward, Mabel May, Lilias Newton, Sarah Robertson, and Annie Savage are also listed as members of the teaching staff; however it appears their names were added for social reasons. They didn't teach at the school. (Interview with Lilias T. Newton, Montreal, 11 September 1973.)
17. Interview with Allan Harrison, Montreal, 13 September 1973.
18. ' "The Atelier"/A School of Modern Art,' *The Montrealer* (October 1932).
19. Thomas Archer, 'Montreal Letter: The Art of Holgate,' *Saturday Night,* vol. xlviii, no. 23 (15 April 1933), p. 7.
20. Interview with Allan Harrison, Montreal, 13 September 1973.
21. 'People Who Do Things: André Biéler,' *Saturday Night,* vol. l, no. 46 (21 September 1935), p. 16.
22. Frances K. Smith, *op cit.*
23. Interview with André Biéler, Glenburnie (Ontario), 18 December 1973.
24. Roland Prévost, 'M. Gérard Morisset,' *La Revue Populaire,* vol. xxviii, no. 4 (April 1935), p. 5.
25. Patrick Morgan was a relative of Cleveland Morgan of the Art Association of Montreal, and of John Lyman.
26. 'The Douanier Rousseau Tradition In French Canada,' *The Art News,* vol. xxxvi, no. 10 (4 December 1937), p. 13.
27. Guy Robert, *Jean Paul Lemieux la poétique de la souvenance* (Quebec: Éditions Garneau, 1968), p. 15.

28. Robert Choquette, *La pension Leblanc* (Montreal, New York: Louis Carrier & Cie., 1927); Régis Roy, *Le manoir hanté* (Montreal, New York: Louis Carrier & Cie., 1928); Cora B. Fortier, *Le petit page de Frontenac* (Montreal: Librairie d'Action canadienne française Ltée, 1930).

29. Guy Robert, *op. cit.,* p. 15.

30. Guy Robert, *op. cit.,* p. 18.

31. See *Soleil d'Après-midi* (1933, oil on canvas; 30 x 34 in., 76.2 x 86.4 cm) in the Musée du Québec; repr. in Guy Robert, *op. cit.,* p. 24.

32. Henri Girard, 'L'École du Meuble,' *La Revue Moderne,* vol. xxi, no. 4 (August 1939), p. 11.

33. Gilles Corbeil, 'Jean Paul Lemieux, Peintre Intimiste,' *Arts et Pensée,* vol. 3, no. 14 (December 1953), p. 39.

34. Guy Robert, *op. cit.,* p. 22.

35. Jean Paul Lemieux, 'La Peinture chez les Canadiens français,' *Le Jour,* vol. i, no. 44 (16 July 1938).

36. Interview with Jori Smith, Montreal, 16 January 1974.

37. Idem.

38. Conversation with Stanley Cosgrove, Montreal, 8 March 1974.

39. Huntley Drummond was president of Redpath Sugar where Stanley Cosgrove's father worked. Stanley himself had worked there for several summers. (Conversation with Stanley Cosgrove, Montreal, 8 March 1974.)

40. Germain Leber, 'Stanley Cosgrove / peinture audacieux,' *La Revue Moderne,* vol. xxvi, no. 3 (July 1944), p. 22. The murals for New York were painted on canvas in Montreal and later installed in the pavilion.

41. Anasthase David had been Minister of Education in the Quebec government and was instrumental in setting up the École des Beaux-Arts in Montreal and Quebec. The David Scholarship, the only one in Canada at this time, was offered for study in France. The first person to receive this prize was Alfred Pellan in 1926.

42. Conversation with Stanley Cosgrove, Montreal, 8 March 1974.

80.
MARC-AURÈLE FORTIN
Landscape at Hochelaga   c. 1931

81.
ANDRÉ BIELÉR
Corpus Christi Procession, Sainte-Adèle   1936

*82.
ANDRÉ BIÉLER
Before the Auction   1936

83.
ANDRÉ BIÉLER
Gatineau Madonna   1940

*84.
JEAN PAUL LEMIEUX
Landscape in the Eastern Townships   1936

85.
JEAN PAUL LEMIEUX
Lazarus   1941

86.
JORI SMITH
Mlle Rose   1936

*87.
STANLEY COSGROVE
Madeleine with Short Hair   1939

7. The Eastern Group and the Contemporary Arts Society

In response to an article lamenting the decline of the Group of Seven,[1] there appeared a letter in *The Canadian Forum*. It read, in part, 'This extreme interest in landscape for its sentimental geography is psychologically of the same essence as the popular predilection for anecdotic and souvenir painting. . . [the] emphasis has been misplaced, has been put on the objective rather than the subjective element of artistic creation. The real adventure takes place in the sensibility and imagination of the individual.'[2] This new voice on the Canadian art scene was that of John Lyman, who, within ten years, was to be largely instrumental in totally transforming the face of art in Canada.

John Lyman first studied art in Paris at the Académie Julian with Jean-Paul Laurens, at which time he came to know James Wilson Morrice, for whom he retained a life-long respect. Two years later, during the summer of 1909, he met the British artist Matthew Smith at Étaples and that autumn the two attended the Académie Matisse, a school run by Matisse's students in Paris.[3] Matthew Smith remained at the school for two months[4] and saw Matisse only three times;[5] however, John Lyman appears to have stayed the entire winter.[6] These contacts with Morrice and Matisse were crucial to John Lyman's art. Their devotion to a pure art of colour, line, and form, an art devoid of all anecdotal details or 'non-artistic' concepts, remained with Lyman throughout his life.

His first exhibition in Canada at the Art Association galleries in May 1913,[7] two months after Randolph Hewton's and A.Y. Jackson's 'daring' exhibition,[8] appeared to the Montreal critics to be adding insult to injury. Taking their cue from the criticism of the Armory Show in New York,[9] the journalists outdid themselves in denouncing his work.[10] Disgusted, John Lyman returned to Paris.

He spent the next eighteen years travelling in the United States, North Africa, Spain, and Southern France though based in Paris. In January of 1927 John Lyman's father died.[11] Lyman returned to Montreal where he held an exhibition of his recent work.[12] To his surprise the critics were favourable. More important, he wrote in his journal, 'before even the flattest Quebec landscape I feel that I have more to say than before the magnificent sites of Europe. Two years ago [I] should have thought this statement impossible.'[13] His exile was almost over.

He returned to Canada in the summer of 1930[14] and in February 1931 held another exhibition of his work in Montreal.[15] That September he returned to Canada for the last time.[16]

In Montreal he sought out people sympathetic to creative ideas in art and literature, holding a weekly *salon* at his Sherbrooke Street apartment.[17] Through these gatherings there grew a core of people familiar with and supportive of contemporary European art.

Soon after settling in Montreal, with Hazen Sise, George Holt, Elizabeth Frost, and André Biéler, Lyman founded the Atelier.[18] In the introductory pamphlet, Hazen Sise[19] wrote, 'The essential qualities of a work of art lie in the relationships of form to form, and of colour to colour. From these the eye, and especially the trained eye derives its pleasure and all artistic emotion must find its expression through these means.'[20] Stressing the importance of classical principles in art, the principles that united the art of the past to the art of the European moderns, Lyman introduced his students to Ingres, Cézanne, and Matisse and the *Journals* of Delacroix.[21] At the same time as he supported French art, John Lyman was opposed to what he felt to be the xenophobic nationalism of Canadian art. To those who feared the taint of foreign art, Lyman replied, 'The talk of the Canadian scene has gone sour. The real Canadian scene is in the consciousness of Canadian painters, whatever the object of their thought.'[22]

The Atelier survived only two winters,[23] though for a few summers, John Lyman ran a school at his Saint-Jovite farm in the Laurentians.[24] He also continued to lecture on art, at one point addressing the Quebec Library Association with Charles Maillard, director of the École des Beaux-Arts. Maillard called for the removal from libraries of all literature hindering 'the true appreciation of art,'[25] and Lyman stressed the necessity of exposure to all new developments.[26]

From 1936 to 1940 John Lyman wrote a monthly art column for *The Montrealer*[27] commenting on developments in Canadian art, linking these with international trends, and offering some of the most intelligent writing on art in Canada at that time. He was especially instrumental in stressing the importance of annual exhibitions of contemporary French art held at the galleries of W. Scott & Sons.[28] These exhibitions, organized in conjunction with Alex. Reid & Lefevre Limited in London and brought to Montreal by John Heaton,[29] offered Montrealers some of the first works by Matisse, Modigliani, Leger, Braque, Derain, Dufy, and Picasso seen in that city. These exhibitions played an important rôle in developing an interest in international developments in painting and determining future trends in Montreal.

John Lyman's own painting during the thirties developed in a sure and logical manner. *Haying by the Lake* (1933, cat. no. 88) is one of a series of landscapes painted at Saint-Jovite which he entitled 'Variations on the Lake.'[30] Confronted by the wilder aspects of the Canadian terrain, he organizes its shapes so that it has almost the aspect of a classical landscape. There is no hint of the more romantic moods of the Group of Seven, but a serene vision of light-modulated forms.

It was above all the human figure, in all its multiplicity of moods and forms, that interested Lyman. The smoothly flowing brush-work and glowing colour asserts the plastic qualities of the forms in *The Card Game* (c. 1935, cat. no. 89). The sombre tones and vibrating colour of *Jori Smith in Costume* (1936, cat. no. 90) contrasts with the severe verticals and horizontals of the patrician *Woman With White Collar* (c. 1936, cat. no. 91). The same, broad, horizontal brushstroke is used in *Lassitude* (c. 1937, cat. no. 92) accentuating the essentially architectonic quality of Lyman's art which is saved from stiffness by the vibrating bronze of the skin.

John Lyman's painting is not easily appreciated. His colour has an almost puritan reticence, his subjects are serious and detached. At times an awkward stiffness does appear in his work; yet at its best, his is an art of sobriety, order, and measure. He builds a solid construction which is made to last.

John Lyman recognized that there were newer artists working in Montreal who were cut off from the 'Canadian scene' painting that dominated in Toronto and who found no support from public institutions. In contrast to the apparent xenophobia of the Group, he found among the newer artists an openness to European art. As he commented, 'In Quebec and generally in the east, possibly because we are accustomed to contacts, painters have never been greatly disturbed by the danger of influence. They have willingly recognized alien qualities and have hoped the example might be of use to them. They have tried to assimilate its fundamental lessons but they have not been inclined to imitation. What they have learned, they have made their own.'[31] Some of these artists were European-born and recent arrivals in Canada. Others had studied in Europe or the United States and were producing work unrelated to the Group tradition.

One of the first artists John Lyman championed was Goodridge Roberts. On visiting an exhibition of Roberts's watercolours at The Arts Club in Montreal,[32] John Lyman wrote him, 'I knew by my elation that I had seen real stuff. I like your work immensely for its terse characterization in drawing and particularly for your rare ability to *see* colour, not merely use it illustratively or as a schematic ornament.'[33] This was important praise for an artist who had been working almost completely unknown and in total poverty for the last two years.

Roberts, nephew of the poet Sir Charles G.D. Roberts and cousin of the poet Bliss Carman, was raised in New Brunswick, except for a period during the First World War

when the family moved to England. He entered the École des Beaux-Arts in Montreal in 1923 and in the fall of 1926 went to New York to study at the Art Students League. Boardman Robinson, John Sloan, and Max Weber introduced him to Cézanne, Giotto, and Masaccio. In the galleries for the first time he saw the works of Matisse and Picasso.[34]

Returning to Canada, Roberts worked for a year in Fredericton and in the summer of 1930 moved to Ottawa. He taught that winter at the Ottawa Art Association and the following summer, with two friends, conducted a school at Wakefield near Hull.[35]

It was in the summer of 1932, working at Kingsmere, near Wakefield, that Roberts 'got beyond the tentative stage of experiment and suddenly found [himself] doing one watercolour after another with feverish speed.'[36] The rapid assessment and simplification demanded by the five-minute sketches in John Sloan's classes now paid off. These watercolours were exhibited later that fall at The Arts Club in Montreal where they attracted the attention of Cleveland Morgan and John Lyman. The latter invited him to participate in the Atelier exhibition the following spring.[37] The exhibition resulted in some of his first sales and brought his work to the attention of a small though interested and knowledgeable public.

These few years in Ottawa were difficult ones for Goodridge Roberts. Living on $1.50 a week left no money for oils, so he confined himself to watercolour. At times, while painting, he would be too weak to continue and would have to lie down in the fields to recoup his strength. However, as Jacques de Tonnancour has written: 'He lost five teeth, his strength for several months . . . and survived. He had supported his painting and had been able to give it life. That had been enough for him and had carried him through. He was a painter; that was his strength.'[38]

During the summer of 1933 he worked just east of Ottawa. The watercolours he produced, such as *Ottawa Valley* (1933, cat. no. 93), are more intricate than those of the previous year. He builds up the space with layers of colour, purples, greens, browns, and blacks so that even the sky becomes a plastic entity. The watercolour suffuses the open landscape with a unity of mood through carefully coordinated tones.

In November 1933, through the assistance of Harry McCurry, Assistant Director of The National Gallery, and with a grant from the Carnegie Corporation, Roberts was appointed resident artist at Queen's University in Kingston and was able to marry. He disliked teaching and had little time to paint.[39] After three years, the Carnegie grant was discontinued[40] and the Robertses moved to Montreal,

13. At Saint-Jovite, Quebec, 1939.
Left to right: John Lyman, Goodridge Roberts, Fritz
Brandtner.

where Goodridge opened a school with Ernst Neumann, whom he had known since his days at the École des Beaux-Arts.[41] Though pupils were few, the school survived two or three winters.

From 1932 to 1940 Goodridge Roberts had twelve solo exhibitions in Montreal, Ottawa, and Toronto[42] and participated in numerous group exhibitions, yet sales were almost non-existent. He had difficulty raising the money even for framing and shipping.[43] In the fall of 1940 he returned to institutional teaching, this time at the Art Association of Montreal.[44]

With the temporary security of money saved while at Queen's, Roberts returned to oil painting with an ever-increasing surety. In *Ontario Landscape in a Red Light* (1936, cat. no. 94), painted on the outskirts of Ottawa in September 1936, he simplifies the shapes of the trees and receding fields and hills, concentrating on the relationship of the forms. As in the earlier watercolours, a single dominant tone pervades the whole picture, creating a feeling of rich melancholy.[45]

As in the work of Giotto, whom he so much admired, Roberts's figures are solemn and monumental. In *Marian* (1937, cat. no. 95) the strongly sculptural quality of the figure is reinforced by the verticals and horizontals of the background playing against the Matisse-like pattern of the dress. The strong division between shadows and light on the face, perhaps derived from John Lyman's work, asserts its plastic solidity.

The silhouette of the *Standing Nude* (1938, cat. no. 96) is less simplified, formed of more subtle curves. The strong contrasts of darks and lights, and of freely brushed forms with flat solid planes, creates dynamic tensions in this complex figure. Comparing this work with John Lyman's *Jori Smith in Costume* (cat. no. 90) opposes intuition and reason. The latter is surely and intelligently constructed with utmost control. Roberts paints with freedom and passion. The shadows are sombre, almost mysterious and, at the same time, beautifully sensuous. As Neufville Shaw has remarked, 'In Lyman, one's eye is directed by the drawing to follow the arabesque of line as it encloses mass or limits colour. In Roberts, one is tossed from mass to mass. The one is all grace and certainty; the other is all imminence and indefiniteness. Lyman leaves little to chance, Roberts everything.'[46]

The sombre moods of Roberts's work take on a quite different character in the paintings of Philip Surrey. Surrey left Vancouver in October 1936[47] to study anatomical drawing at Johns Hopkins University in Baltimore;[48] however, unable to enter the class, he went to the Art Students League in New York where he studied three months with Frank Vincent Dumond and painting tech-

niques with Alexander Abels. He moved to Montreal that spring, doing freelance commercial work for a year until he found employment with the Montreal *Standard* as photograph editor.[49]

Philip Surrey's painting in Montreal changed considerably from his earlier Vancouver work. *The Boardwalk* (c. 1938, cat. no. 97) still retains much of the Varley lyricism with its misty blues and greens. The solidly painted shadows on the boardwalk, abruptly projecting from the foreground, similar to the mast of Varley's *Night Ferry, Vancouver* (cat. no. 40), catches some of the menacing quality of his later work.

Surrey's New York experience, the Depression, and his contacts in Montreal, pulled him away from lyrical painting to more socially involved themes. With Jean Paul Lemieux and Jori Smith he shared a concern for political developments both in Quebec and Spain. His recognition of a growing malaise and the imminence of conflict is reflected in his art. The gaunt and awkward figures in *Sunday Afternoon* (1939, cat. no. 98), painted from memory of a *veillée* at Saint-Hilarion which he attended with the Palardys, are isolated, each caught in his or her own tragic situation. He paints with less fluidity and more concern for structure, accentuating the macabre reality of the individual sitters.

In *The Red Portrait* (1939, cat. no. 99), a Gothic arch of light emanates from the window framing the sitter. The rough texture of the paint, the isolation of the figure, and the hollow space of the empty room express the feeling of dislocation and tension felt by many on the eve of war. The simplified forms of the buildings and increased solidity of the forms reflect Surrey's debt to Goodridge Roberts.

Fritz Brandtner, born and educated in Danzig, emigrated to Canada in 1928. In Winnipeg he first worked as a house-painter but soon found employment with the T. Eaton Co. and from there with Brigden's of Winnipeg Limited working on the Eaton's catalogues. With his savings and the sponsorship of LeMoine FitzGerald he was able to bring out his fiancée the following year.[50]

While Winnipeg offered steady employment, Brandtner found few outlets for his work. Being paid so little, he couldn't afford the cost of framing and shipping his work east for exhibition.[51] FitzGerald recommended he go to Montreal recognizing that Montreal would be more open to experimental art than Toronto which was still so strongly tied to the Group of Seven.[52]

The Brandtners arrived in Montreal in March 1934[53] and he soon found work in window display for the T. Eaton Co.[54] FitzGerald had given him an introduction to Robert Ayre, art critic for the Montreal *Gazette* and, through the Ayres, Fritz met many of the newer Montreal artists.[55]

The first work Fritz Brandtner exhibited in Montreal was purchased by Norman Bethune;[56] he made contact with the artist and from there developed a close friendship. Brandtner for several years had been doing drawings and watercolours, similar to *Men of 1939* (1939, cat. no. 100), in a style often reminiscent of George Grosz. Drawings in vivid coloured inks of unemployed men on park benches, blind fiddlers, workers locked out of factories, families in gas masks, victims of chemical warfare – all these appealed to Bethune, both in their subject matter and their intensity of expression. He arranged an exhibition of Brandtner's work at Morgan's department store in February 1936 under the sponsorship of The Canadian League Against War and Fascism.[57] The exhibition received a mixed reaction. Robert Ayre in *The Gazette* praised his inventiveness and strength.[58] Henri Girard in *Le Canada* called Brandtner, 'one of the most remarkable artists, the artists worthy of our respect, who have ever lived in Montreal.'[59] However, Reynald of *La Presse*, in a long article entitled 'The Nightmares of F. Brandtner,' raised a cry of horror: 'Brandtner rejects the canons of drawing, the rules of colouring, conventions and fixed laws. For him the world exists only in an image, and as a resemblance of nightmares and hallucinations.'[60] Fritz Brandtner had arrived.

Brandtner's work at this time shows a great variety both in subject-matter and style with an intensity of colour and line that is very personal. Much of it is small in format, as he had little money for materials and drew continuously. However, it is often these small works that are most successful, for they retain the directness of expression and strength of line sometimes lost in larger works. He absorbed, reproduced and transformed themes and styles of many different artists, mostly from artists whose work he knew in Germany, such as George Grosz, Erich Waske, Heinrich Naven, or Wilhelm Morgener.[61] The gas-masked figures from Diego Rivera's Detroit Institute murals reappear in his drawings.

His familiarity with modern European art as well as the speed of execution and inventiveness, which he also incorporated into his commercial art, gave his work a great freedom and strength. In his representational works, such as *The Riders* (1939, cat. no. 101), as well as in *Abstraction* (1936, cat. no. 102), totally devoid of all figurative references, he organizes flat planes, geometric patterns, and Expressionist line into a dynamically integrated whole.

This same daring and freedom he passed on to the children in his classes. Late in the summer of 1936 Norman Bethune invited Fritz Brandtner to set up children's classes in his apartment on Beaver Hall Square.[62] Bethune paid for the materials and the Children's Art Centre was opened. However, Bethune soon left for Spain;[63] the Brandtners moved into the apartment, and Fritz supported the Centre himself. He conducted classes for children from the poorer areas of the city and in the hospitals,[64] offering them their first opportunity to work with freedom, breaking away from mechanical reproduction.

Marian Scott taught with Fritz Brandtner at the Children's Art Centre for two years.[65] She had studied at the École des Beaux-Arts in Montreal for one year and then for a term at the Slade School of Art in London. Returning to Canada in 1928 she married Frank Scott. The birth of a son the following year prevented her from devoting herself to her art.[66] It was only after the mid-thirties that she had time to paint.

Marian Scott's earliest works consisted of geometrically organized landscapes. These were followed by formal studies of plants and buds in various stages of growth, inspired by the work of Georgia O'Keeffe. Through the exhibitions at W. Scott & Sons and periodicals she developed an interest in the linear stylization of Modigliani's figures and the ambiguous, spatial relationships of Juan Gris' cubist works.

At the same time, Marian Scott, like so many other artists in the thirties, felt a need somehow to relate her work to the social issues of the day, to break down the barrier between contemporary art and the people and be integrated with the society at large.[67] She turned away from landscape and organic subjects to urban scenes, ships in harbour, people on escalators, and workers in the streets. In *Escalator* (1937, cat. no. 103) the environment is mechanized, the people shifted on conveyor belts. The concern for the movement of figures in space and differing spatial relationships is also seen in *Tenants* (c. 1940, cat. no. 104) where the figures retain a greater individuality, even in their anonymity. Just as in the work of Oskar Schlemmer, the human figure becomes a symbol of a humanist philosophy within a rational environment.

If Marian Scott's reaction to her urban environment was based on a rationalist faith, Louis Muhlstock's derived from a more immediate sensuous and romantic identification. Born in the province of Galicia in Poland, Louis Muhlstock came to Canada with his family in 1911 at the age of seven. He first took drawing lessons in evening courses at the Monument National in Montreal under Edmond Dyonnet and later at the École des Beaux-Arts, all this time working for his family's fruit importing firm, saving money to enable him to study in Paris. He spent three years in France, from 1928 to 1931, studying with Louis François Biloul in Paris, with summers in Brittany

(1929) and Belgium and the Alps (1930).[68]

Returning to Canada at the outset of the Depression, Louis Muhlstock again found employment with his family's firm. Having little money for materials, he drew during his free time – studies of unemployed men he picked up on the street, men sleeping in the parks or ill or elderly people. For a period around 1932 he frequented the public wards of hospitals drawing patients with incurable diseases.[69] Interpreted with compassion and love, Louis Muhlstock transforms their suffering into symbols of human dignity and pride in the face of destruction. Death and suffering are always present but also an enduring faith in life.

With the materials available, Louis Muhlstock did continue to paint the back lanes in the area around his Sainte-Famille Street apartment, dead trees on Mount Royal, or empty rooms in abandoned houses. In Sainte-Famille Street (1939, cat. no. 105), the streets and lanes are devoid of people, expressing the quiet calm of early summer mornings. Of the empty rooms, Muhlstock wrote, 'What intrigued me was the feeling of rooms that had been lived in. To try to express the silence of a room that was something I wanted very much to arrive at and at the same time to play with shapes on canvas, to create a composition and to play with structures and textures.'[70] The musty drabness of Open Door of Third House, Groubert Lane, Montreal (c. 1939, cat. no. 106) is transformed by the fluid texture and play of light. The compassionate humanism of his figure drawings pervades these empty urban scenes, evoking their former inhabitants by their very abandonment.

Alexandre Bercovitch and Eric Goldberg both arrived in Canada via Germany and Palestine. Bercovitch was born in Cherson in the Ukraine and studied four years in Palestine and one year in Munich under Franz von Stuck.[71] He returned to Russia and designed stage sets for the Moscow Art Theatre under Leon Bakst.[72] In 1924 he moved to Turkestan where he opened an art school in Ashkabad.[73] However, famines and political strife forced him to leave Russia two years later to join his wife's family in Montreal.

At first he supported his family in Montreal by painting signs and decorations for cabarets, churches, and synagogues. However, jobs were harder and harder to find. When he was about to be evicted from his apartment, his social worker, Regina Shoolman,[74] put him in touch with Sidney Carter who offered him an exhibition and temporary reprieve.[75] He later found work teaching at the Y.W.H.A.

He continued to design stage sets for Yiddish theatre groups and for productions put on by various leftist political groups, though more from an interest in theatre than political conviction.[76] In 1935, with financial assistance from Vincent Massey,[77] he made his first trip to the Gaspé, to which he was often to return.

Alexandre Bercovitch's work at this time consisted of naturalistic depictions of city streets, Expressionist stage sets, Impressionist Gaspé landscapes, and dramatic portraits and character studies of his family and friends. In The Artist's Family (1934, cat. no. 107) the roughly applied paint has an Expressionist intensity, accentuated by the confinement and monumentality of the figures.

The forceful plastic and Expressionist qualities of Bercovitch's work contrasts with the gentle romanticism of Eric Goldberg's paintings. Born in Berlin, Goldberg studied first with Lovis Corinth and later at the Académie Julian in Paris from 1906 to 1910, at the same time as John Lyman, A.Y. Jackson, and Randolph Hewton.[78] He returned to Berlin and after the war travelled and painted in France, Spain, and Palestine. In 1928 he married the Montreal artist Regina Seiden and for the next eight years alternated between Montreal and Europe.

Eric Goldberg's painting has a very lyrical quality, reminiscent of Jules Pascin. In Tossa del Mar (c. 1934, cat. no. 108) all is suggestion rather than statement. Reducing the elements to their basic shapes, he creates a colour poem of misty forms and spacious landscapes.

Despite the high quality of their work, these artists had little chance to exhibit. Their paintings were consistently rejected by the juries for Montreal exhibitions, the Royal Canadian Academy, and the Spring Exhibition at the Art Association, and, unlike the Toronto community, there was little cooperative effort among Montreal artists.

John Lyman first brought the newer artists together in an exhibition at The Arts Club in February 1937.[79] That autumn Fritz Brandtner arranged another Salon des Indépendants at the annual Produced in Canada Exhibition.[80] In the spring of 1938, the Eastern Group of Painters was formed, the first exhibition being held at the galleries of W. Scott & Sons in November.[81]

The members of the new group included John Lyman, Alexandre Bercovitch, Eric Goldberg, Goodridge Roberts, Jack Humphrey,[82] and Jori Smith. As John Lyman had stated in his column in The Montrealer, what characterized the 'eastern' artists was their openness to European influence. At the same time there is a pervasive mood in the work of all these artists, be it the colour-saturated landscapes of Roberts and Goldberg or the moody figure studies and portraits by Lyman, Bercovitch, Humphrey, Smith, and Roberts. A similar tone pervades the work of Philip Surrey who replaced Jack Humphrey as the sixth member of the group the following year.[83]

John Lyman was not alone in supporting more international developments in Canada. Maurice Gagnon, Ottawa-born and graduate of the University of Paris and the École du Louvre, returned to teach in Montreal in 1935.[84] In *La Revue Moderne*,[85] and in lectures [86] he outlined and publicized the development of contemporary French art. He began teaching art history at the École du Meuble in 1937, joining Marcel Parizeau, also Paris-trained and professor of architecture, and Paul-Émile Borduas, the newly appointed instructor of drawing and decoration.[87]

Born in Saint-Hilaire near Montreal, Paul-Émile Borduas first discovered the world of art through the decorations of Ozias Leduc in the village church. In 1920, at the age of fifteen, he apprenticed himself to Ozias Leduc and for the next seven years assisted him in his work, at the same time attending the École des Beaux-Arts in Montreal. Graduating in 1927, he taught for a year and, in November 1928, with financial assistance from Monseigneur Olivier Maurault and Ozias Leduc, left for France.[88]

In Paris he studied five months at the École des Arts Sacrés, the school directed by Maurice Denis and George Desvallières, and, in April 1929, left Paris to travel in Brittany, Alsace, and Lorraine. After a winter assisting in various church decorations, including the installations of the windows by the Dominican Marie-Alain Couturier at Chaillon, he returned to Montreal in June 1930.[89]

After two years of fruitless attempts to obtain commissions for church decorations,[90] he returned to teaching at the Collège André Grasset and for the Catholic School Commission.[91] In 1937 he sought a teaching position at the École des Beaux-Arts in Quebec. However, Jean Paul Lemieux obtained the post and Borduas replaced him at the École du Meuble.[92]

Teaching long hours left little time for his own work. Of his painting in the thirties, Borduas wrote, 'Studio work is soul-destroying. Out of six years of determined work only ten canvases are worth a thing. And I recognize that those ten are happy accidents impossible to repeat.'[93] His early work shows a strong influence of Maurice Denis, very decorative with a gentle romanticism. However by 1937 there is greater concern for structure and for the plastic qualities of paint. In the *Portrait of Maurice Gagnon* (1937, cat. no. 109),[94] the structure of the vest and broad lapels, and the richness of brown becoming sensuous texture in the background, show Borduas slowly progressing to a more personal and studied expression.

Teaching children guided Borduas to the freedom of creative painting.[95] At the same time, with John Lyman,[96] Marcel Parizeau, and Maurice Gagnon he studied the history of art, seeking the principles and forms that unite the art of the past to the present.[97] In his own work to 1941

there occurs a form of *rattrapage* ('catching up') from Maurice Denis to Cézanne to Picasso and Braque and finally to Surrealism.[98] However, it is only with the arrival of Pellan in 1940 that Borduas was to accelerate his development leading to the gouaches of 1941 – 1942.

With the increasing artistic activity in Montreal and the large number of artists excluded from the Eastern Group,[99] it was apparent that a larger society was needed to incorporate progressive artists of divergent trends and to further the cause of modern art.

John Lyman first mentioned the idea for such an organization in an article published in the fall of 1938 in which he lamented the lack of financial and moral support given the finest contemporary artists.[100] In the unpublished closing line, he wrote, 'We badly need active organizations in support of creative art such as the Contemporary Arts [sic] Society in England and numerous ones in the United States.'[101]

The British Contemporary Art Society[102] had been formed in 1910 'to bring to light young and rising talent . . .; to purchase, for the benefit of the public, works by artists of acknowledged power who are not properly represented in the [public] Galleries; and by its loan and presentations to spread throughout the country the knowledge and appreciation of modern art.'[103] John Lyman recognized that a similar organization in Montreal could further the cause of contemporary art and financially assist the artists.

In January 1939[104] the Contemporary Arts Society[105] was formed and by May had twenty-six artist members.[106] John Lyman was president, Paul-Émile Borduas, vice-president, Fritz Brandtner, secretary, and Philip Surrey, treasurer.[107] All the artist members were from Montreal except for Jack Humphrey, though Fritz Brandtner did invite André Biéler,[108] Paraskeva Clark,[109] and LeMoine FitzGerald[110] to join. All refused.

The Contemporary Arts Society was not solely an artists' organization. It also sought to foster the development of a living, progressive art alive to contemporary life. 'It took exactly the position of an anti-academy, putting emphasis on the living quality of art – on imagination, sensitivity, intuition, and spontaneity as opposed to conventional proficiency, regarding membership in an academy as merely a consolation for having died during one's own lifetime.'[111] An associate membership was created for non-artists 'to give support to contemporary trends in art and to further the artistic interests of its members . . . .'[112] To encourage sales of works, a discount was available to members and a picture-loan system organized.[113]

To fulfill its educational rôle, the first exhibition arranged by the Contemporary Arts Society was entitled *Art of Our Day*[114] and consisted of non-Canadian modern works borrowed from Montreal collectors.[115] The works in the exhibition reflected Lyman's preferences in contemporary art – Derain, Dufy, Frances Hodgkins, Modigliani, and Matthew Smith – as well as the limitations of local collections.[116] While not 'the first adequate representation in Canada of Modern work by leading foreign artists,'[117] it did signal the beginnings of a united effort for contemporary art and the invasion of the conservative halls of the Art Association.

The following autumn an exhibition of paintings by artist-members of the Contemporary Arts Society was held at the Stevens Art Gallery,[118] and in November 1940 a third exhibition of works by members of the Canadian Group of Painters and Contemporary Arts Society.[119] However, the battle was not to be fought without some token opposition. Even before the opening of *Art of Our Day* Clarence Gagnon lashed out in a talk entitled 'The Grand Bluff – Modernistic Art' given to the conservative Pen and Pencil Club,[120] drawing an assertive reply from John Lyman full of references to heavy-weight supporters of contemporary art and a more reasoned response from Marcel Parizeau.[121] Most of the journalistic response, however, was extremely favourable.

Apart from Robert Ayre, most of the coverage and interest in the development of the Contemporary Arts Society was coming from French-language writers,[122] who soon commented on the lack of French-Canadian artists in the group.[123] Of all the members only four were French-speaking: Paul-Émile Borduas, Stanley Cosgrove, Louise Gadbois, and Jean Palardy. However, political, literary, and artistic developments were eventually to transform the Contemporary Arts Society into one of the leading forces in French-Canadian cultural life.

Jean-Charles Harvey founded the newspaper *Le Jour* in 1937 with a nationalist ideology designed to bring the culture of Quebec out of its provincialism into the mainstream of world developments. He denounced the soul-destroying education of the École des Beaux-Arts and the isolationism of its director, Charles Maillard,[124] calling upon the artists to break away from regionalist local colour, *ceinture flèchée,* and *habitants,* to seek a non-colonial universal expression. 'If French Canadians have been so mediocre in arts and letters, it is not for want of talent but from a lack of freedom. They have been subjugated. For one hundred years they have been subjected to an intellectual fascism which has annihilated them . . . .'[125] 'Art must be revolutionary or nothing, in the sense that, at the risk of dying, it must incessantly search for all the formulas of beauty and all aspects of beauty.'[126]

In contrast to the 'lack of audacity, of personality, and genuine sensitivity' of the Anciens de l'École des Beaux-Arts[127] was Alfred Pellan, a rising Quebec star in France. In the two years before his return from France, large Pellan exhibitions were periodically predicted.[128] Here was not only a local boy who made good, but a Quebecker who had left behind regionalist clichés to discover 'a Paris enriched by centuries of refinement.'[129] To the critics of internationalism, Jean Paul Lemieux wrote, 'Pellan is reproached for being an internationalist, for not having remained Canadian. Why should he be content with folklore images when he could go further? Why confine art within petty limits? Is not art universal?'[130]

To find the universal through subjective expression, to link the intellectual life of Quebec to the source of twentieth-century ideas in France, not in colonial servitude but in an alliance of spirit, this was the direction of the forties. With the arrival of Père Marie-Alain Couturier in March 1940[131] and Alfred Pellan in May [132] the stage was set.

NOTES TO CHAPTER 7

1. Jehanne Biétry Salinger, 'The Group of Seven,' *The Canadian Forum*, vol. XII, no. 136 (January 1932), pp. 142–143.

2. John Lyman, 'Letter to the Editor: Canadian Art,' *The Canadian Forum*, vol. XII, no. 140 (May 1932), p. 313.

3. Edward P. Lawson, 'Chronology,' *John Lyman* (exhibition catalogue) (Montreal: The Montreal Museum of Fine Arts, 1963).

4. Philip Hendy, *Matthew Smith* (Harmondsworth: Penguin, 1944), p. 7.

5. *Matthew Smith* (London: George Allen and Unwin Limited, 1962).

6. Edward P. Lawson, *op. cit.* John Lyman stated he attended the school during its final year. See John Lyman, 'Adieu Matisse,' *Canadian Art*, vol. XII, no. 2 (Winter 1955), p. 45. However, the school did not close until the summer of 1911. See Alfred H. Barr, Jr, *Matisse: His Art And His Public* (New York: The Museum of Modern Art, 1951), p. 117.

7. Montreal, Art Association of Montreal, 21–31 May 1913, *Exhibition of Paintings & Drawings by John G. Lyman*.

8. Montreal, Art Association of Montreal, to 7 March 1913, [*R.S. Hewton and A.Y. Jackson*].

9. New York, Sixty-Ninth Regiment Armory, 17 February–15 March 1913, *International Exhibition of Modern Art*.

10. They had also bitterly denounced John Lyman's works included in the Annual Spring Exhibition the previous month. For excerpts from the critical reaction, see Edward P. Lawson, *op. cit.*; also Paul Dumas, 'Lyman,' *Le Quartier Latin*, vol. XXVI, no. 11 (17 December 1943), p. III.

11. Edward P. Lawson, *op. cit.*

12. Montreal, the Johnson Art Galleries Ltd., 1–15 October 1927, *Exhibition of Recent Paintings and Drawings by John Lyman*.

13. John Lyman, 'Journal,' vol. I, entry for 3 August [1927]; in the Bibliothèque Nationale du Québec, Montreal.

14. John Lyman, 'Journal,' vol. II, entries for 17 August [1930] at Sainte-Pétronille, Île d'Orléans; 5 September [1930] at Montreal; in the Bibliothèque nationale du Québec, Montreal.

15. Montreal, W. Scott & Sons, [February 1931], *Exhibition of Paintings by John Lyman*.

16. John Lyman, 'Journal,' vol. II, entry for 28 September [1931] at Outremont; in the Bibliothèque nationale du Québec, Montreal.

17. Among others attending these weekly gatherings were Frank and Marian Scott, Jeannette and André Biéler, Hazen Sise, Elizabeth Frost, Ronald McCall, Cleveland Morgan, John and Florence Byrd, Jacques Biéler, and John Humphrey.

18. 'School Of Art Is Formed By Group,' Montreal *Gazette* (17 November 1931).

19. Hazen Sise graduated in 1929 from the Massachusetts Institute of Technology and received his degree in February 1930. He went to Paris and worked for a short period in Le Corbusier's architectural office. In the fall of 1930 he went to New York and worked for Howe and Lescaze, returning to Montreal in the autumn of 1931. (Interview with Hazen Sise, Ottawa, 1 February 1974).

20. *The Atelier: A School of Drawing Painting Sculpture* (pamphlet, n.d.).

21. Interview with Allan Harrison, Montreal, 13 September 1973. Allan Harrison was *massier* at the Atelier – responsible for arranging the classes and timing the poses of the models.

22. John Lyman, 'Art,' *The Montrealer* (1 February 1938).

23. Two exhibitions of works by staff members and invited contributors were held: Montreal, Henry Morgan & Company, 29 March–9 April 1932, *André Biéler, Marc-Aurèle Fortin, Elizabeth Frost, Edwin H. Holgate, George Holt, John Lyman*; Montreal, Henry Morgan & Company, 1–13 May 1933, *André Biéler, Elizabeth Frost, George Holt, John Lyman, Goodridge Roberts*.

24. *The Lyman Summer Art Class, 2 July to 10 September 1935*, Pamphlet. Harold Beament also taught with John Lyman this summer.

25. Montreal *Gazette* (23 January 1934).

26. The typescript of John Lyman's talk is among the Lyman Papers in the Bibliothèque nationale du Québec, Montreal.

27. See section Selected Bibliography: John Lyman in Bibliography.

28. Montreal, W. Scott & Sons, December 1934, *French Paintings by the Impressionists and Modern Artists*; Montreal, W. Scott & Sons, March 1936, *Exhibition of French Paintings / Renoir and His Contemporaries*; Montreal, W. Scott & Sons, October 1936, *Exhibition of Modern French Paintings / The School of Paris*; Montreal, W. Scott & Sons, October 1937, *Exhibition of Paintings by French Masters of the Nineteenth and Twentieth Centuries*; Montreal, W. Scott & Sons, October 1938, *Paintings By French Masters, 'Delacroix to Dufy.'*

29. John Heaton took over W. Scott & Sons about 1930 from his father Frank Heaton, the son-in-law of William Scott. See 'Frank R. Heaton Dies in 74th Year,' Montreal *Gazette* (23 October 1939). The firm held an auction of their stock in April 1938 (Montreal, Fraser Bros., Ltd., [April 1938], *Greatest Art Auction in Montreal's History . . . Comprising The Entire Stock of Messrs. W. Scott & Sons*), moving to new quarters that fall and closing permanently the next spring. See St. George Burgoyne, 'W. Scott & Sons Leaving Business as Art Dealers in Firm's 80th Year,' Montreal *Gazette* (4 March 1939).

30. 'Variations on the Lake' exhibited Montreal, W. Scott & Sons, 6–20 February 1937, *Exhibition of Paintings by John Lyman*, nos. 36–42.

31. John Lyman, 'Art,' *The Montrealer* (1 February 1938).

32. Montreal, The Arts Club, 31 October–18 November 1932, *Exhibition of Water Color Paintings by Goodridge Roberts*.

33. Jacques G. de Tonnancour, *Roberts* (Montreal: L'Arbre, 1944), p. 15, n. 1.

34. James Borcoman, *Goodridge Roberts* (exhibition catalogue) (Ottawa: The National Gallery of Canada, 1969), pp. 44–45.

35. *Idem.*

36. Goodridge Roberts, 'From This Point I Looked Out,' *Queen's Quarterly* (Autumn 1953), p. 320. Reprinted in James Borcoman, *op. cit.*, p. 188. All references will be to the reprint edition.

37. Montreal, Henry Morgan & Company, 1–13 May 1933, *André Biéler, Elizabeth Frost, George Holt, John Lyman, Goodridge Roberts*.

38. Jacques G. de Tonnancour, *op. cit.*, p. 14.

39. Goodridge Roberts, *op. cit.*, p. 192.

40. Marian Roberts, Kingston, to Kathleen Fenwick, Ottawa, 27 August [1936]; in The National Gallery of Canada.

41. Ernst Neumann, 'Canadian Artists of Today / Wm. Goodridge Roberts,' *New Frontier*, vol. I, no. 4 (July 1936), p. 30.

42. James Borcoman, *op. cit.*, pp. 45–46.

43. Goodridge Roberts, Montreal, to H.O. McCurry, Ottawa, 15 June 1940; in The National Gallery of Canada.

44. Robert Ayre, 'Art in Montreal is Given New and Vigorous Life,' *Saturday Night*, vol. LVI, no. 10 (16 November 1940), p. 19.

45. This melancholia appears in Roberts's poetry also. 'Beneath my feet the spring of life is gushing; Above my head the bird of death is winging.' (Goodridge Roberts, *op. cit.*, p. 189.)

46. Neufville Shaw, 'Goodridge Roberts – 1949,' *Northern Review*, vol. III, no. 1 (October–November 1949), p. 27.

47. Interview with Philip Surrey, Montreal, 14 September 1973.

48. Robert Ayre, 'The City and the Dream of Philip Surrey,' *Canadian Art*, vol. XXI, no. 5 (September–October 1964), p. 284.

49. Interview with Philip Surrey, Montreal, 14 September 1973.

50. Interview with Mrs Mieze Brandtner, Montreal, 12 September 1973.

51. Fritz Brandtner, Winnipeg, to Eric Brown, Ottawa, 27 December 1932; in The National Gallery of Canada.

52. J. Russell Harper, *Fritz Brandtner 1896 – 1969* (exhibition catalogue) (Montreal: Sir George Williams University, 1971), p. 15.

53. Fritz Brandtner, Montreal, to L.L. FitzGerald, Winnipeg, 4 April 1934; private property.

54. Interview with Mrs Mieze Brandtner, Montreal, 12 September 1973.

55. Fritz Brandtner, Montreal, to L.L. FitzGerald, Winnipeg, 4 April 1934; private property.

56. Interview with Mrs Mieze Brandtner, Montreal, 12 September 1973. The painting was *Sunflower* and was exhibited at the Art Association of Montreal, 19 April – 13 May 1934, *51st Spring Exhibition*, no. 38. It is presently in the collection of Mr Edward Schneerer, Montreal.

57. Montreal, Henry Morgan & Company, 15 — 29 February 1936, *Exhibition of Paintings by Fritz Brandtner*.

58. R.H.A. [Robert Ayre], 'Fritz Brandtner's Work is Exhibited,' Montreal *Gazette* (15 February 1936). Reprinted as 'Art-Expressionist in Montreal,' *New Frontier*, vol. i, no. 2 (May 1936), pp. 29 – 30.

59. Henri Girard, 'La Vie Artistique – Fritz Brandtner,' *Le Canada* (26 February 1936).

60. Reynald [E.R. Bertrand], 'Les cauchemars de F. Brandtner,' *La Presse* (22 February 1936).

61. Fritz Brandtner brought with him to Canada a series of monograph booklets on modern German and French artists through which he continually refamiliarized himself with their work. There was no contemporary German art being exhibited in Canada at this time.

62. Graham C. McInnes, 'The World of Art,' *Saturday Night,* vol. lii, no. 6 (12 December 1936), p. 19.

63. Roderick Stewart, *Bethune* (Toronto: New Press, 1973), p. 91. Norman Bethune left for Spain on 24 October 1936.

64. 'Kids and Paints,' Montreal *Standard* (10 September 1938).

65. Interview with Marian Scott, Montreal, 15 September 1973.

66. *Idem.*

67. Marian Scott, 'Science as an Inspiration to Art,' *Canadian Art*, vol. i, no. 1 (October – November 1943), p. 19.

68. Interview with Louis Muhlstock, Montreal, 15 September 1973.

69. The 'Paranka' drawings were done at this time.

70. Laurence Sabbath, 'Artists in Action Series: 1, Louis Muhlstock with Lawrence Sabbath,' *Canadian Art*, vol. xvii, no. 4 (July 1960), p. 219.

71. 'Alexandre Bercovitch,' The National Gallery of Canada Information Form, [received 9 May 1932]. According to John Lyman, Bercovitch also studied under Eric Goldberg's father, a portrait painter in Berlin. See John Lyman, 'Art,' *The Montrealer* (15 April 1938).

72. Interview with Sylvia (Bercovitch) Ary, Montreal, 11 September 1973.

73. 'Alexandre Bercovitch,' The National Gallery of Canada Information Form, 16 June 1942.

74. Regina Shoolman later married Charles Slatkin, owner of the Slatkin Gallery in New York City. They co-authored *The Enjoyment of Art in America* (Philadelphia, New York: Lippincott, 1942).

75. 'Eviction of Artist Brings Recognition,' *Montreal Daily Herald* (7 April 1933).

76. Interview with Sylvia (Bercovitch) Ary, Montreal, 11 September 1973.

77. Alexandre Bercovitch, Montreal, to Mrs Vincent Massey, Ottawa, 22 November 1935; in The National Gallery of Canada.

78. John Lyman, 'Art,' *The Montrealer* (15 April 1938). Eric Goldberg is the blond boy with glasses seated second from the right in the second row in the photograph of the Académie Julian reproduced in Dennis Reid, *The Group of Seven* (exhibition catalogue) (Ottawa: The National Gallery of Canada, 1970), p. 23.

79. Robert Ayre, 'Two Exhibitions,' *The Montrealer* (February 1937). This exhibition included works by Prudence Heward, Sarah Robertson, Mabel Lockerby, Jack Humphrey, Jori Smith, Jean Palardy, Goodridge Roberts, Fritz Brandtner, and Marian Scott.

80. [Montreal, Sun Life Building, National Produced in Canada Exhibition, November 1937], *Art Exhibition*. The catalogue lists the following artists: Alexandre Bercovitch, Sam Borenstein, Fritz Brandtner, Marian Scott, Allan Harrison, Prudence Heward, Jack Humphrey, John Lyman, Carl Mangold, Louis Muhlstock, Goodridge Roberts, Sarah Robertson, Jori Smith, and Philip Surrey.

81. Robert Ayre, 'The Eastern Group Has a Show,' *Saturday Night*, vol. liv, no. 7 (17 December 1938), p. 36.

82. Jack Humphrey had contacted the Montreal artists during his stay in 1933. It is also possible he visited Montreal in 1937. (Interview with Jori Smith, Montreal, 16 January 1974.)

83. John Lyman, Montreal, to H.O. McCurry, Ottawa, 29 November 1939; in The National Gallery of Canada. 'Jack Humphrey, who felt he was at a material disadvantage, compared with the other members, on account of living so far away, has, on our advice, dropped out, and has been replaced by Philip Surrey.'

84. 'La Peinture Moderne par Maurice Gagnon,' *La Revue Populaire*, vol. xxxiii, no. 11 (November 1940).

85. Maurice Gagnon, 'Initiation à la peinture moderne,' *La Revue Moderne*, vol. xviii, no. 5 (March 1937), pp. 16 – 17; vol. xviii, no. 6 (April 1937), pp. 6 – 7; vol. xviii, no. 7 (May 1937), pp. 6 – 7; vol. xviii, no. 8 (June 1937), pp. 8 – 9.

86. Paul-Émile Borduas, 'Projections libérantes,' (annotated edition prepared under the direction of François Gagnon), *Études françaises*, vol. viii, no. 3 (August 1972), p. 265, n. 61.

87. *Ibid.*, p. 261, n. 45.

88. Guy Robert, *Borduas* (Quebec: Les presses de l'Université du Québec, 1972), pp. 15 – 21.

89. Guy Robert, *op. cit.*, p. 21.

90. Paul-Émile Borduas, *op. cit.*, p. 258.

91. *Ibid.*, p. 259, nn. 39 – 41.

92. *Ibid.*, pp. 261 – 263.

93. *Ibid.*, p. 260.

94. In 1937, the year the portrait was painted, Maurice Gagnon published the first article on Borduas. See Maurice Gagnon, 'Paul-Émile Borduas/Peintre montréalais,' *La Revue Moderne*, vol. xviii, no. 11 (September 1937), pp. 10 – 11.

95. Paul-Émile Borduas, *op. cit.*, p. 260.

96. Paul-Émile Borduas met John Lyman in the spring of 1938. See John Lyman, 'Borduas and the Contemporary Arts Society,' in Evan H, Turner, *Paul-Émile Borduas 1905 – 1960* (exhibition catalogue) (Montreal: The Montreal Museum of Fine Arts, 1962), p. 40.

97. Maurice Gagnon published *Peinture Moderne* (Montreal: Éditions Bernard Valiquette) in 1940, in which he traced the development of art, predominantly French, from the Renaissance to the present day with its manifestations in the contemporary art of Quebec.

98. It is probably not coincidental that Maurice Gagnon published Pablo Picasso's *Femme à la mandoline* in *Peinture Moderne* in 1940 (fig. 29), and that in 1941 Borduas was to paint a similar work with the same title (oil on canvas; 32 x 26 in., 81.3 x 66.1 cm, Musée d'art contemporain, Montreal, repr. in colour in Guy Robert, *op. cit.*, p. 250). George Braque's *Nature morte* reproduced in *Peinture Moderne* (fig. 30) bears many similarities to Borduas' still lifes of 1941, not-

ably *Nature morte aux ananas et poirs* (oil on canvas; 19-5/8 x 23-5/8 in., 49.8 x 59.9 cm, The National Gallery of Canada).

99. The Eastern Group continued to exhibit intermittently up to 1950 though Alexandre Bercovitch resigned in 1942 ('Alexandre Bercovitch,' The National Gallery of Canada Information Form, 16 June 1942).

100. John Lyman, 'Art,' *The Montrealer* (1 October 1938).

101. John Lyman, 'Five Tons,' Typescript for 'Art,' *The Montrealer* (1 October 1938); in the Bibliothèque nationale du Québec, Montreal. In a letter to H.O. McCurry, Ottawa, 8 October 1938; in The National Gallery of Canada, John Lyman quoted the omitted line as, 'We in Canada badly need something in the nature of a Contemporary Arts [sic] Society which would give encouragement to artists who have not the material advantages given by regimentation.'

102. An exhibition of works loaned by the Contemporary Art Society was exhibited at the Art Association of Montreal, 15 – 30 April 1938. See Art Association of Montreal, *Annual Report 1938*, p. 26.

103. *Contemporary Art Society Report 1936 – 7* (London: The Curwen Press, [1937]), p. 3.

104. John Lyman, 'Borduas and the Contemporary Arts Society,' in Evan H. Turner, *op. cit.*, p. 40.

105. The English name of the organization was originally 'Contemporary Arts Society,' though by 1946 the Society's letterhead read 'Contemporary Art Society.' In French the singular 'Société d'art contemporain' or abbreviation 'C.A.S.' was used.

106. 'Contemporary Arts Society. List of Artist Members. 16 May 1939'; in The Montreal Museum of Fine Arts. Artist members included Jack Beder, Alexandre Bercovitch, Paul-Émile Borduas, Sam Borenstein, Fritz Brandtner, Stanley Cosgrove, Henry Eveleigh, Charles Fainmel, Louise Gadbois, Eric Goldberg, Eldon Grier, Allan Harrison, Prudence Heward, Jack Humphrey, John Lyman, Louis Muhlstock, Jean Palardy, Marguerite Paquette, Goodridge Roberts, Anne Savage, Marian Scott, Regina Seiden, Jori Smith, Philip Surrey, Cambell Tinning, and Bernard Mayman.

107. Fritz Brandtner, Montreal, to H.O. McCurry, Ottawa, 15 April 1939; in The National Gallery of Canada.

108. Fritz Brandtner, Montreal, to André Biéler, Kingston, 6 March 1939; property of André Biéler. As one of the conditions of membership was that artists not participate in the activities of any academy, André Biéler refused membership in the C.A.S. ,feeling it to be useless to revive the conflict with the Royal Canadian Academy. See André Biéler, Kingston, to Fritz Brandtner, Montreal, 21 April 1939; copy property of André Biéler. My thanks to Frances Smith for bringing these letters to my attention.

109. Interview with Paraskeva Clark, Toronto, 18 October 1973.

110. Fritz Brandtner, Montreal, to L.L. FitzGerald, Saint James (Manitoba), 8 March 1939; private property.

111. John Lyman, 'Borduas and the Contemporary Arts Society,' in Evan H. Turner, *op. cit.*, p. 40.

112. 'Contemporary Arts Society Constitution,' [1939], paragraph 2; private property.

113. [Foreword], *Contemporary Arts Society/Exhibition of Paintings by Members* (exhibition catalogue) [Montreal: Frank Stevens Gallery, December 1939].

114. Montreal, Art Association of Montreal, 13 – 28 May 1939, *Loan Exhibition/Art of Our Day*. The exhibition's title was probably chosen with one eye on the opening exhibition at the new (1939) Museum of Modern Art in New York, *Art in Our Time*.

115. The collectors included friends of John Lyman who had purchased works from the exhibitions at W. Scott & Sons, Jewish refugees from Europe, Europeans working in Montreal, and artist members of the Contemporary Arts Society.

116. This exhibition was shown with deletions and additions from Toronto and Buffalo collections at The Art Gallery of Toronto the following autumn. See Toronto, The Art Gallery of Toronto, November – December 1939, *20th Century European Paintings*.

117. [Foreword], *Contemporary Arts Society Exhibition of Paintings By Members* (exhibition catalogue) [Montreal: Frank Stevens Gallery, December 1939]. Toronto had had more consistent exposure to contemporary art including the Société Anonyme exhibition in 1927 and a large surrealist exhibition at the Canadian National Exhibition in 1938 (Toronto: Canadian National Exhibition, 26 August – 10 September 1938, *Surrealist Art*).

118. Sam Borenstein, Charles Fainmel, Eldon Grier, Jack Humphrey, Jean Palardy, Marguerite Paquette, Anne Savage, Regina Seiden, and Campbell Tinning were not included in this exhibition. Three new members were added: Mabel Lockerby, Ethel Seath, and Piercy Younger.

119. Montreal, Art Association of Montreal, 22 November – 15 December 1940, *Contemporary Arts Society*. This was dubbed 'Art of Our Day in Canada' by Robert Ayre in *Saturday Night*, vol. LVI, no. 16 (28 December 1940), p. 26.

120. Roy Kerwin, 'Gagnon Lashes Out At False Values In Modernistic Art,' Montreal *Standard* (29 April 1939). This talk was translated into French and published after Clarence Gagnon's death. See Clarence Gagnon, 'L'Immense Blague de l'Art Moderniste,' *Amérique française* (September 1948), pp. 60 – 65; (December 1948), pp. 44 – 48; (March 1949), pp. 67 – 71; (June 1949), pp. 30 – 33.

121. 'Gagnon's Talk On Art Draws Spirited Reply,' Montreal *Standard* (6 May 1939).

122. Especially from 1940 these included Marcel Parizeau and Henri Girard in *Le Canada*; Charles Doyon, Émile-Charles Hamel, and Jean-Charles Harvey in *Le Jour*; and Jacques de Tonnancour in *Le Quartier Latin*.

123. Maurice Gagnon, *Peinture Moderne* (1940), p. 127.

124. Jean-Charles Harvey, 'Les Bourses d'Europe et M. Maillard,' *Le Jour*, vol. I, no. 37 (28 May 1938).

125. Jean-Charles Harvey, 'En lettres, en art, être libre ou ne pas être,' *Le Jour*, vol. I, no. 6 (23 October 1937).

126. Jean-Charles Harvey, 'La pire obstacle à l'art canadien,' *Le Jour*, vol. I, no. 28 (26 March 1938).

127. Paul Riverin, 'Écoliers ou professionnels?,' *Le Jour*, vol. I, no. 33 (30 April 1938).

128. Jean Paul Lemieux, 'Notes sur quelques toiles de Pellan,' *Le Jour*, vol. I, no. 35 (14 May 1938); J. Picart-Ledoux, 'Un jeune peintre, Pellan,' *Le Jour*, vol. II, no. 18 (14 January 1939); Juliette Cabana, 'Chez Alfred Pellan peintre moderne,' *La Revue Populaire*, vol. XXXII, no. 11 (November 1939), pp. 8 – 9.

129. Jean Paul Lemieux, *ibid.*

130. *Idem.*

131. 'Des leçons pratiques sur l'art religieux,' Montreal *La Presse* (30 March 1940).

132. Maurice Gagnon, *Pellan* (Montreal: L'Arbre, 1943), p. 11.

*88.
JOHN LYMAN
Haying by the Lake   1933

89.
JOHN LYMAN
The Card Game   c. 1935

90.
JOHN LYMAN
Jori Smith in Costume   1936

91.
JOHN LYMAN
Woman with White Collar   c. 1936

*92.
JOHN LYMAN
Lassitude   c. 1937

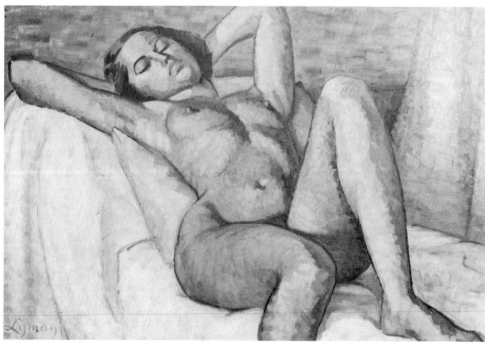

*93.
GOODRIDGE ROBERTS
Ottawa Valley   1933

94.
GOODRIDGE ROBERTS
Ontario Landscape in a Red Light   1936

*95.   96.
GOODRIDGE ROBERTS   GOODRIDGE ROBERTS
Marian   1937   *Standing Nude*   1938

97.
PHILIP SURREY
The Boardwalk   *c.* 1938

*98.
PHILIP SURREY
Sunday Afternoon   1939

97.
PHILIP SURREY
The Boardwalk   *c.* 1938

*98.
PHILIP SURREY
Sunday Afternoon   1939

99.
PHILIP SURREY
The Red Portrait   1939

100.
FRITZ BRANDTNER
Men of 1939   1939

*101.
FRITZ BRANDTNER
The Riders 1939

*102.
FRITZ BRANDTNER
Abstraction 1936

103.
MARIAN SCOTT
Escalator   1937

*104.
MARIAN SCOTT
Tenants   c. 1940

*105.
LOUIS MUHLSTOCK
Sainte-Famille Street   1939

106.
LOUIS MUHLSTOCK
Open Door of Third House, Groubert Lane,
Montreal   c. 1939

*107.
ALEXANDRE BERCOVITCH
The Artist's Family   1934

108.
ERIC GOLDBERG
Tossa del Mar   *c. 1934*

109.
PAUL-ÉMILE BORDUAS
Portrait of Maurice Gagnon   1937

49.   DAVID MILNE, *Palgrave (I)* (1931)

Catalogue

Abbreviations

AAM   Art Association of Montreal. Became The Montreal Museum of Fine Arts in 1948.

AGO   Art Gallery of Ontario, Toronto.

AGT   The Art Gallery of Toronto, Toronto.

Bradfield AGO   Helen Pepall Bradfield, *Art Gallery of Ontario: The Canadian Collection* (Toronto: McGraw-Hill Company of Canada Limited, 1970).

~*CNE*   The Canadian National Exhibition, Toronto. Annual exhibitions held in the Fine Arts Pavilion (exhibition catalogues).

~*CSPWC*   Canadian Society of Painters in Water Colour. Annual exhibitions held at The Art Gallery of Toronto (exhibition catalogues).

~*Group of Seven 1936*   *Retrospective Exhibition of Paintings by Members of the Group of Seven 1919 – 1933* (exhibition catalogue; Ottawa: The National Gallery of Canada, 1936). Exhibited at Ottawa, The National Gallery of Canada, March 1936; Montreal, Art Asoociation of Montreal, until 5 May 1936; Toronto, The Art Gallery of Toronto, from 15 May 1936.

Hubbard NGC   Robert H. Hubbard, ed., *The National Gallery of Canada. Catalogue. Paintings and Sculpture. Volume III: Canadian School* (Toronto: University of Toronto Press, 1960).

MMFA   The Montreal Museum of Fine Arts.

NGC   The National Gallery of Canada, Ottawa.

~*OSA*   Ontario Society of Artists. Annual exhibitions held at The Art Gallery of Toronto (exhibition catalogues).

~*RCA*   Royal Canadian Academy of Arts. Annual exhibitions held alternately at The Art Gallery of Toronto and the Art Association of Montreal (exhibition catalogues).

Southern Dominions Exhibition   *Exhibition of Contemporary Canadian Painting Arranged on Behalf of the Carnegie Corporation of New York for Circulation in the Southern Dominions of the British Empire* (exhibition catalogue; Ottawa: The National Gallery of Canada, 1936).

Summer 1935   *Catalogue of the portion of the permanent collection of oil and water colour paintings as arranged for exhibition* (exhibition catalogue; Toronto: The Art Gallery of Toronto, Summer 1935).

VAG   The Vancouver Art Gallery, Vancouver.

Unless otherwise specified, all works are oil on canvas. Dimensions are given in inches and centimeters, height preceding width.

Catalogue entries that are starred will not be exhibited outside Ottawa, Vancouver, and Toronto.

*1

Arthur Lismer   1885 – 1969
Baie Saint-Paul, Quebec   1931
24 x 32 in. (61.0 x 81.3 cm)

INSCRIPTION: Signed and dated l.r., *A. LISMER '31.*

PROVENANCE: Acquired from the artist.

EXHIBITION: (?) Toronto, The Galleries of J. Merritt Malloney, 4 – 25 May 1935, *Exhibition of Paintings, Sketches and Drawings by Arthur Lismer, A.R.C.A., O.S.A.,* no. 6 (as *Quebec Landscape*).

Probably painted from the same sketch as *Quebec Uplands* (1926, oil on canvas; 32 x 40 in., 81.3 x 101.6 cm) in The National Gallery of Canada, Ottawa (5056).

Another version is in a private collection, Edmonton.

Power Corporation of Canada, Limited

NOT IN EXHIBITION

2

Arthur Lismer   1885 – 1969
Pine Wrack   1933
36-1/2 x 42 in. (92.8 x 106.7 cm)

INSCRIPTION: Signed and dated l.r., *A. Lismer 1933.*

PROVENANCE: Royal Canadian Academy Diploma Deposit, 1948.

EXHIBITIONS: Toronto, AGT, November 1933, *Exhibition of Paintings by Canadian Group of Painters,* no. 43; Montreal, AAM, 1 – 21 January 1934, *Exhibition of Paintings by Canadian Group of Painters,* no. 35; (?) Toronto, The Galleries of J. Merritt Malloney, 4 – 25 May 1935, *Exhibition of Paintings, Sketches and Drawings by Arthur Lismer, A.R.C.A., O.S.A.,* no. 20 (as *Pine-wrack, Georgian Bay*); Pittsburgh, Carnegie Institute, 17 October – 8 December 1935, *The 1935 International Exhibition of Paintings,* no. 237; London, Royal Institute Galleries, 8 – 29 May 1937, *Exhibition of Paintings Drawings and Sculpture by Artists of the British Empire Overseas,* no. 49; Liverpool, Walker Art Gallery, 16 October 1937 – 8 January 1938, *The Sixty-Third Autumn Exhibition,* no. 519; Buffalo, Albright Art Gallery, November 1938, *Great Lakes Exhibition,* no. 160; Toronto, AGT, January 1950, *Arthur Lismer Paintings 1913 – 1945,* no. 35; Montreal, MMFA, 19 November – 19 December 1954, *75th RCA Retrospective Exhibition,* no. 35.

BIBLIOGRAPHY: Lawren Harris, 'Different Idioms in Creative Art,' *Canadian Comment,* vol. 2, no 12 (December 1933), p. 6 repr.; Walter Abell, 'Canadian Aspirations in Painting,' *Culture,* vol. III (1942), pp. 172 – 173, repr. fig. I; E. Robert Hunter, 'Arthur Lismer,' *Maritime Art,* vol. 3, no. 5 (July – August 1943), p. 140 repr.; *Hubbard NGC* (1960), p. 397, repr.; John A.B. McLeish, *September Gale* (1973), pp. 185, 206.

A watercolour version, entitled *Pine Wrack* (1939, watercolour on paper; 21-1/2 x 30 in., 54.6 x 76.2 cm) is in The McMichael Canadian Collection, Kleinburg. See Paul Duval, *A Vision of Canada* (1973), p. 163 repr.

The National Gallery of Canada, Ottawa (4873)

*3

Arthur Lismer   1885 – 1969
Bright Morning   1935
32 x 40 in. (81.3 x 101.6 cm)

INSCRIPTION: Signed and dated, 1.1., *A. Lismer '35.*

PROVENANCE: Donated by graduates.

EXHIBITIONS: Toronto, AGT, January 1936, *Exhibition of Paintings by the 'Canadian Group of Painters,'* no. 50; Ottawa, NGC, 1936, *Canadian Group of Painters Travelling Exhibition* (Western Tour), no. 22; Ottawa, NGC, 1936, *Canadian Group of Painters Travelling Exhibition* (Eastern Tour), no. 24; Toronto, AGT, January 1950, *Arthur Lismer Paintings 1913 – 1945,* no. 38.

BIBLIOGRAPHY: John A.B. McLeish, *September Gale* (1973), p. 206.

The sketch, entitled *McGregor Bay* (1935, oil on board; 11 x 15-1/2 in., 27.9 x 39.4 cm), is in The McMichael Canadian Collection, Kleinburg. See Paul Duval, *A Vision of Canada* (1973), p. 163 repr.

St. Hilda's College, University of Toronto

4

A.Y. Jackson   1882 – 1974
A Quebec Farm   1930
32-1/4 x 40 in. (81.9 x 101.6 cm)

INSCRIPTION: Signed 1.1., *A.Y. JACKSON.*

PROVENANCE: Acquired from the artist by Vincent Massey, Port Hope, Ontario; Bequest of the Right Hon. Vincent Massey, 1968.

EXHIBITIONS: Toronto, CNE, 22 August – 7 September 1930, no. 90 repr.;(?) Ottawa, NGC, 1931, *Annual Exhibition of Canadian Art,* no. 138 (as *Farm on a Hill*); College Art Association, 1933, *International 1933* (Travelling Exhibition), no. 171 repr.; Toronto, AGT, December 1934, *Canadian Paintings, The Collection of Hon. Vincent and Mrs. Massey,* no. 122 repr.; London, The Tate Gallery, 1938, *A Century of Canadian Art,* no. 110; Ottawa, NGC, 20 September – 20 October 1968, *Vincent Massey Bequest/ The Canadian Paintings,* no. 14.

BIBLIOGRAPHY: Frederick H. Brigden, 'Exhibition of Fine and Graphic Arts Canadian National Exhibition – 1930,' *Journal Royal Architectural Institute of Canada,* vol. VII, no. 10 (October 1930), p. 353 repr.; 'Pastoral Painting in the Machine Age,' *Parnassus,* vol. V, no. 1 (January 1933), p. 26 repr.; *Magazine of Art,* vol. 26 (March 1933), p. 133 repr.; Hugo McPherson, 'The Resonance of Batterwood House,' *Canadian Art,* vol. XXI, no. 2 (March – April 1964), p. 102, repr. p. 103; J. Russell Harper, *Painting in Canada* (1966), p. 296 repr.; Irene Heywood, 'Vers une identité nationale,' *Vie des Arts,* no. 61 (Winter 1970 – 1971), p. 20 repr.; Jean-René Ostiguy, *Un siècle de peinture canadienne* (1971), repr. pl. 85.

The National Gallery of Canada, Ottawa (15481)

*5

A.Y. Jackson 1882 – 1974
Winter, Charlevoix County c. 1933
25 x 32 in. (63.5 x 81.3 cm)

INSCRIPTION: Signed l.l centre, *A.Y. JACKSON.*

PROVENANCE: Purchased from the artist (*Canadian Group of Painters*, 1933).

EXHIBITIONS: Toronto, AGT, November 1933, *Exhibition of Paintings by Canadian Group of Painters*, no. 39 repr. (as *Winter Morning, Charlevoix County*); Montreal, AAM, 1 – 21 January 1934, *Exhibition of Paintings by Canadian Group of Painters*, no. 32; Toronto, AGT, *Summer 1935*, no. 113; Rio de Janeiro, Museu Nacional de Belas Artes, November – December 1944, *Pintura canadense contemporanea*, no. 100; London (Ontario), London Public Library and Art Museum, 20 September – 29 October 1946, *The Group of Seven 1919 – 1933*, no. 13; London, Royal Academy of Arts, 1965, *Commonwealth Arts Festival*, no. 342 repr.

BIBLIOGRAPHY: Toronto, AGT, *Bulletin* (November 1933), repr.; Lawren Harris, 'Different Idioms in Creative Art,' *Canadian Comment*, vol. 2, no. 12 (December 1933), p. 6 repr. (as *Charlevoix County, P.Q.*); Toronto, AGT, *Bulletin and Annual Report* (April 1934), p. 8 repr.; Albert H. Robson, *A.Y. Jackson* (1938), p. 11; Donald W. Buchanan, *Canadian Painters from Paul Kane to the Group of Seven* (1945), repr. pl. 51; Wyndham Lewis, 'Canadian Nature and Its Painters,' *Listener* (29 August 1946), p. 267, repr.; *Maclean's Magazine*, vol. 60 (15 February 1947), p. 17, repr. in colour; J. Russell Harper, *Painting in Canada* (1966), p. 293, repr. p. 297; Naomi Jackson Groves, *A.Y.'s Canada* (1968), pp. 70, 235; *Bradfield AGO* (1970), p. 210 repr.

According to the artist's statement, 1947, the painting was done in July after a preliminary sketch painted in March near St. Urbain, about fifteen years earlier. Naomi Jackson Groves (*A.Y.'s Canada*, p. 235) points out that this is a sunny version of a drawing, *The Old Road Northward* (*A.Y.'s Canada*, pl. 34 repr.; The McMichael Canadian Collection, Kleinburg). Another version, *Grey Day, Laurentians* (c. 1930, oil on canvas; 25 x 32 in., 63.5 x 81.3 cm) is in the collection of The Montreal Museum of Fine Arts. See A.Y. Jackson, *A Painter's Country* (1967), Centennial Edition, repr. opp. p. 146.

Art Gallery of Ontario, Toronto (2156)

*6

A.Y. Jackson 1882 – 1974
Iceberg 1930
25 x 32-1/2 in. (63.5 x 82.6 cm)

INSCRIPTION: Signed l.r., *A.Y. JACKSON.*

PROVENANCE: Acquired from the artist.

EXHIBITIONS: (?) Montreal, W. Scott & Sons, 16 – 30 November 1935, *A.Y. Jackson Exhibition*, no. 27; Toronto, AGT, October 1947, *Pictures from the Collection of Mr. & Mrs. Charles S. Band*, [no cat. no.]; Ottawa, NGC, 1953, *Paintings and Drawings from the Collection of Mr. & Mrs. C.S. Band*, no. 27; Buffalo, Albright Art Gallery, 1 October – 2 November 1958, *The Collection of Mr. & Mrs. Charles S. Band*, no. 20 (as *Iceberg Arctic*); Ottawa, NGC, 19 June – 8 September 1970, *The Group of Seven*, no. 199 repr. (not in ex.).

The sketch, *Iceberg at Godhavn* (1930, oil on board; 8-1/2 x 10-1/2 in., 21.6 x 26.7 cm), is in The McMichael Canadian Collection, Kleinburg. See Paul Duval, *A Vision of Canada* (1973), p. 157 repr.

Mrs Charles S. Band, Toronto

7

A.Y. Jackson   1882 – 1974
Algoma, November   1935
31-3/8 x 39-3/8 in. (79.7 x 100.0 cm)

PROVENANCE: Gift of H.S. Southam, Esq., C.M.G., LL.D., Ottawa, 1945.

EXHIBITIONS: Montreal, W. Scott & Sons, 16 – 30 November 1935, *A.Y. Jackson Exhibition*, no. 3; Toronto, AGT, January 1936, *Exhibition of Paintings by the 'Canadian Group of Painters,'* no. 47; Ottawa, NGC, *Group of Seven 1936*, no. 119 repr.; London, Royal Institute Galleries, 8 – 29 May 1937, *Exhibition of Paintings Drawings and Sculpture by Artists of the British Empire Overseas*, no. 22; Liverpool, Walker Art Gallery, 16 October 1937 – 8 January 1938, *The Sixty-Third Autumn Exhibition*, no. 498; New Haven, Yale University Art Gallery, 11 March – 16 April 1944, *Canadian Art 1760 – 1943*, [no cat. no.]; Toronto, AGT, October – November 1953, *A.Y. Jackson Paintings 1902 – 1953*, no. 60; Bordeaux, 'Le Mai de Bordeaux,' 11 May – 31 July 1962, *L'art au Canada*, no. 46, repr. pl. XVII; Stratford (Ontario), Shakespearean Festival, 1963, [no cat. avail.]; Victoria, Art Gallery of Greater Victoria, 25 April – 14 May 1967, *Ten Canadians – Ten Decades*, no. 17, repr.; Spokane, International Exposition, 1974, 4 May – 3 November 1974, *Our Land, Our Sky, Our Water*, no. 116.

BIBLIOGRAPHY: Walter Abell, 'Canadian Aspirations in Painting,' *Culture*, vol. III (1942), repr. fig. 2; Graham C. McInnes, *Canadian Art* (1950) repr. in colour; H.O. McCurry, 'The Emerging Art of Canada,' *United Nations World* (July 1950), p. 67 repr.; 'A.Y. Jackson – A Retrospective Exhibition,' *Canadian Art*, vol. XI, no. 1 (Autumn 1953), p. 5; A.Y. Jackson, 'Box-car Days in Algoma, 1919 – 20,' *Canadian Art*, vol. XIV, no. 4 (Summer 1957), repr. p. 141; *Hubbard NGC* (1960), p. 140, repr.; J. Russell Harper, *Painting in Canada* (1966), p. 302, repr. in colour; Peter Mellen, *The Group of Seven* (1970), p. 215, repr.; Dennis Reid, *A Concise History of Canadian Painting* (1973), p. 175, repr. p. 176.

The sketch, *Algoma, November* (1934, oil on board; 10-3/4 x 13-3/4 in., 27.3 x 34.9 cm), is in The McMichael Canadian Collection, Kleinburg. See Paul Duval, *A Vision of Canada* (1973), p. 158 repr.

The National Gallery of Canada, Ottawa (4611)

*8

A.Y. Jackson   1882 – 1974
Blood Indian Reserve, Alberta   1937
25-1/8 x 32 in. (63.8 x 81.3 cm)

INSCRIPTION: Signed l.r., *A Y JACKSON*.

PROVENANCE: Purchased from the artist, 1946.

EXHIBITIONS: Toronto, CNE, 1952, no. 70; Toronto, AGT, October – November 1953, *A.Y. Jackson Paintings 1902 – 1953*, no. 62, repr. pl. 13; Edmonton Art Gallery, 1973, *Art in Alberta*, [no cat. no.], repr.

BIBLIOGRAPHY: A.Y. Jackson, *A Painter's Country* (1958), p. 121 (says sketch done in the foothills of Alberta in 1937); Naomi Jackson Groves, *A.Y.'s Canada* (1968), pp. 136, 238; Peter Mellen, *The Group of Seven* (1970), p. 193 repr.; *Bradfield AGO* (1970), p. 211.

The sketch, *Mokowan Butte* (1937, oil on panel; 10-1/4 x 13-1/2 in., 26.0 x 34.3 cm), is on loan to the Art Gallery of Ontario from the Ontario Heritage Foundation, gift of the J.S. McLean Collection, 1970.

The drawing, *Blood Indian Reserve, Alberta* (1937, graphite on paper; 8-5/8 x 11-1/4 in., 21.9 x 28.6 cm), is in The McMichael Canadian Collection, Kleinburg. See Naomi Jackson Groves, *A.Y.'s Canada* (1968), p. 136, repr. pl. 64.

Art Gallery of Ontario, Toronto (2828)

*9

A.Y. Jackson   1882 – 1974
Northern Landscape   1939
32 x 40 in. (81.3 x 101.6 cm)

INSCRIPTION: Signed l.r., *AY JACKSON.*

PROVENANCE: H.S. Southam, Esq., C.M.G., LL.D., Ottawa; Laing Galleries, Toronto.

EXHIBITIONS: New York, World's Fair, 1 August – 15 September 1939, *Canadian Group of Painters*, no. 31; Toronto, AGT, November 1939, *Canadian Group of Painters*, [no cat. no.]; Ottawa, NGC, from 27 May 1944, *Paintings Lent by H.S. Southam, Esq.*, C.M.G., *Ottawa*, no. 49; Halifax, Nova Scotia Museum of Fine Arts, Centennial Art Gallery, 5 – 28 March 1969, *Sobey Collections/ Canadian Paintings*, no. 7, repr.; Pictou County, Nova Scotia, 'Crombie', 14 – 16 September 1973, *Exhibition of the Sobey Collection of Canadian Art*, no. 21.

Another version, *Rocky Pool with Jackpines* (oil on canvas; 24-3/4 x 32-3/4 in., 62.9 x 83.2 cm) was sold at Montreal, Christie, Manson and Woods (Canada) Ltd., with Montreal Book Auctions, 26 March 1970, lot 153 (repr. in cat.).

A related work, *Canada's Rugged Northland*, was commissioned by the International Business Machines Corporation and exhibited at the San Francisco Golden Gate International Exposition (*Contemporary Art of 79 Countries*, The International Business Machines Corporation, 1939, no. 19, repr.). This work is now entitled *Sunlit Tapestry* (1939, oil on canvas; 28 x 36 in., 71.1 x 91.4 cm) and is in The McMichael Canadian Collection, Kleinburg. See Paul Duval, *A Vision of Canada* (1973), p. 158, repr.

The sketch is in the collection of Paraskeva Clark, R.C.A., Toronto, and was painted in the fall of 1938 at Great Bear Lake. A related sketch is in the collection of Mrs J.P. Barwick, Ottawa. A related drawing, *Arctic Lake*, is reproduced in *The Canadian Forum*, vol. XIX, no. 221 (June 1939), p. 85.

Frank H. Sobey, Sobeys Stores Limited, Stellarton, Nova Scotia.

*10

Lawren S. Harris   1885 – 1970
Icebergs, Davis Strait   1930
48 x 60 in. (121.9 x 152.4 cm)

PROVENANCE: Roberts Gallery, Toronto; Mr & Mrs H. Spencer Clark, Toronto.

EXHIBITIONS: Toronto, AGT, December 1931, *An Exhibition by The Group of Seven*, no. 59 (as *Icebergs, Smith Sound*); Ottawa, NGC, 1932, *Annual Exhibition of Canadian Art*, no. 96 (as *Icebergs, Smith Sound*); Toronto, CNE, 25 August – 9 September 1933, no. 105, repr. (as *Icebergs, Smith Sound*); Pittsburgh, Carnegie Institute, 17 October – 8 December 1935, *The 1935 International Exhibition of Paintings*, no. 230; Ottawa, NGC, 7 June – 8 September 1963, *Lawren Harris Retrospective Exhibition, 1963*, no. 44.

BIBLIOGRAPHY: *Canadian Review of Music and Art*, vol. 1, no. 6 (October 1942), p. 11 repr. (with the sketch entitled *Iceberg – Baffin Bay*, repr. p. 10); *Canadian Art*, vol. XIX, no. 3 (May – June 1962), p. 179 repr.; Bess Harris and R.G.P. Colgrove, *Lawren Harris* (1969), p. 83 repr.; *Canadian Antiques Collector*, vol. 4, no. 11 (November 1969), p. 73 repr.; *Canadian Antiques Collector*, vol. 6, no. 5 (May 1971), p. 90 repr.; *Artscanada*, vol. XXVIII, no. 6 (December 1971 – January 1972), p. 67 repr.; Paul Duval, *A Vision of Canada* (1973), repr. in colour p. 72, p. 153 repr.

The sketch, *Iceberg, Baffin Bay North* (1930, oil on board; 12 x 15 in., 30.5 x 38.1 cm), is in the collection of Mrs Charles S. Band, Toronto. See J. Russell Harper, *Painting in Canada* (1966), p. 295 repr.

This work was slightly altered at a later date.

The McMichael Canadian Collection, Kleinburg (790).

*11

Lawren S. Harris   1885 – 1970
Grounded Icebergs   c. 1931
31-1/2 x 40 in. (80.01 x 101.6 cm)

INSCRIPTION: on *verso,* signed lower corner, *LS HARRIS.*

PROVENANCE: Dr & Mrs Thomas Ingledow, Vancouver;
The Warwick Gallery, Vancouver.

EXHIBITIONS: Toronto, AGT, January 1936, *Exhibition of
Paintings by the 'Canadian Group of Painters,'* no. 33 (as
Icebergs, Disco Island); Ottawa, NGC, *Group of Seven 1936,*
no. 81 (as *Icebergs, Disco Island*); Ottawa, NGC, 1942,
Canadian Group of Painters Travelling Exhibition, no. 11
(as *Icebergs, Disco Island*); Toronto, AGT, October –
November 1948, *Lawren Harris Paintings 1910 – 1948* (not
in cat.); Ottawa, NGC, 7 June – 8 September 1963, *Lawren
Harris Retrospective Exhibition, 1963,* no. 40.

A.Y. Jackson, in *A Painter's Country* (1967), Centennial
Edition, p. 106 writes, 'at Godhavn . . . Harris and I
hurried along the shore to paint some stranded icebergs
. . . .' Disco Island is near Godhavn, Greenland.

Mr Stuart H. Wallace, Vancouver

12

Lawren S. Harris   1885 – 1970
Icebergs and Mountains, Greenland   c. 1932
36 x 45 in. (91.4 x 114.3 cm)

PROVENANCE: Gift of H.S. Southam, Esq., C.M.G., LL.D.,
1953.

EXHIBITIONS: Ottawa, NGC, *Group of Seven 1936,* no. 85;
Johannesburg, *Empire Exhibition,* 15 September 1936 – 15
January 1937, no. 830, repr.; Ottawa, NGC, 1936, *Southern
Dominions Exhibition,* no. 31; Ottawa, NGC, from 27 May
1944, *Paintings Lent by H.S. Southam Esq., C.M.G., Ottawa,*
no. 37 (as *Icebergs*); Toronto, AGT, October – November
1948, *Lawren Harris Paintings 1910 – 1948,* no. 57, repr. pl.
14; Toronto, O'Keefe Centre, 4 January – 4 March 1963,
[no cat.]; Ottawa, NGC, 7 June – 8 September 1963, *Lawren
Harris Retrospective Exhibition, 1963,* no. 43; Windsor,
Willistead Art Gallery, 21 March – 18 April 1962,
Hamilton Collects, no. 12.

BIBLIOGRAPHY: Art Gallery of Hamilton, *Handbook* (1964),
p. 18, repr.; Bess Harris and R.G.P. Colgrove, *Lawren
Harris* (1969), p. 85 repr.; Peter Mellen, *The Group of Seven*
(1970) p. 180 repr.; McClelland & Stewart Limited,
Group of Seven. A Fine Art Calendar (1973), repr. in colour.

Art Gallery of Hamilton (53-66)

*13

Yvonne McKague Housser b. 1898
Cobalt 1931
44-1/4 x 54-1/4 in. (112.4 x 137.8 cm)

INSCRIPTION: Signed l.r., *YVONNE McKAGUE.*

PROVENANCE: Purchased from the artist (*Annual Exhibition of Canadian Art*, 1932).

EXHIBITIONS: Toronto, AGT, December 1931, *An Exhibition by The Group of Seven*, no. 126; Ottawa, NGC, 1932, *Annual Exhibition of Canadian Art*, no. 183; New York, Roerich Museum, 5 March – 5 April 1932, *Exhibition of Paintings by Contemporary Canadian Artists*, no. 43; Johannesburg, *Empire Exhibition*, 15 September 1936 – 15 January 1937, no. 861; Ottawa, NGC, 1936, *Southern Dominions Exhibition*, no. 62; Toronto, AGT, January 1945, *The Development of Painting in Cnada 1665 – 1945*, no. 166; Stratford (Ontario), Shakespearean Festival, 1963, [no cat. avail.].

BIBLIOGRAPHY: Eric Brown, 'Canada's National Painters,' *The Studio*, vol. CIII (June 1932), p. 313 repr.; ' "The Best Old Town I Know" Painting by Yvonne McKague,' *Gold Magazine* (December 1933), repr.; Edward Buckman, 'Cobalt and the Artists,' *Gold Magazine* (April 1934); W.J. Gorman, 'Grab Samples,' *Northern Miner* (5 April 1934); *Hubbard NGC* (1960), p. 131, repr.; Peter Mellen, *The Group of Seven* (1970), p. 186 repr.; Dennis Reid, *A Concise History of Canadian Painting* (1973), p. 177.

The National Gallery of Canada, Ottawa (3984)

14

Anne Savage 1896 – 1971
Dark Pool, Georgian Bay 1933
31 x 40 in. (78.7 x 101.6 cm)

PROVENANCE: Gift of Arthur B. Gill, October 1970.

EXHIBITIONS: Toronto, AGT, November 1933, *Exhibition of Painting by Canadian Group of Painters*, no. 72 (as *A Pool, Georgian Bay*); Montreal, AAM, January 1934, *Exhibition of Paintings by Canadian Group of Painters*, no. 62 (as *A Pool, Georgian Bay*); (?) Montreal, AAM, 21 March – 14 April 1935, *Spring Exhibition*, no. 292 (as *The Still Pond, Georgian Bay*); Montreal, Sir George Williams University, 4 – 30 April [1969], *Anne Savage/A Retrospective*, no. 21 (dated '1930's').

BIBLIOGRAPHY: Paul Duval, *Four Decades* (1972), p. 43 repr. (dated c.1945).

Art Gallery of Hamilton (70-111-37)

15

Sarah Robertson   1891 – 1948
Coronation   1937
33 x 24 in. (83.8 x 61.0 cm)

INSCRIPTION: Signed l.r., *S.M. Robertson.*

PROVENANCE: Purchased from the artist (*Canadian Group of Painters*, 1937); H.S. Southam, Ottawa; Gift of H.S. Southam, Esq., C.M.G., LL.D., March 1951.

EXHIBITIONS: Toronto, AGT, November 1937, *Canadian Group of Painters*, no. 68 repr.; Ottawa, NGC, 1938, *Canadian Group of Painters*, no. 65; London, The Tate Gallery, 1938, *A Century of Canadian Art*, no. 189; New York, World's Fair, 1 August – 15 September 1939, *Canadian Group of Painters*, no. 52; New Haven, Yale University Art Gallery, 11 March – 16 April 1944, *Canadian Art 1760 – 1943*, [no cat. no.]; Toronto, AGT, January 1945, *The Development of Painting in Canada 1665 – 1945*, no. 174; New York, Riverside Museum, 1947, *Canadian Women Artists*, no. 62; Ottawa, NGC, 1947, *Exhibition of Paintings by Canadian Women Artists*, no. 50; Ottawa, NGC, 1951, *Memorial Exhibition/Sarah Robertson*, no. 48 repr.

BIBLIOGRAPHY: A.Y. Jackson, 'Sarah Robertson,' *Canadian Art*, vol. VI, no. 3 (Spring 1949), p. 126 repr.; Art Gallery of Hamilton, *Handbook* (1964), p. 46 repr.; Paul Duval, *Four Decades* (1972), p. 37 repr. in colour.

Art Gallery of Hamilton (51-105-A)

*16

Sarah Robertson   1891 – 1948
Village, Isle of Orleans   1939
22-1/4 x 26-1/4 in. (56.5 x 66.7 cm)

INSCRIPTION: Signed l.r., *S.M. Robertson.*

EXHIBITIONS: Toronto, AGT, November 1939, *Canadian Group of Painters*, [no cat. no.]; Ottawa, NGC, 1951, *Memorial Exhibition/Sarah Robertson*, no. 33.

Private collection

*17

Edwin H. Holgate   b. 1892
Ludovine   c. 1930
30 x 25 in. (76.2 x 63.5 cm)

INSCRIPTION: Signed l.l., *E. Holgate.*

PROVENANCE: Vincent Massey, Port Hope; Bequest of the Right Hon. Vincent Massey, 1968.

EXHIBITIONS: Toronto, AGT, November 1930, *51st RCA*, no. 90; Ottawa, NGC, 1931, *Annual Exhibition of Canadian Art*, no. 120; New York, Roerich Museum, 5 March – 5 April 1932, *Exhibition of Paintings by Contemporary Canadian Artists*, no. 21; Toronto, AGT, December 1934, *Canadian Paintings/The Collection of Hon. Vincent and Mrs Massey*, no. 115; London, The Tate Gallery, 1938, *A Century of Canadian Art*, no. 102 repr.; Ottawa, NGC, 1953, *Exhibition of Canadian Painting to Celebrate the Coronation of Her Majesty Queen Elizabeth II*, no. 25, repr.; Hamilton, Art Gallery of Hamilton, December 1953 – January 1954, *Inaugural Exhibition*, no. 23, repr.; Vancouver, VAG, 29 March – 25 April 1954, *Group of Seven*, no. 31; Ottawa, NGC, 15 May – 15 September 1967, *Three Hundred Years of Canadian Art*, no. 240, repr.; Ottawa, NGC, 20 September – 20 October 1968, *Vincent Massey Bequest/The Canadian Paintings*, no. 11, repr. pl. 11; Halifax, Dalhousie University Art Gallery, 15 October – 5 December 1971, *Selected Works from the Massey Bequest of Canadian Painting*, [no cat.].

BIBLIOGRAPHY: Blodwen Davies, 'Annual Canadian Art Show,' *Saturday Night*, vol. XLVI, no 13 (7 February 1931), p. 3 repr.; Donald W. Buchanan, 'Canada,' *The Studio*, vol. CXXV (April 1943), p. 123 repr.; Donald W. Buchanan, *The Growth of Canadian Painting* (1950), p. 46, repr. pl. 34; Ottawa, NGC, *A Portfolio of Canadian Paintings* (1950), repr.; Julian Park, ed., *The Culture of Contemporary Canada* (1957), p. 132; Robert H. Hubbard, *The Development of Canadian Art* (1963), p. 112, repr. pl. 193; Hugo McPherson, 'The Resonance of Batterwood House,' *Canadian Art*, vol. XXI, no. 2 (March/April 1964), p. 99 repr.; Jean-René Ostiguy, *Un siècle de peinture canadienne* (1971), repr. pl. 76.

The National Gallery of Canada, Ottawa (15478)

18

Edwin H. Holgate   b. 1892
Interior   c. 1933
30 x 25 in. (76.2 x 63.5 cm)

INSCRIPTION: Signed l.r., *E. Holgate.*

PROVENANCE: Purchased from the artist (*Canadian Group of Painters*, 1933).

EXHIBITIONS: Toronto, AGT, November 1933, *Exhibition of Paintings by Canadian Group of Painters*, no. 30, repr.; Montreal, AAM, 1 – 21 January 1934, *Exhibition of Paintings by Canadian Group of Painters*, no. 26; Toronto, AGT, Summer 1935, no. 35; Toronto, AGT, November 1935, *Loan Exhibition of Paintings*, no. 111; Ottawa, NGC, *Group of Seven 1936*, no. 91, repr.; London, The Tate Gallery, 1938, *A Century of Canadian Art*, no. 100; Toronto, AGT, April 1940, *Edwin Holgate, A.Y. Jackson, Arthur Lismer, Lilias Torrance Newton*, [no cat. no.]; New Haven, Yale University Art Gallery, 11 March – 16 April 1944, *Canadian Art 1760 – 1943* (as *Interior with Nude*), [no cat. no.]; London (Ontario), London Public Library and Art Museum, 20 September – 29 October 1946, *The Group of Seven 1919 – 1933*, no. 39; Mexico City, Museo Nacional de Arte Moderna, November 1960, *Arte Canadiense*, no. 135; St. Catharines (Ontario), Rodman Hall Arts Centre, 6 – 29 December 1963, *The Figure Form*, [no cat.]; Toronto, AGO, 1967 – 1968, *Canadian Paintings of the 1930s* (Travelling Exhibition), no. 10.

BIBLIOGRAPHY: Donald W. Buchanan, *Canadian Painters From Paul Kane to the Group of Seven* (1945), repr. pl. 83; Paul Duval, 'Human Form More Inspiring than Landscapes,' *Saturday Night*, vol. LXIII (13 September 1947), p. 2 repr.; AGT, *Paintings and Sculpture* (1959), p. 73 repr.; *Bradfield AGO* (1970), p. 176, repr. p. 177.

Art Gallery of Ontario, Toronto (2155)

*19

Edwin H. Holgate   b. 1892
Early Autumn   c. 1938
28-1/2 x 28-1/2 in. (72.4 x 72.4 cm)

INSCRIPTION: Signed l.r., *E. Holgate.*

PROVENANCE: Royal Canadian Academy Diploma Deposit, 1939.

EXHIBITIONS: Toronto, AGT, 18 November – 18 December 1938, *59th RCA,* no. 102; Montreal, MMFA, 19 November – 19 December 1954, *75th RCA, Retrospective Exhibition,* no. 43.

BIBLIOGRAPHY: *Hubbard NGC* (1960), p. 390, repr.

The National Gallery of Canada, Ottawa (4355)

*20

Lilias Torrance Newton   b. 1896
Portrait of Frances McCall   c. 1931
32 x 26 in. (81.3 x 66.0 cm)

INSCRIPTION: Signed l.r., *L.T. NEWTON.*

PROVENANCE: Acquired from the artist.

EXHIBITIONS: Ottawa, NGC, 1932, *Annual Exhibition of Canadian Art,* no. 213; Toronto, AGT, November 1933, *Exhibition of Paintings by Canadian Group of Painters,* no. 63; Montreal, AAM, 1 – 21 January 1934, *Exhibition of Paintings by Canadian Group of Painters,* no. 52.

Dr G.R. McCall, Montreal

21

Lilias Torrance Newton   b. 1896
Portrait of Louis Muhlstock   *c.* 1937
24 x 25-1/4 in. (61.0 x 64.1 cm)

INSCRIPTION: Signed l.r., *L. Torrance Newton.*

PROVENANCE: Royal Canadian Academy Diploma Deposit, 1940.

EXHIBITIONS: Montreal, AAM, 18 March – 11 April 1937, *54th Spring Exhibition,* no. 217; Toronto, AGT, November 1937, *Canadian Group of Painters,* no. 58; Ottawa, NGC, 1938, *Canadian Group of Painters,* no. 56; New York, World's Fair, 1 May – 15 June 1939, *The Royal Canadian Academy of Arts,* no. 52; Montreal, AAM, October 1939, *Portraits by Lilias T. Newton,* [no cat.]; Ottawa, NGC, 1942, *Canadian Group of Painters Travelling Exhibition,* no. 31; Montreal, MMFA, 19 November – 19 December 1954, *75th RCA, Retrospective Exhibition,* no. 52.

BIBLIOGRAPHY: *Hubbard NGC* (1960), p. 404, repr.

The National Gallery of Canada, Ottawa (4552)

22

Lilias Torrance Newton   b. 1896
Maurice   1939
30-1/4 x 24-1/4 in. (76.8 x 61.6 cm)

INSCRIPTION: Signed l.r., *L. Torrance Newton.*

PROVENANCE: Purchased with income from the Murray and Harold Wrong Memorial Fund, 1940.

EXHIBITION: Toronto, AGT, April 1940, *Edwin Holgate, A.Y. Jackson, Arthur Lismer, Lilias Torrance Newton,* [no cat. no.].

BIBLIOGRAPHY: J. Russell Harper, *Canadian Paintings in Hart House* (1955), p. 56; Jeremy Adamson, *The Hart House Collection of Canadian Paintings* (1969), p. 101, repr. p. 49.

Hart House, University of Toronto

*23

Lawren P. Harris   b. 1910
Decorative Nude   1937
30-1/4 x 25-1/4 in. (76.8 x 64.1 cm)

INSCRIPTION: Signed and dated l.l., *HARRIS/ – 1937 – .*
Inscribed *verso*, u.l., *NEGRESS – 1937 – Lawren Harris
1937 Toronto – Can.*

PROVENANCE: Presented by the artist.

EXHIBITIONS: Toronto, AGT, March 1938, *66th OSA*, no.
76; *OSA Travelling Exhibition*, 1938 – 1939, [no cat. no.];
Montreal, AAM, 16 November – 16 December 1939, *60th
RCA*, no. 96; Fredericton, Beaverbrook Art Gallery, 9
February – 1 March 1965, *The Figure in Contemporary Art*,
no. 20; Halifax, The Dalhousie University Art Gallery,
1972, *Lawren P. Harris 37/72*, no. 3, repr. (as *Negress*);
Fredericton, Beaverbrook Art Gallery, 1973, *Nine New
Brunswick Artists*, no. 15, p. 21 repr. (as *Negress*).

BIBLIOGRAPHY: Robert Percival, 'Lawren P. Harris: The
Man and His Art,' *Art Magazine*, vol. 4, no. 4 (Spring/
Summer 1973), p. 24 repr. (as *Negress*).

Beaverbrook Art Gallery, Fredericton (65-1)

*24

Prudence Heward   1896 – 1947
Sisters of Rural Quebec   1930
62 x 42 in. (157.5 x 106.7 cm)

INSCRIPTION: Signed and dated l.r., *P. Heward '30.*

PROVENANCE: Purchased from the family of the artist,
1962; Gift of the Women's Committee, 1962.

EXHIBITIONS: Baltimore, Baltimore Museum of Art,
15 January–28 February 1931, *First Baltimore Pan-American
Exhibition of Contemporary Paintings*, no. 36 repr. (as *Portrait of Roliandi* [sic] *and Pierrette*); Montreal, W. Scott &
Sons, April 1932, [*Prudence Heward Exhibition*], [no cat.].

BIBLIOGRAPHY: Willistead Art Gallery of Windsor, *Catalogue of the Permanent Collection* (1964) [n.p.]; The Art
Gallery of Windsor, *A Checklist of the Permanent Collection to December 31, 1971*, p. 10, repr. in colour p. 13; Paul
Duval, *Four Decades* (1972), p. 69, repr. in colour.

The Art Gallery of Windsor (62:16)

25

Prudence Heward 1896 – 1947
Girl Under a Tree 1931
48 x 76 in. (121.9 x 193.0 cm)

PROVENANCE: Gift of the family of the artist, June 1961.

EXHIBITIONS: Toronto, AGT, December 1931, *An Exhibition By The Group of Seven*, no. 73; Ottawa, NGC, 1932, *Annual Exhibition of Canadian Art*, no. 119; Montreal, W. Scott & Sons, April 1932, [*Prudence Heward Exhibition*], [no cat.].

BIBLIOGRAPHY: 'Modernistic In Tone,' *Bridle and Golfer* (October 1932), repr.; Jerrold Morris, *The Nude in Canadian Painting* (1972), p. 12, repr. pl. 34.

Art Gallery of Hamilton (61-72-4)

26

Prudence Heward 1896 – 1947
Dark Girl 1935
36-1/4 x 40-1/4 in. (92.1 x 102.2 cm)

INSCRIPTION: Signed l.l., *P.H.*

PROVENANCE: Purchased with income from the Murray and Harold Wrong Memorial Fund, 1936.

EXHIBITIONS: Toronto, AGT, January 1936, *An Exhibition of Paintings by the 'Canadian Group of Painters,'* no. 34 repr.; London, The Tate Gallery, 1938, *A Century of Canadian Art*, no. 96 repr.; Toronto, AGT, January 1945, *The Development of Painting in Canada 1665 – 1945*, no. 170; Ottawa, NGC, 1948, *Memorial Exhibition/Prudence Heward 1896 – 1947*, no. 97 repr.; Hamilton, Art Gallery of Hamilton, December 1953 – January 1954, *Inaugural Exhibition*, no. 21 repr.; Toronto, CNE, 1960, *A Tribute to Women*, [no cat. no.]; London (Ontario), London Public Library and Art Museum, February 1961, *The Face of Early Canada/Milestones of Canadian Painting*, [no cat. no.]; London (Ontario), London Public Library and Art Museum, 1970, *Approaches to Figure Painting*, no. 18.

BIBLIOGRAPHY: Bertram Brooker, ed., *Yearbook of the Arts in Canada, 1936* (1936), repr. pl. 56; J. Russell Harper, *Canadian Paintings in Hart House* (1955), p. 55; Jeremy Adamson, *The Hart House Collection of Canadian Paintings* (1969), p. 93, repr. p. 47; Dennis Reid, *A Concise History of Canadian Painting* (1973), p. 188 repr.

Hart House, University of Toronto

*27

Prudence Heward   1896 – 1947
Fruit in the Grass   *c.* 1939
17 x 22 in. (43.2 x 55.9 cm)

PROVENANCE: Gift of the family of the artist, 1948.

EXHIBITIONS: (?) Toronto, AGT, November 1939, *Canadian Group of Painters,* [no cat. no.] (as *Fruit*); Ottawa, NGC, 1948, *Memorial Exhibition/Prudence Heward 1896 – 1947,* no. 10; London, The Women's International Art Club, 1951, *The Festival of Britain Exhibition,* no. 92; Stratford (Ontario), Shakespearean Festival, 1954, [no cat. avail.]; Columbo, Ceylon, Art Gallery, 17 – 29 May 1955, *An Exhibition of Canadian Painting from The National Gallery of Canada,* no. 13; Ottawa, NGC, 1966, *Beaver Hall Hill Group* (Travelling Exhibition), no. 5.

BIBLIOGRAPHY: *Hubbard NGC* (1960), p. 123, repr.

The National Gallery of Canada, Ottawa (4952)

*28

Emily Carr   1871 – 1945
Grey   *c.* 1931
44 x 27-1/2 in. (111.8 x 69.9 cm)

PROVENANCE: Purchased from the artist, *c.* 1937.

EXHIBITIONS: Toronto, AGT, March – April 1937, [*Emily Carr*], [no cat.]; Toronto, AGT, February 1943, *Paintings by Emily Carr,* [no cat. no.]; Toronto, AGT, 1945, *Emily Carr/Her Paintings and Sketches,* no. 51; Toronto, AGT, October 1947, *Pictures from the Collection of Mr. & Mrs. Charles S. Band,* [no cat. no.]; Toronto, CNE, 27 August – 11 September 1948, *Canadian Painting and Sculpture Owned by Canadians,* no. 45; Buffalo, Albright Art Gallery, 1 October – 2 November 1958, *The Collection of Mr. and Mrs. Charles S. Band,* no. 10; Toronto, CNE, 1959, *Private Collectors' Choice in Canadian Art,* [no cat. no.]; Vancouver, VAG, 1 – 29 March 1960, *Paintings & Drawings from the Collection of Mr. & Mrs. Charles S. Band,* no. 9; Windsor, Willistead Art Gallery, 28 April – 29 May 1961, *Canadian Paintings and Drawings from the C.S. Band Collection,* no. 7; Toronto, AGT, 15 February – 24 March 1963, *The Collection of Mr. and Mrs. Charles S. Band,* no. 15; Vancouver, VAG, September 1966, *Images for a Canadian Heritage,* no. 63; Montreal, Expo '67, Canadian Pavilion, 1967, *Painting in Canada,* no. 7, repr.; Vancouver, VAG, 18 May – 29 August 1971, *Emily Carr,* no. 69, repr., repr. in colour p. 37.

BIBLIOGRAPHY: Paul Duval, *Four Decades* (1972), p. 27 repr. in colour.

This work was shipped to The National Gallery of Canada, 6 January 1933, for selection for the *Annual Exhibition of Canadian Art.*

Mrs Charles S. Band, Toronto.

29

Emily Carr   1871 – 1945
Tree   c. 1931
50-3/4 x 22 in. (128.9 x 55.9 cm)

INSCRIPTION: Signed l.l., *M. EMILY CARR.*

PROVENANCE: The Emily Carr Trust, 1942.

EXHIBITIONS: (?) Victoria, Island Arts and Crafts Society, 11 – 22 October 1932, *23rd Annual Exhibition*, Modern Room, no. 2; Toronto, AGT, February 1943, *Paintings by Emily Carr*, [no cat. no.]; Toronto, AGT, 1945, *Emily Carr/ Her Paintings and Sketches*, no. 41 (incorrectly measured: '40-1/4 x 21-1/2 in.'); Seattle, Henry Gallery, University of Washington, 1 December 1949 – 2 January 1950, *Emily Carr Memorial Exhibition*, no. 18; Vancouver, VAG, 1958, *100 Years of B.C. Art*, no. 283, repr.; Ottawa, NGC, 1967, *Canadian Painting 1850 – 1950*, no. 27 (incorrectly measured: '40-1/4 x 21-1/2 in.'); Vancouver, VAG, 18 May – 29 August 1971, *Emily Carr*, no. 64, repr. (dated 'c. 1929 – 30').

The Vancouver Art Gallery (42.3.2)

30

Emily Carr   1871 – 1945
A Rushing Sea of Undergrowth   c. 1932 – 1934
44 x 27 in. (111.8 x 68.6 cm)

INSCRIPTION: Signed l.l., *EMILY CARR.*

PROVENANCE: The Emily Carr Trust, 1942.

EXHIBITIONS: Vancouver, VAG, 12 – 23 October 1938, *Exhibition by Emily Carr*, no. 18 (as *Sea of Growth [a woodscape]*); Vancouver, The University of British Columbia, 1 – 4 November 1938, *Exhibition by Emily Carr*, no. 18 (as *Sea of Growth [a woodscape]*); New York, World's Fair, 1 August – 15 September 1939, *Canadian Group of Painters*, no. 10; Toronto, AGT, November 1939, *Canadian Group of Painters*, [no cat. no.]; Toronto, AGT, March 1940, *Emily Carr, Lawren Harris, Fritz Brandtner, Charles Comfort*, [no cat. no.]; Toronto, AGT, February 1943, *Paintings by Emily Carr*, [no cat. no.]; Toronto, AGT, 1945, *Emily Carr/Her Paintings and Sketches*, no. 66, repr. pl. 22; Seattle, Henry Gallery, University of Washington, 1 December 1949 – 2 January 1950, *Emily Carr Memorial Exhibition*, no. 14; Vancouver, VAG, 1958, *100 Years of B.C. Art*, no. 293; Ottawa, NGC, 15 May – 15 September 1967, *Three Hundred Years of Canadian Art*, no. 245, repr.; Vancouver, VAG, 18 May – 29 August 1971, *Emily Carr*, no. 84, repr.; Madison, Wisconsin, Elvehjem Art Center, University of Wisconsin, 1973, *Canadian Landscape Painting, 1670 – 1930*, no. 39, repr.

BIBLIOGRAPHY: Graham C. McInnes, 'The Canadian Artist and His Country,' *The Geographical Magazine*, vol. XVI, no. 8 (December 1943), p. 401 repr.; Robert H. Hubbard, *An Anthology of Canadian Art* (1960), repr. pl. 99; Emily Carr, *Hundreds and Thousands* (1966), repr. in colour opp. p. 134 (opp. p. 126 in deluxe ed.); *Emily Carr. A Canadian Art Calendar* (1973), repr. in colour.

The sketch, *Untitled (Forest Landscape)* (c. 1932 – 1934, oil on paper; 34-7/8 x 23-1/2 in., 88.6 x 59.7 cm) is in the collection of University College, University of Toronto. See Doris Shadbolt, *Emily Carr* (exhibition catalogue) (Vancouver: VAG, 1971), p. 81 repr.

The Vancouver Art Gallery (42.3.17)

*31

Emily Carr   1871 – 1945
Tree   c. 1932 – 1933
Oil on paper, 35 x 23-3/8 in. (88.9 x 59.4 cm)

INSCRIPTION: Signed 1.1., *EMILY CARR.*

PROVENANCE: The Emily Carr Trust, 1942.

EXHIBITIONS: Toronto, AGT, 1945, *Emily Carr / Her Paintings and Sketches,* no. 160; Vancouver, VAG, 18 May – 29 August 1971, *Emily Carr,* no. 87, repr.

The Vancouver Art Gallery (42.3.63)

*32

Emily Carr   1871 – 1945
Overhead   c. 1935
Oil on paper, 24 x 36 in. (61.0 x 91.4 cm)

INSCRIPTION: Signed 1.1., *EMILY CARR.*

PROVENANCE: The Emily Carr Trust, 1942.

EXHIBITIONS: Vancouver, VAG, 16 September – 9 October 1938, *7th Annual B.C. Artists' Exhibition,* no. 18; Toronto, AGT, 1945, *Emily Carr/Her Paintings and Sketches,* no. 170; Windsor, Willistead Art Gallery, January 1958, *Emily Carr,* no. 9; Vancouver, VAG, 18 May – 29 August 1971, *Emily Carr,* no. 105, repr.

The Vancouver Art Gallery (42.3.69)

33

34

Emily Carr   1871 – 1945
Scorned as Timber, Beloved of the Sky   c. 1936
44 x 27 in. (111.8 x 68.6 cm)

INSCRIPTION: Signed l.r., *ME CARR.*

PROVENANCE: The Emily Carr Trust, 1942.

EXHIBITIONS: Vancouver, VAG, 12 – 23 October 1938, *Exhibition by Emily Carr,* no. 23; Vancouver, The University of British Columbia, 1 – 4 November 1938, *Exhibition by Emily Carr,* no. 23; Toronto, AGT, February 1943, *Paintings by Emily Carr,* [no cat. no.]; Toronto, AGT, 1945, *Emily Carr/Her Paintings and Sketches,* no. 69, repr. pl. 24; Seattle, Henry Gallery, University of Washington, 1 December 1949 – 2 January 1950, *Emily Carr Memorial Exhibition,* no. 21; Vancouver, VAG, 1958, *100 Years of B.C. Art,* no. 291, repr.; Vancouver, VAG, September 1966, *Images for a Canadian Heritage,* no. 65; Vancouver, VAG, 18 May – 29 August 1971, *Emily Carr,* no. 108, repr., repr. in colour p. 49.

BIBLIOGRAPHY: Elizabeth Kilbourn, ed., *Great Canadian Painting* (1966), p. 121 repr. in colour.

The Vancouver Art Gallery (42.3.15)

F.H. Varley   1881 – 1969
Dhârâna   c. 1932
34 x 40 in. (86.4 x 101.6 cm)

PROVENANCE: Acquired from the artist; Gift from the Albert H. Robson Memorial Subscription Fund, 1942.

EXHIBITIONS: Vancouver, VAG, 5 – 30 October 1932, *First Annual B.C. Artists' Exhibition,* no. 47; Toronto, AGT, 4–30 November 1932, *53rd RCA,* no. 194; Ottawa, NGC, 1933, *Annual Exhibition of Canadian Art,* no. 268; Atlantic City, Heinz Art Salon, 1933, *Paintings by the Canadian Group of Painters,* no. 58; Ottawa, NGC, *Group of Seven 1936,* no. 190; Johannesburg, *Empire Exhibition,* 15 September 1936 – 15 January 1937, no. 897; Ottawa, NGC, 1936, *Southern Dominions Exhibition,* no. 98, repr; London (Ontario), London Public Library and Art Museum, 20 September – 29 October 1946, *Group of Seven 1919 – 1933,* no. 31; Vancouver, VAG, 1954, *The Group of Seven,* no. 74; Mexico City, Museu Nacional de Arte Moderno, November 1960, *Arte Canadiense,* no. 119; London (Ontario), London Public Library and Art Museum, 1963 – 1964, *Master Canadian Painters and Sculptors,* no. 46, repr.; Windsor, Willistead Art Gallery, 12 April – 17 May 1964, *F.H. Varley Retrospective,* no. 23; Thunder Bay, Lakehead College, 19 November – 12 December 1964, *The Group of Seven and Lake Superior,* no. 32; Toronto, O'Keefe Centre, 1971 – 1972, *Group of Seven and Contemporaries,* [no cat.]; Burnaby, Burnaby Art Gallery, 1 May – 2 June 1974, *Varley/The Middle Years,* no. 21.

BIBLIOGRAPHY: 'Canada Holds Its Largest And Best Annual Exhibition At Ottawa,' *Art Digest,* vol. VII (15 March 1933), p. 6; 'Directions in British Columbia Painting,' *Canadian Art,* vol. V, no. 1 (October – November 1947), p. 3 repr.; Donald W. Buchanan, *The Growth of Canadian Painting* (1950), p. 43; George Elliott, 'F.H. Varley – Fifty Years of His Art,' *Canadian Art,* vol. XII, no. 1 (Autumn 1954), p. 8; AGT, *Painting and Sculpture* (1959), p. 56 repr.; J. Barry Lord, 'In Search of the Figure in Canadian Painting,' *Canadian Art,* vol. XXI, no. 4 (July – August 1964), p. 195 repr.; J. Russell Harper, *Painting in Canada* (1966), p. 299 repr.; Elizabeth Kilbourn, ed., *Great Canadian Painting* (1966), p. 81 repr. in colour; Peter Mellen, *The Group of Seven* (1970), p. 170, repr.; *Bradfield AGO* (1970), pp. 489 – 490, repr. in colour p. 544; Dennis Reid, *A Concise History of Canadian Painting* (1973), p. 190 repr.

Art Gallery of Ontario, Toronto (2593)

35

*36

F.H. Varley   1881 – 1969
Open Window   c. 1932
40 x 43 in. (101.6 x 109.2 cm)

Philip Surrey   b. 1910
Going to Work   1935
24 x 30 in. (61.0 x 76.2 cm)

INSCRIPTION: Signed l.r., *VARLEY,* with thumbprint.

INSCRIPTION: Signed l.l., *Surrey.*

PROVENANCE: Purchased with income from the Murray
and Harold Wrong Memorial Fund, 1944.

EXHIBITIONS: Toronto, AGT, November 1937, *Canadian
Group of Painters,* no. 102; Ottawa, NGC, 1938, *Canadian
Group of Painters,* no. 70.

EXHIBITIONS: Toronto, CNE, 25 August – 9 September
1933, no. 176; Toronto, AGT, November 1933, *Exhibition
of Paintings by Canadian Group of Painters,* no. 77a; Montreal, AAM, January 1934, *Exhibition of Paintings by Canadian Group of Painters,* no. 65; Ottawa, NGC, *Group of
Seven 1936,* no. 193; Montreal, W. Scott & Sons, from 26
May 1937, *Fredrick H. Varley, A.R.C.A.,* no. 34; Ottawa,
James Wilson & Company, November 1937, [*Frederick
H. Varley*], [no cat.]; Toronto, Eaton's Fine Art Galleries,
30 October – 11 November 1944, *Paintings and Drawings
by F.H. Varley,* [no cat.]; Toronto, AGT, October – November 1954, *F.H. Varley Paintings 1915 – 1954,* no. 19.

Philip Surrey, Montreal

BIBLIOGRAPHY: J. Russell Harper, *Canadian Paintings in
Hart House* (1955), p, 36 repr.; J. Russell Harper, *Painting
in Canada* (1966), p. 295; Jeremy Adamson, *The Hart
House Collection of Canadian Paintings* (1969), p. 100, repr.
p. 35.

A photograph by John Vanderpant shows Fred Varley
with *Complementaries* (collection of the Art Gallery of
Ontario, Toronto) in an incomplete state and *Open
Window* completed. Thus *Open Window* predates *Com-
plementaries* which was first exhibited at The National
Gallery of Canada, January 1933, *Annual Exhibition of
Canadian Art,* no. 269. The watercolour study, *Dawn*
(private collection, Vancouver), was first exhibited at The
Vancouver Art Gallery, 5 – 30 October 1932, *First Annual
B.C. Artists' Exhibition,* no. 102.

Another version, *View from the Artist's Studio, Jericho
Beach* (n.d., oil on canvas; 43-3/4 x 37-3/4 in., 111.1 x
95.9 cm) is in the collection of The Winnipeg Art Gallery,
Winnipeg. The same subject appears in *Sea Music* (c. 1945,
oil on canvas; 28 x 24 in., 71.1 x 61.0 cm) in the collection
of Mr George Trim, Montreal.

Hart House, University of Toronto

*37

J.W.G. Macdonald   1897 – 1960
The Black Tusk, Garibaldi Park, B.C.   1932
28 x 35-1/4 in. (71.1 x 89.5 cm)

INSCRIPTION: Signed and dated l.r., *J.W.G. Macdonald '32.*

PROVENANCE: Estate of the Artist; Mrs William Davenport, Ventura, California; Paul Duval, Toronto.

EXHIBITIONS: Vancouver, VAG, 5 – 30 October 1932, *First Annual B.C. Artists' Exhibition,* no. 22; Toronto, AGT, 4 – 30 November 1932, *53rd RCA,* no. 125; Ottawa, NGC, 1933, *Annual Exhibition of Canadian Art,* no. 165; (?) Atlantic City, Heinz Art Salon, 1933, *Paintings by the Canadian Group of Painters,* no. 37 (as *The Black Tusk*); Vancouver, VAG, 26 June – 12 July 1936, *26th Annual Exhibition, B.C. Society of Fine Arts,* no. 22 (as *The Black Tusk*); Johannesburg, *Empire Exhibition,* 15 September 1936 – 15 January 1937, no. 855; Ottawa, NGC, 1936, *Southern Dominions Exhibition,* no. 56, repr.; New York, World's Fair, 1 August – 15 September 1939, *Canadian Group of Painters,* no. 39; Vancouver, VAG, May 1941, *J.W.G. Macdonald,* [no cat.]; Ottawa, NGC, 1942, *Canadian Group of Painters Travelling Exhibition,* no. 23; Ottawa, NGC, 1969 – 1970, *Jock Macdonald Retrospective Exhibition,* no. 2, repr.

BIBLIOGRAPHY: Eric Brown, 'New Art on the Horizon,' *The Christian Science Monitor,* Weekly Magazine Section (13 January 1937), p. 8.

Reta and Max Merkur, Toronto

38

J.W.G. Macdonald   1897 – 1960
Indian Burial, Nootka   1937
36-1/4 x 28-1/4 in. (92.1 x 71.8 cm)

INSCRIPTION: Signed and dated l.l., *J.W.G. MACDONALD/1937.*

PROVENANCE: Purchased from the artist, 1938.

EXHIBITIONS: London, Royal Institute Galleries, 8 – 29 May 1937, *Exhibition of Paintings Drawings And Sculpture By Artists Of The British Empire Overseas,* no. 15; Liverpool, Walker Art Gallery, 16 October 1937 – 8 January 1938, *The 63rd Autumn Exhibition,* no. 524; San Francisco, Golden Gate International Exposition, 1939, *Contemporary Art,* [Canadian section], no. 18; Toronto, AGT, April 1941, *Miller Brittain, Adrien Hébert, J.W.G. Macdonald, Bernard Middleton,* [no cat. no.]; Toronto, AGT, January 1945, *The Development of Painting in Canada 1665 – 1945,* no. 173, repr. p. 39; Toronto, AGT, May 1960, *Jock W.G. Macdonald / A Retrospective Exhibition,* no. 9.

BIBLIOGRAPHY: VAG, *The Art Gallery Bulletin,* vol. 6, no. 1 (September 1938), repr.; VAG, *Illustrated Catalogue* (1941), no. 243.

The Vancouver Art Gallery (38.1)

39

J.W.G. Macdonald   1897 – 1960
Pilgrimage   1937
31 x 24 in. (78.7 x 61.0 cm)

INSCRIPTION: Signed and dated u.1., *J W G MACDONALD /1937.*

PROVENANCE: Estate of the artist.

EXHIBITIONS: Vancouver, VAG, 17 September – 10 October 1937, *6th Annual B.C. Artists' Exhibition*, no. 37; Toronto, AGT, November 1937, *Canadian Group of Painters*, no. 48; Ottawa, NGC, 1938, *Canadian Group of Painters*, no. 47; London, The Tate Gallery, 1938, *A Century of Canadian Art*, no. 147.

Roberts Gallery, Toronto

*40

F.H. Varley   1881 – 1969
Night Ferry, Vancouver   1937
32-1/4 x 40-1/4 in. (81.9 x 102.2 cm)

INSCRIPTION: Signed 1.r., *VARLEY*, with thumbprint.

PROVENANCE: Acquired from the artist.

EXHIBITIONS: Montreal, W. Scott & Sons, from 26 May 1937, *Frederick H. Varley, A.R.C.A.*, no. 24; Ottawa, James Wilson & Company, November 1937, [*Frederick H. Varley*], [no cat.]; Toronto, AGT, October 1947, *Pictures from the Collection of Mr. & Mrs. Charles S. Band*, [no cat. no.]; Toronto, CNE, 27 August – 11 September 1948, *Canadian Painting and Sculpture Owned by Canadians*, no. 43; Ottawa, NGC, 1953, *Paintings and Drawings from the Collection of Mr. and Mrs. C.S. Band*, no. 44, repr.; Hamilton, Art Gallery of Hamilton, December 1953 – January 1954, *Inaugural Exhibition*, no. 59, repr.; Toronto, AGT, October – November 1954, *F.H. Varley Paintings 1915 – 1954*, no. 24, repr. pl. 7; Buffalo, Albright Art Gallery, 1 October – 2 November 1958, *The Collection of Mr. and Mrs. Charles S. Band*, no. 28; Toronto, CNE, 1959, *Private Collectors' Choice in Canadian Art*, [no cat. no.]; Vancouver, VAG, 1 – 21 March 1960, *Paintings & Drawings from the Collection of Mr. & Mrs. Charles S. Band*, no. 29; Mexico City, Museo Nacional de Arte Moderno, November 1960, *Arte Canadiense*, no. 120; Windsor, Willistead Art Gallery, 28 April – 29 May 1961, *Canadian Paintings and Drawings from the C.S. Band Collection*, no. 20; St Catharines (Ontario), Rodman Hall Arts Centre, November 1962, *F.H. Varley Paintings & Drawings from the C.S. Band Collection*, [no cat.]; Toronto, AGT, 15 February – 24 March 1963, *The Collection of Mr. and Mrs. Charles S. Band*, no. 40, repr.; Vancouver, VAG, September 1966, *Images for a Canadian Heritage*, no. 75; Ottawa, NGC, 15 May – 15 September 1967, *Three Hundred Years of Canadian Art*, no. 247, repr.; Burnaby, Burnaby Art Gallery, 1 May – 2 June 1974, *Varley / The Middle Years*, no. 40.

BIBLIOGRAPHY: Robert H. Hubbard, *An Anthology of Canadian Art* (1960), repr. in colour pl. 95; Robert H. Hubbard, *The Development of Canadian Art* (1963), p. 98; J. Russell Harper, *Painting in Canada* (1966), p. 296; Paul Duval, *Four Decades* (1972), p. 21 repr. in colour.

Mrs Charles S. Band, Toronto

*41

F.H. Varley   1881 – 1969
Summer in the Arctic   c. 1939
34 x 40 in. (86.4 x 101.6 cm)

INSCRIPTION: Signed l.r., *VARLEY*, with thumbprint.

PROVENANCE: Acquired from the artist.

EXHIBITIONS: New York, World's Fair, 1 August – 15 September 1939, *Canadian Group of Painters*, no. 59; Toronto, AGT, November 1939, *Canadian Group of Painters*, [no cat. no.]; Montreal, AAM, 6 November – 4 December 1941, *62nd RCA*, no. 191; Toronto, AGT, October – November 1954, *F.H. Varley Paintings 1915 – 1954*, no. 25; Toronto, Royal Ontario Museum, April 1958, *Up North*, [not in cat.]; Toronto, Laing Galleries, 27 January – 8 February 1959, *A Loan Exhibition, One Hundred Years of Canadian Painting*, no. 23, repr. p. 16; Toronto, CNE, 1959, *Private Collectors' Choice in Canadian Art*, [no cat. no.], repr.

BIBLIOGRAPHY: Donald W. Buchanan, 'The Paintings and Drawings of F.H. Varley,' *Canadian Art*, vol. VII, no. 1 (Autumn 1949), p. 5 repr.; 'A Gallery of Northern Painting,' *Maclean's Magazine*, Vol. 67 (15 November 1954), p. 26, repr. in colour.

The sketch, *Summer in the Arctic*, (1938, watercolour; 9 x 12 in., 22.9 x 30.5 cm) is in the collection of Mrs Dyde, Edmonton. See Edmund S. Carpenter, Frederick H. Varley, and Robert Flaherty, *Eskimo* (1959), p. 22 repr.

Private collection.

*42

L.L. FitzGerald   1890 – 1956
Doc Snider's House   1931
29-1/2 x 33-1/2 in. (74.9 x 85.1 cm)

INSCRIPTION: Signed and dated l.l., *L.L. FITZGERALD 1931*.

PROVENANCE: Purchased from the artist (*Annual Exhibition of Canadian Art, 1932*); Gift of P.D. Ross, LL.D., Ottawa, 1932.

EXHIBITIONS: Toronto, AGT, December 1931, *An Exhibition by the Group of Seven*, no. 53; Ottawa, NGC, 1932, *Annual Exhibition of Canadian Art*, no. 60; New York, Roerich Museum, 5 March – 5 April 1932, *Exhibition of Paintings by Contemporary Canadian Artists*, no. 13 (incorrectly listed as lent by the Hon. Vincent Massey); Ottawa, NGC, *Group of Seven 1936*, no. 44, repr.; Johannesburg, *Empire Exhibition*, 15 September 1936 – 15 January 1937, no. 822; Ottawa, NGC, 1936, *Southern Dominions Exhibition*, no. 23 repr.; New Haven, Yale University Art Gallery, 11 March – 16 April 1944, *Canadian Art 1760 – 1943*, [no cat. no.]; Toronto, AGT, January 1945, *The Development of Painting in Canada 1665 – 1945*, no. 165, repr. p. 338; Albany (New York), Albany Institute of History and Art, 10 January – 10 March 1946, *Painting in Canada*, no. 66; London (Ontario), London Public Library and Art Museum, 20 September – 20 October 1946, *The Group of Seven 1919 – 1933*, no. 38; Richmond (Virginia), Virginia Museum of Fine Arts, 1949, *Exhibition of Canadian Painting 1668 – 1948*, no. 23; Toronto, AGT, October – November 1949, *Fifty Years of Painting in Canada*, no. 46; Washington, National Gallery of Art, 1950 – 1951, *Canadian Painting*, no. 27, repr.; Vancouver, VAG, 1954, *Group of Seven*, no. 19 repr.; Winnipeg, The Winnipeg Art Gallery, 1958, *L.L. FitzGerald 1890 – 1956 / A Memorial Exhibition*, no. 7, repr.; Madison, Wisconsin, Elvehjem Art Center, University of Wisconsin, 1973, *Canadian Landscape Painting 1670 – 1930*, no. 74 repr.

BIBLIOGRAPHY: *Arts Weekly*, vol. 1, no. 2 (18 March 1932), p. 28, repr; Eric Brown, 'Canada's National Painters,' *The Studio*, vol. CIII (June 1932), p. 315 repr.; 'Moderne Malerei in Kanada,' *Die Kunst Für Alle*, vol. 48, no. 11 (August 1933), p. 347 repr.; 'Two recent acquisitions by the National Gallery,' *The Curtain Call*, vol. 7, no. 3 (December 1935), p. 6, repr. p. 11; Bertram Brooker, ed., *Yearbook of the Arts in Canada 1936* (1936), repr. pl. 1; Graham C. McInnes, 'Art of Canada,' *The Studio*, vol.

CXIV (August 1937), p. 60 repr.; Donald W. Buchanan, *Canadian Painters from Paul Kane to the Group of Seven* (1945), repr. pl. 80; Robert Ayre, 'Lionel LeMoine FitzGerald 1890 – 1956,' *Canadian Art*, vol. XIV, no. 1 (Autumn 1956), p. 14 repr.; Julian Park, ed., *The Culture of Contemporary Canada* (1957), p. 131; Ferdinand Eckhardt, 'The Technique of L.L. FitzGerald,' *Canadian Art*, vol. XV, no. 2 (April 1958), p. 116 repr. in colour; *Hubbard NGC* (1960), p. 84, repr.; Elizabeth Kilbourn, ed., *Great Canadian Painting* (1966), p. 71 repr. in colour; Peter Mellen, *The Group of Seven* (1970), p. 183 repr.; Jean Sutherland Boggs, *The National Gallery of Canada* (1971), repr. pl. 140; Jean-René Ostiguy, *Un siècle de peinture canadienne 1870 – 1970* (1971), repr. pl. 79; Dennis Reid, *A Concise History of Canadian Painting* (1973), p. 161, repr. p. 162.

The National Gallery of Canada, Ottawa (3993)

43

L.L. FitzGerald   1890 – 1956
Farm Yard   1931
Oil on canvas mounted on board, 13-3/4 x 16-3/4 in. (34.9 x 42.6 cm)

INSCRIPTION: Signed and dated l.l., *L.L. FITZGERALD 1931.*

PROVENANCE: Acquired from the artist; Vincent Massey, Port Hope, Ontario; Bequest of the Right Hon. Vincent Massey, 1968.

EXHIBITIONS: Toronto, AGT, December 1931, *An Exhibition By The Group of Seven*, no. 54 (as *Farm Buildings*); Toronto, AGT, December 1934, *Canadian Paintings, The Collection of Hon. Vincent and Mrs. Massey*, no. 106; London, The Tate Gallery, 1938, *A Century of Canadian Art*, no. 55; Hamilton, Art Gallery of Hamilton, December 1953 – January 1954, *Inaugural Exhibition*, no. 14, repr. (as *Western Farm*); Winnipeg, The Winnipeg Art Gallery, 1958, *L.L. FitzGerald 1890 – 1956/A Memorial Exhibition*, no. 9; Ottawa, NGC, 20 September – 20 October 1968, *Vincent Massey Bequest/The Canadian Paintings*, no. 7 repr.

A related work, *Prairie Farm* (1931), formerly in the collection of the International Business Machine Corporation, was exhibited at Toronto, C.N.E., September 1941, *Contemporary Art of the Western Hemisphere*, no. 35, repr. This work is presently in a private collection, Toronto.

The National Gallery of Canada, Ottawa (15474)

*44

L.L. FitzGerald 1890 – 1956
Broken Tree in Landscape 1931
14 x 16-13/16 in. (35.6 x 42.7 cm)

INSCRIPTION: Signed and dated l.l., *L.L. FITZGERALD 1931.*

PROVENANCE: Donated by the Women's Committee of The Winnipeg Art Gallery, 1956.

EXHIBITIONS: Atlantic City, Heinz Art Salon, 1933, *Paintings by the Canadian Group of Painters,* no. 11 (as *Dead Tree*); Toronto, AGT, November 1933, *Exhibition of Paintings by the Canadian Group of Painters,* no. 19 (as *Dead Tree*); Montreal, AAM, January 1934, *Exhibition of Paintings by Canadian Group of Painters,* no. 16 (as *Dead Tree*); Winnipeg, The Winnipeg Art Gallery, 30 March 1957, *Memorial Room for LeMoine FitzGerald 1890 – 1956,* no. 4; Portage-La-Prairie, The Brush & Palette Club, October 1958, *FitzGerald 1890 – 1956,* no. 4.

BIBLIOGRAPHY: *The Winnipeg Art Gallery 1912 – 1962* (n.d.), p. 31.

The Winnipeg Art Gallery (G-56-29)

45

L.L. FitzGerald 1890 – 1956
The Pool 1934
Oil on board, 14-1/4 x 17-1/4 in. (36.2 x 43.8 cm)

INSCRIPTION: Signed and dated l.l. centre, *L.L. FITZGERALD/1934.*

PROVENANCE: Acquired from the artist; Purchased from Harry Adaskin, Vancouver, 1973.

EXHIBITION: Toronto, AGT, January 1936, *Exhibition of Paintings by the 'Canadian Group of Painters,'* no. 22.

The National Gallery of Canada, Ottawa (17612)

46

L.L. FitzGerald   1890 – 1956
Jar   1938
24 x 21-1/8 in. (61.0 x 53.7 cm)

INSCRIPTION: Signed and dated l.l., *L.L.F./'38.*

PROVENANCE: The estate of the artist; Donated by the
Women's Committee of The Winnipeg Art Gallery, 1956.

EXHIBITIONS: London, The Tate Gallery, 1938, *A Century
of Canadian Art,* no. 56; New York, World's Fair, 1 August – 15 September 1939, *Canadian Group of Painters,* no.
18; Toronto, AGT, November 1939, *Canadian Group of
Painters,* [no cat. no.]; The American Federation of Arts,
24 April 1944 – 28 April 1946, *Canadian Painting* (Travelling Exhibition), no. 7 (incorrectly measured 26 x 30 in.);
New York, The Canadian Club of New York, 1948, *Exhibition of Contemporary Canadian Painting,* no. 12; Winnipeg, The Winnipeg Art Gallery, 30 March 1957, *Memorial
Room for LeMoine FitzGerald 1890 – 1956,* no. 5 (as *Still
Life – Jug*); Winnipeg, The Winnipeg Art Gallery, 1958,
L.L. FitzGerald 1890 – 1956/A Memorial Exhibition, no. 15,
repr.; Stratford (Ontario), Shakespearean Festival, 1962,
Paintings at Stratford/Lionel LeMoine FitzGerald, no. 4;
Vancouver, VAG, September 1966, *Images for a Canadian
Heritage,* no. 88; Ottawa, NGC, 15 May – 15 September
1967, *Three Hundred Years of Canadian Art,* no. 250, repr.
(as *The Jar*).

BIBLIOGRAPHY: Donald W. Buchanan, 'The Story of Cana-
dian Art,' *Canadian Geographical Journal,* vol. XVII, no. 6
(December 1938), p. 279 repr.; Lawren Harris, 'LeMoine
FitzGerald – Western Artist,' *Canadian Art,* vol. III, no. 1
(October – November 1945), p. 10 repr.; *The Winnipeg
Art Gallery 1912 – 1962* (n.d.), p. 31; Dennis Reid, *A Con-
cise History of Canadian Painting* (1973), p. 163, repr. p. 164.

The Winnipeg Art Gallery (G-56-25)

*47

David Milne   1882 – 1953
Blind Road   1930
16 x 20 in. (40.6 x 50.8 cm)

INSCRIPTION: Signed and dated l.l., *David B. Milne 1930.*

PROVENANCE: Mellors Galleries, Toronto; Vincent Massey, Port Hope, Ontario; Laing Galleries, Toronto.

EXHIBITIONS: Toronto, Mellors Galleries, 27 November –
8 December 1934, *Exhibition of Paintings by David B. Milne,*
no. 14 (as *Across the Fields*); Toronto, Hart House, University of Toronto, 9 – 22 January 1962, *David Milne,* [no
cat.].

This is one of a series of landscapes painted near Palgrave,
Ontario. Related works include *Contours and Elm Trees*
(1930, oil on canvas; 16 x 24 in., 40.7 x 61.0 cm), in The
National Gallery of Canada (4258) and *Late Afternoon*
(1930, oil on canvas; 16 x 20 in., 40.6 x 50.8 cm), in the
Art Gallery of Ontario (51/88).
David Milne also produced a three-colour dry-point
(5 x 6-7/8 in., 12.7 x 17.4 cm) entitled *Blind Road.* The
dry-point is of a related, though not identical, subject.

Mr and Mrs W.A. Manford, Toronto

*48

David Milne 1882 – 1953
Splendour Touches Hiram's Farm 1932
20-1/4 x 24-1/4 in. (51.4 x 61.6 cm)

INSCRIPTION: Signed and dated u.l., *David Milne 1932.*

PROVENANCE: Acquired from the artist; Vincent Massey, Port Hope, Ontario; Bequest of the Right Hon. Vincent Massey, 1968.

EXHIBITIONS: Toronto, AGT, December 1934, *Canadian Paintings, The Collection of Hon. Vincent and Mrs. Massey,* no. 143; Ottawa, NGC, 20 September – 20 October 1968, *Vincent Massey Bequest/The Canadian Paintings,* no. 62.

This is one of three paintings of this subject including, *Spring on Hiram's Farm,* originally entitled *The Cold and Rain Grip Hiram's Farm* (1932, oil on canvas; 20-1/4 x 24-1/8 in., 51.4 x 61.3 cm), in The Winnipeg Art Gallery (G-70-519) and *Maple Blooms on Hiram's Farm* (1933, oil on canvas; 20 x 28 in., 50.8 x 71.1 cm), in the London Public Library and Art Museum (70.A.56).

The National Gallery of Canada, Ottawa (15530)

49

David Milne 1882 – 1953
Palgrave (I) 1931
18-1/8 x 22-3/8 in. (46.0 x 56.8 cm)

INSCRIPTION: Signed and dated u.r., *David Milne 1931.* Inscribed on the stretcher, '*The House is a Square Red Cloud/Palgrave 1931.*'

PROVENANCE: Acquired from the artist; Vincent Massey, Port Hope, Ontario; Bequest of the Right Hon. Vincent Massey, 1968.

EXHIBITION: Ottawa, NGC, 20 September – 20 October 1968, *Vincent Massey Bequest/The Canadian Paintings,* no. 54.

This is part of one of two groups of works depicting this house at Palgrave, Ontario. One group has a cloudless sky. Related works with a cloud-filled sky include *House and Clouds* (c. 1930 – 1932) in the collection of Mrs J.P. Barwick, Ottawa, *Palgrave (II)* (1931), in The National Gallery of Canada (15522), and *House, Palgrave* (c. 1930 – 1932) in the Beaverbrook Art Gallery, Fredericton.

The National Gallery of Canada, Ottawa (15521)

50

David Milne   1882 – 1953
Young Poplars Among Driftwood   1937
18-1/4 x 24-1/4 in. (46.4 x 61.6 cm)

INSCRIPTION: Signed and dated u.1., *David Milne 1937.*

PROVENANCE: Purchased from the estate of the artist, per Douglas M. Duncan, 1955.

EXHIBITION: Toronto, Mellors Galleries, 15 – 29 January 1938, *Exhibition of Recent Pictures by David B. Milne*, no. 31.

BIBLIOGRAPHY: Alan Jarvis, *David Milne* (1962), p. 23 repr.; *Hubbard NGC* (1960), p. 217, repr.

The National Gallery of Canada, Ottawa (6369)

51

David Milne   1882 – 1953
Raspberry Jam   1936
18-1/8 x 22-1/8 in. (46.0 x 56.2 cm)

INSCRIPTION: Signed and dated 1.1., *David Milne 1936.*

PROVENANCE: Mellors Galleries, Toronto; Douglas M. Duncan, Toronto; Gift from the Douglas M. Duncan Collection, 1970.

EXHIBITIONS: Toronto, Mellors Galleries, 24 October – 7 November 1936, *Exhibition of Little Pictures by David B. Milne*, no. 5; New York, World's Fair, 1 August – 15 September 1939, *Canadian Group of Painters*, no. 43; Kingston, Agnes Etherington Art Centre, Queen's University, 3 February – 2 March 1967, *David Milne 1882 – 1953*, no. 32; Ottawa, NGC, 5 March – 4 April 1971, *Gift from the Douglas M. Duncan Collection and the Milne-Duncan Bequest*, no. 136.

BIBLIOGRAPHY: Donald W. Buchanan, 'Canada,' *The Studio*, vol. cxxv (April 1943), p. 124 repr.

The National Gallery of Canada, Ottawa (16601)

*52

David Milne   1882 – 1953
Red Nasturtiums   1937
Watercolour on paper, 14 x 20-3/4 in. (35.6 x 52.7 cm)

INSCRIPTION: Signed and dated l.r., *David Milne 1937*.

PROVENANCE: Mellors Galleries, Toronto; Douglas M. Duncan, Toronto; Gift from the Douglas M. Duncan Collection, 1970.

EXHIBITIONS: Toronto, Mellors Galleries, 15 – 29 January 1938, *Exhibition of Recent Pictures by David B. Milne*, no. 37; Kingston, Agnes Etherington Art Centre, Queen's University, 3 February – 2 March 1967, *David Milne 1882 – 1953*, no. 34; Ottawa, NGC, 5 March – 4 April 1971, *Gift from the Douglas M. Duncan Collection and the Milne-Duncan Bequest*, no. 156.

A related watercolour *Red Nasturtium* (1937) is in the collection of Carleton University, Ottawa (Gift from the Douglas M. Duncan Collection, 1970).

The National Gallery of Canada, Ottawa (16429)

*53

Lawren S. Harris   1885 – 1970
Riven Earth I   c. 1936
30-1/2 x 36 in. (77.5 x 91.4 cm)

PROVENANCE: Acquired from the artist.

EXHIBITIONS: Toronto, AGT, November 1937, *Canadian Group of Painters*, no. 31, repr. (as *Composition 8*); Ottawa, NGC, 1938, *Canadian Group of Painters*, no. 25 (as *Composition 8*); Toronto, AGT, October – November 1948, *Lawren Harris Paintings 1910 – 1948*, no. 68 (as *Abstract Painting*); Ottawa, NGC, 7 June – 8 September 1963, *Lawren Harris Retrospective Exhibition, 1963*, no. 50 (as *Abstraction*); Ottawa, NGC, 15 May – 15 September 1967, *Three Hundred Years of Canadian Art*, no. 249, repr. (as *Composition No. 8*).

BIBLIOGRAPHY: H.A. Mulligan, 'The Canadian Painters,' *Canadian Comment*, vol. 6, no. 12 (December 1937), pp. 25-26, repr.; Robert H. Hubbard, *The Development of Canadian Art* (1963), p. 103, repr. pl. 172 (as *Composition No. 8*); Bess Harris and R.G.P. Colgrove, *Lawren Harris* (1969), p. 108 repr. (as *Abstraction*).

A related work *Riven Earth II* (c. 1936, oil on masonite; 22 x 26 in., 55.9 x 66.0 cm), is in the collection of Mrs Charles S. Band, Toronto. See Bess Harris and R.G.P. Colgrove, *Lawren Harris* (1969), p. 124 repr.

Miss Isabel McLaughlin, Toronto

*54

Lawren S. Harris   1885 – 1970
Resolution   c. 1937
36 x 28 in. (91.4 x 71.1 cm)

INSCRIPTION: On stretcher *verso, RESOLUTION / INTER-LOCKING FORMS – SYMBOL OF STEADFAST-NESS, COURAGE.*

PROVENANCE: Acquired from the artist.

EXHIBITIONS: Toronto, AGT, November 1937, *Canadian Group of Painters*, no. 29 (as *Composition 2*); Ottawa, NGC, 1938, *Canadian Group of Painters*, no. 23 (as *Composition 2*); Ottawa, NGC, 7 June – 8 September 1963, *Lawren Harris Retrospective Exhibition, 1963*, no. 55.

The sketch, *Abstract Sketch* (c. 1937, oil on wood; 12 x 15 in., 30.5 x 38.1 cm) is in The McMichael Canadian Collection, Kleinburg. See Paul Duval, *A Vision of Canada* (1973), p. 154 repr. horizontal. This sketch was formerly in the collection of Jock and Barbara Macdonald.

Mrs Leslie J. Kerr, Vancouver

55

Lawren S. Harris   1885 – 1970
White Triangle   c. 1939
51-1/8 x 36-5/8 in. (129.9 x 93.0 cm)

INSCRIPTION: *Verso, PAINTING I/owned by Bess Harris/ 1946.*

PROVENANCE: Gift of the artist to Bess Harris, Vancouver; Gift of the estate of Bess Harris and of the three children of Lawren S. Harris, 1972.

EXHIBITIONS: Toronto, AGT, November 1939, *Canadian Group of Painters*, [no cat. no.] (as *Painting I*); New York, Museum of Non-Objective Painting, 6 August – 30 September 1940, *Six American Non-Objective Painters*, [no cat.] (as *Painting I*); Toronto, AGT, October – November 1948, *Lawren Harris Paintings 1910 – 1948*, no. 59 (as *Abstract Painting*); Ottawa, NGC, 7 June – 8 September 1963, *Lawren Harris Retrospective Exhibition, 1963*, no. 47 (as *Abstraction*).

BIBLIOGRAPHY: Bess Harris and R.G.P. Colgrove, *Lawren Harris* (1969), p. 103 repr. (dated 1945).

A drawing for this work is in the collection of Howard Harris, Vancouver.

The National Gallery of Canada, Ottawa (17159)

56

Carl Schaefer   b. 1903
Ontario Farmhouse   1934
41-7/8 x 49-1/4 in. (106.4 x 125.1 cm)

INSCRIPTION: Signed and dated 1.1., *Carl Schaefer 1934.*

PROVENANCE: Mr and Mrs Bertram Tate, Toronto; Gift of
Mr Floyd S. Chalmers, Toronto, 1969.

EXHIBITIONS: Toronto, AGT, March 1935, *63rd OSA*, no.
174; Toronto, CNE, 23 August – 5 September 1935, no. 271,
repr.; Toronto, AGT, October – November 1949, *Fifty
Years of Painting in Canada*, no. 86; Montreal, Sir George
Williams University, 1969, *Carl Schaefer Retrospective
Exhibition*, no. 13, repr. in colour.

BIBLIOGRAPHY: Andrew Bell, 'Contemporary Canadian
Water-Colours,' *The Studio*, vol. CXLIII (April 1952), p.
109 repr. (incorrectly as a watercolour); NGC, *Second
Annual Review of the National Gallery of Canada, Ottawa
1969-1970*, p. 74, repr. pl. 74; Dennis Reid, *A Concise
History of Canadian Painting* (1973), p. 179, repr. in colour
pl. xxv.

A watercolour painting of the same subject, *The Felzing
House, Hanover* (watercolour on paper; 14-1/2 x 17-1/2 in.,
36.8 x 44.5 cm), painted on 12 July 1934, is in the collection of the artist.

The National Gallery of Canada, Ottawa (15845)

57

Carl Schaefer   b. 1903
Storm over the Fields   1937
27-3/16 x 37 in. (69.1 x 94.0 cm)

INSCRIPTION: Signed and dated 1.1., *Carl Schaefer/1937.*

PROVENANCE: Acquired from the artist; Gift from
J.S. McLean, Canadian Fund, 1954.

EXHIBITIONS: Toronto, AGT, March 1938, *66th OSA*, no.
156; Toronto, AGT, 26 March – 25 April 1954, *Paraskeva
Clark and Carl Schaefer*, no. 15; Stratford (Ontario),
Shakespearean Festival, 1963, *Canada on Canvas*, [no cat.
avail.]; Toronto, AGO, 1967 – 1968, *Canadian Paintings of
the 1930s* (Travelling Exhibition), no. 21; Montreal,
Sir George Williams University, 1969, *Carl Schaefer
Retrospective Exhibition*, no. 21, repr.

BIBLIOGRAPHY: George Johnston, 'Carl Schaefer,' *Canadian Art*, vol. XVII, no. 2 (March 1960), pp. 66 – 67;
Dennis Reid, *A Concise History of Canadian Painting* (1973),
p. 179, repr.; Paul Duval, *Four Decades* (1972), p. 38 repr. in
colour; *Bradfield AGO*, p. 410, repr. p. 411.

A watercolour painting of the same subject, *Storm over the
Fields* (watercolour on paper; 15 x 22-1/2 in, 38.1 x 57.2
cm), painted at Hanover, Ontario, on 11 July 1937 is in
the J.S. McLean Collection, Toronto. See J. Russell Harper,
'Three Centuries of Canadian Painting,' *Canadian Art*,
vol. XIX, no. 6 (November – December 1962), p. 445 repr.

Art Gallery of Ontario, Toronto (53/51)

*58

Carl Schaefer   b. 1903
Fields with Stubble   1937
Watercolour on paper, 15-3/8 x 22-5/8 in. (39.0 x 57.5 cm)

INSCRIPTION: Signed and dated 1.r., *Carl Schaefer 1937*.

PROVENANCE: Purchased from the artist, 1951.

EXHIBITIONS: Toronto, AGT, April 1938, CSPWC, no. 137;
Toronto, CNE, 25 August – 9 September 1939, no. 328
repr.; Ottawa, NGC, 1961 – 1962, *The Group of Seven and
After* (Travelling Exhibition), [no cat.] (as *Stubble Fields*).

BIBLIOGRAPHY: *Hubbard NGC* (1960), p. 277, repr. (as
Stubble Fields).

Painted at Schomberg, Ontario, on 29 September 1937.

The National Gallery of Canada, Ottawa (5793)

*59

Carl Schaefer   b. 1903
Yellow Apples on a Fall Landscape   1939
Watercolour on paper, 16-1/2 x 23-1/2 in. (41.9 x 59.7 cm)

INSCRIPTION: Signed and dated l.r., C. *Schaefer/39*.

PROVENANCE: Acquired from the artist.

EXHIBITIONS: Brooklyn, Brooklyn Museum, 28 March –
11 May 1941, *11th Biennial International Water Color Exhibition*, no. 225; Ottawa, NGC, 1951, *CSPWC Retrospective
Exhibition 1926 – 1951*, no. 92; Toronto, AGT, 26 March –
25 April 1954, *Paraskeva Clark and Carl Schaefer*, no. 11;
Montreal, Sir George Williams University, 1969, *Carl
Schaefer Retrospective Exhibition*, no. 31, repr. p. 25.

BIBLIOGRAPHY: J. Russell Harper, *Painting in Canada*
(1966), p. 326 repr.

Mrs Carl F. Schaefer, Toronto

*60

Charles Comfort   b. 1900
Portrait of John Creighton   1931 – 1933
30 x 24 in. (76.2 x 61.0 cm)

INSCRIPTION: Signed and dated l.r., *Comfort 1933.*

PROVENANCE: Acquired from the artist.

EXHIBITIONS: Montreal, AAM, 19 November – 20 December 1931, *52nd RCA*, no. 32; Toronto, AGT, 4 – 30 November 1932, *53rd RCA*, no. 32; Ottawa, NGC, 1933, *Annual Exhibition of Canadian Art*, no. 44; Atlantic City, Heinz Art Salon, 1933, *Paintings by the Canadian Group of Painters,* no. 10.

Originally a full-length portrait, the work was cut down by the artist *c.* 1933. The original version can be seen in a photograph of the installation of the Canadian Group of Painters exhibition at Atlantic City. See Frank Bagnall, 'Canadian Artists' Show,' *Saturday Night*, vol. XLVIII, no. 50 (21 October 1933), p. 16 repr.

John H. Creighton, Vancouver

*61

Charles Comfort   b. 1900
Young Canadian   1932
Watercolour on paper, 35-1/2 x 41-1/2 in. (90.2 x 105.4 cm)

INSCRIPTION: Signed and dated l.r., *Comfort/1932*

PROVENANCE: Purchased from the artist by the Sketch Committee, 1934.

EXHIBITIONS: Toronto, AGT, April 1933, *CSPWC*, no. 71; Toronto, CNE, 24 August – 8 September 1934, no. 381, repr.; Toronto, AGT, November 1935, *Loan Exhibition of Paintings*, no. 225; London, The Tate Gallery, 1938, *A Century of Canadian Art*, no. 39; New York, World's Fair, 10 June – 31 July 1939, *CSPWC*, no. 30; Toronto, AGT, March 1940, *Emily Carr, Lawren Harris, Fritz Brandtner, Charles Comfort*, [no cat. no.]; Andover, Addison Gallery of American Art, Phillips Academy, 18 September – 8 November 1942, *Aspects of Contemporary Painting in Canada*, no. 15, repr. p. 7; New Haven, Yale University Art Gallery, 11 March – 16 April 1944, *Canadian Art 1760 – 1943*, [no cat. no.], repr.; Toronto, AGT, January 1945, *Development of Painting in Canada 1665 – 1945*, no. 167; Toronto, CNE, 27 August – 11 September 1948, *Canadian Painting and Sculpture Owned by Canadians*, no. 89; Washington, National Gallery of Art, 1950 – 1951, *Canadian Painting*, no. 19, repr.; Ottawa, NGC, 1951, *CSPWC Retrospective Exhibition 1926 – 1951*, no. 35; Mexico City, Museo Nacional de Arte Moderno, November 1960, *Arte Canadiense*, no. 138, repr.; Stratford (Ontario), Festival Arena, 11 June – 12 September 1964, *Faces of Canada*, [no cat. no.]; Vancouver, VAG, September 1966, *Images for a Canadian Heritage*, no. 91, repr.; Winnipeg, The Winnipeg Art Gallery, 19 October – 20 November 1972, *Charles Fraser Comfort / Fifty Years*, no. 10, repr.

BIBLIOGRAPHY: H.M. Jackson, *Charles Comfort / The Man and the Artist* [Christmas 1935, New Year 1936], repr.; *Magazine of Art*, vol. 32, no. 8 (August 1939), p. 483, repr.; Graham C. McInnes, 'The Canadian Artist and His Country,' *The Geographical Magazine*, vol. XVI, no. 8 (December 1943), p. 406 repr.; 'Portrait of an Artist,' *Canadian Art*, vol. II, no. 2 (December 1944 – January 1945), p. 84 repr.; Donald W. Buchanan, *The Growth of Canadian Painting* (1950), p. 58, repr. pl. 38; Paul Duval, *Canadian Water Colour Painting* (1954), p. 39 repr.; J. Russell Harper, *Canadian Paintings in Hart House* (1955), p. 53; J. Barry Lord, 'In Search of the Figure in Canadian

Painting,' *Canadian Art,* vol. XXI, no. 4 (July – August 1964), p. 198 repr.; J. Russell Harper, *Painting in Canada* (1966), p. 335, repr. p. 337; Jeremy Adamson, *The Hart House Collection of Canadian Paintings* (1969), p. 27, repr. p. 41; Dennis Reid, *A Concise History of Canadian Painting* (1973), p. 181, repr. p. 182.

Young Canadian is one of three portraits of Carl Schaefer painted by Charles Comfort. The other two portraits are *Flight Lieut. Carl Schaefer, R.C.A.F.* (1948, watercolour on paper; 32-3/8 x 30-3/8 in., 82.2 x 77.1 cm) in the Art Gallery of Ontario (*Bradfield AGO*, p. 78 repr.), and *Carl Schaefer at Bond Head* (1969, oil on canvas; 60 x 50 in., 152.4 x 127.0 cm) in the collection of Mr Bruce Pierce, Toronto.

Hart House, University of Toronto

62

Charles Comfort   b. 1900
Tadoussac   1935
30 x 36 in. (76.2 x 91.4 cm)

INSCRIPTION: Signed and dated l.r., COMFORT / '35.

PROVENANCE: Purchased from the artist, 1935; Vincent Massey, Port Hope, Ontario; Bequest of the Right Hon. Vincent Massey, 1968.

EXHIBITIONS: Toronto, AGT, January 1936, *An Exhibition of Paintings by the 'Canadian Group of Painters,'* no. 19, repr.; London, The Tate Gallery, 1938, *A Century of Canadian Art,* no. 40, repr.; Washington, National Gallery of Art, 1950 – 1951, *Canadian Painting,* no. 18; Ottawa, NGC, 1953, *Exhibition of Canadian Painting to Celebrate the Coronation of Her Majesty Queen Elizabeth II,* no. 16; Ottawa, NGC, 15 May – 15 September 1967, *Three Hundred Years of Canadian Art,* no. 243, repr.; Ottawa, NGC, 20 September – 20 October 1968, *Vincent Massey Bequest / The Canadian Paintings,* no. 4; Halifax, Dalhousie University Art Gallery, 15 October – 5 December 1971, *Selected Works from the Massey Bequest of Canadian Painting,* [no cat.].

BIBLIOGRAPHY: Bertram Brooker, ed., *Yearbook of the Arts in Canada, 1936* (1936), repr. pl. 2; Julian Park, ed., *The Culture of Contemporary Canada* (1957), p. 131; Robert H. Hubbard, *An Anthology of Canadian Art* (1960), repr. pl. 102; Robert H. Hubbard, *The Development of Canadian Art* (1963), p. 111, repr. pl. 189; Hugo McPherson, 'The Resonance of Batterwood House,' *Canadian Art,* vol. XXI, no. 2 (March – April 1964), p. 100 repr.; Peter Mellen, *The Group of Seven* (1970), p. 187 repr.; Jean Sutherland Boggs, *The National Gallery of Canada* (1971), pp. 55, 63, repr. pl. 141.

This work was commissioned by Vincent Massey in the fall of 1935.

The sketch, *Tadoussac* (1935, oil on board; 9-3/4 x 11-3/4 in., 24.8 x 29.9 cm) is in the collection of The National Gallery of Canada (17163) and was purchased from Harry Adaskin, Vancouver, 1973.

The National Gallery of Canada, Ottawa (15471)

*63

Bertram Brooker   1888 – 1955
Portrait of Morley Callaghan   1932
30 x 24 in. (76.2 x 61.0 cm)

INSCRIPTION: Signed and dated l.r., *BERTRAM /
BROOKER / 1932.*

PROVENANCE: Acquired from the artist.

EXHIBITION: Toronto, AGT, March 1932, *60th OSA,*
no. 15.

Morley Callaghan, Toronto

64

Bertram Brooker   1888 – 1955
Ski Poles   1936
24 x 30 in. (61.0 x 76.2 cm)

INSCRIPTION: Signed l.r., *BERTRAM / BROOKER.*

PROVENANCE: The artist; M. A. Brooker, Toronto.

EXHIBITIONS: Toronto, AGT, from 6 November 1936, *57th
RCA,* no. 33; Ottawa, NGC, 1937, *RCA Travelling Exhibition,* no. 11; Toronto, AGT, 17 February – 18 March 1956,
84th OSA / Bertram Brooker Memorial Exhibition, no. 11
(as *Ski Boots*); Ottawa, NGC, 1972 – 1973, *Bertram
Brooker (1888 – 1955) / A Retrospective Exhibition* (Travelling Exhibition), no. 18.

BIBLIOGRAPHY: Dennis Reid, *Bertram Brooker 1888 – 1955*
(1973), p. 20, repr. pl. 29.

Estate of M.A. Brooker

65

Bertram Brooker   1888 – 1955
Torso   1937
24-1/4 x 18 in. (61.6 x 45.7 cm)

INSCRIPTION: Signed and dated l.r., *BERTRAM/ BROOKER / 1937.*

PROVENANCE: The artist; Purchased from the estate of M.A. Brooker, Toronto, per Jerrold Morris Gallery, Toronto, 1971.

EXHIBITIONS: Toronto, AGT, March 1937, *65th OSA*, no. 24; Toronto, CNE, 27 August – 11 September 1937, no. 144; Toronto, Hart House, University of Toronto, November 1937, *[Bertram Brooker]*, [no. cat.]; Toronto, AGT, 17 December 1937 – 2 January 1938, *Exhibition of Little Pictures by Members of the OSA*, no. 15; Toronto, Hart House, University of Toronto, January 1942, *[Bertram Brooker]*, [no. cat.]; Ottawa, NGC, 1972 – 1973, *Bertram Brooker (1888 – 1955) / A Retrospective Exhibition* (Travelling Exhibition), no. 22.

BIBLIOGRAPHY: Dennis Reid, *Bertram Brooker 1888 – 1955* (1973), p. 20, repr. pl. 33; Dennis Reid, *A Concise History of Canadian Painting* (1973), p. 184, repr. p. 185.

The National Gallery of Canada, Ottawa (16877)

66

Paraskeva Clark   b. 1898
Self-Portrait   1933
40 x 30 in. (101.6 x 76.2 cm)

INSCRIPTION: Signed and dated l.r., *PARASKEVA CLARK / 33.*

EXHIBITIONS: Toronto, AGT, November 1933, *Exhibition of Paintings by Canadian Group of Painters*, no. 89 (as *Myself*); Montreal, AAM, January 1934, *Exhibition of Paintings by Canadian Group of Painters*, no. 74 (as *Myself*); Toronto, Galleries of J. Merritt Malloney, 4 – 18 January 1936, *Rody Keny Courtice, Isabel McLaughlin, Kathleen Daly, Yvonne McKague, Paraskeva Clark*, no. 44 (as *Woman in Black*); Montreal, MMFA, 29 December 1954 – 16 January 1955, *Paraskeva Clark and Henri Masson*, [no cat. no.].

Paraskeva Clark, R.C.A., Toronto

*67

Paraskeva Clark   b. 1898
Wheat Field   1936
26-3/4 x 30-3/8 in. (68.0 x 77.2 cm)

INSCRIPTION: Signed and dated l.r., *paraskeva clark 36.*

PROVENANCE: Purchased from the artist by Douglas M. Duncan, Toronto; Gift from the Douglas M. Duncan Collection, 1970.

EXHIBITIONS: Toronto, AGT, November 1937, *Canadian Group of Painters*, no. 18; Ottawa, NGC, 1938, *Canadian Group of Painters*, no. 12; London, The Tate Gallery, 1938, *A Century of Canadian Art*, no. 35; Toronto, AGT, November – December 1939, *Paraskeva Clark, Carl Schaefer, Caven Atkins, David Milne*, [no cat. no.]; Ottawa, NGC, 5 March – 4 April 1971, *Gift from the Douglas M. Duncan Collection and the Milne-Duncan Bequest*, no. 9.

BIBLIOGRAPHY: Graham C. McInnes, 'Contemporary Canadian Artists No. 7 – Paraskeva Clark,' *The Canadian Forum*, vol. XVII, no. 199 (August 1937), pp. 166 – 167, repr.; Graham C. McInnes, 'Art of Canada,' *The Studio*, vol. CXIV (August 1937), p. 62 repr.; Alan Jarvis, ed., *Douglas Duncan* (1974), repr. in colour opp. p. 60.

The National Gallery of Canada, Ottawa (16452)

68

Paraskeva Clark   b. 1898
Petroushka   1937
48 x 32 in. (121.9 x 81.3 cm)

INSCRIPTION: Signed and dated l.r., *Paraskeva Clark 37.*

EXHIBITIONS: Toronto, AGT, November 1937, *Canadian Group of Painters*, no. 16; Ottawa, NGC, 1938, *Canadian Group of Painters*, no. 11; Buffalo, Albright Art Gallery, November 1938, *Great Lakes Exhibition*, no. 153; New York, World's Fair, 1 August – 15 September 1939, *Canadian Group of Painters*, no. 13; Montreal, MacDonald College, McGill University, January 1956 (information from the artist).

BIBLIOGRAPHY: Janice Cameron and others, *Eclectic Eve* (1973), repr.

Attached to the stretcher is a newspaper clipping: 'Five Steel Strikers Killed In Clash With Chicago Police,' *Toronto Daily Star* (1 June 1937).

Paraskeva Clark, R.C.A., Toronto

*69

Paraskeva Clark   b. 1898
Trout   1940
19-3/4 x 23-3/4 in. (50.2 x 60.3 cm)

INSCRIPTION: Signed and dated l.l., *paraskeva clark/40.*

PROVENANCE: Acquired from the artist; J.S. McLean, Toronto.

EXHIBITIONS: Toronto, AGT, 7 – 31 March 1941, *69th OSA,* no. 22; Andover, Addison Gallery of American Art, Phillips Academy, 18 September – 8 November 1942, *Aspects of Contemporary Painting in Canada,* no. 14, repr. p. 37; Ottawa, NGC, 1952, *Paintings and Drawings from the Collection of J.S. McLean,* no. 11; Toronto, AGT, 26 March – 25 April 1954, *Paraskeva Clark and Carl Schaefer,* no. 12.

Canada Packers Limited

70

Pegi Nicol MacLeod   1904 – 1949
School in a Garden   c. 1934
44-1/2 x 39 in. (113.0 x 99.1 cm)

PROVENANCE: Purchased from the artist, 1939; Vincent Massey, Port Hope, Ontario; Bequest of the Right Hon. Vincent Massey, 1968.

EXHIBITIONS: London, The Tate Gallery, 1938, *A Century of Canadian Art,* no. 168; Ottawa, NGC, 20 September – 20 October 1968, *Vincent Massey Bequest/The Canadian Paintings,* no. 41.

BIBLIOGRAPHY: Donald W. Buchanan, 'The Story of Canadian Art,' *Canadian Geographical Journal,* vol. XVII, no. 6 (December 1938), p. 281 repr.; Donald W. Buchanan, 'Pegi Nicol MacLeod 1904 – 49,' *Canadian Art,* vol. VI, no. 4 (Summer 1949), p. 162, repr.; 'Pegi Nicol, Two Paintings,' *Northern Review,* vol. 3, no. 3 (February – March 1950), p. 29 repr.; Donald W. Buchanan, *The Growth of Canadian Painting* (1950), p. 67, repr. pl. 45.

The National Gallery of Canada, Ottawa (15506)

*71

Pegi Nicol MacLeod   1904 – 1949
Descent of Lilies   1935
48 x 36 in. (121.9 x 91.4 cm)

INSCRIPTION: Signed l.r., *PEGI/NICOL.*

PROVENANCE: Acquired from the artist.

EXHIBITIONS: Toronto, AGT, December 1935, *Exhibition of Paintings by John Alfsen, Caven Atkins, Thoreau MacDonald, Pegi Nicol, Robert Ross, Carl Schaefer,* no. 268; Ottawa, NGC, 1949, *Memorial Exhibition/Pegi Nicol MacLeod 1904 – 1949,* no. 30.

BIBLIOGRAPHY: Walter Abell, 'Some Canadian Moderns,' *Magazine of Art,* vol. 30, no. 7 (July 1937), p. 422 repr.; Graham C. McInnes, 'Contemporary Canadian Artists No. 8 – Pegi Nicol,' *The Canadian Forum,* vol. XVII, no. 200 (September 1937), pp. 202 – 203, repr.; Paul Duval, *Four Decades* (1972), p. 51 repr. in colour.

Mr and Mrs T.E. Nichols, Dundas

*72

Pegi Nicol MacLeod   1904 – 1949
Jarvis Street Sidewalk   c. 1936
Watercolour on paper, 22-3/4 x 29-3/4 in. (57.8 x 75.6 cm)

INSCRIPTION: Signed l.r., *PEGI.*

PROVENANCE: Purchased from the artist (*CSPWC, 1939*).

EXHIBITIONS: Toronto, AGT, April 1939, CSPWC, [no cat. no.]; New York, World's Fair, 10 June – 31 July 1939, CSPWC, no 71; Rio de Janeiro, Museu Nacional de Belas Artes, November – December 1944, *Pintura Canadense Contemporanea,* no. 35; Ottawa, NGC, 1951, *CSPWC Retrospective Exhibition 1926 – 1951,* no. 72.

BIBLIOGRAPHY: *Bradfield AGO* (1970), p. 293.

Art Gallery of Ontario, Toronto (2525)

73

Pegi Nicol MacLeod   1904 – 1949
Children in Pliofilm   1939
31-3/4 x 41-7/8 in. (80.7 x 106.4 cm)

PROVENANCE: Purchased from the estate of the artist,
1950.

EXHIBITIONS: New York, World's Fair, 1 August –
5 September 1939, *Canadian Group of Painters*, no. 46;
Toronto, AGT, February 1942, *Canadian Group of Painters*,
no. 30; Ottawa, NGC, 1942, *Canadian Group of Painters
Travelling Exhibition*, no. 24; Ottawa, NGC, 1949, *Memorial
Exhibition/Pegi Nicol MacLeod 1904 – 1949*, no. 41.

BIBLIOGRAPHY: *Hubbard NGC* (1960), p. 205, repr.

The National Gallery of Canada, Ottawa (5020)

*74

Jack Humphrey   1901 – 1967
Studio Chair and Still-Life   1932
24 x 20 in. (61.0 x 50.8 cm)

PROVENANCE: Acquired from the artist.

The Honourable Milton Gregg and Erica Deichmann
Gregg, Fredericton.

*75

Jack Humphrey 1901 – 1967
Untitled (Houses) 1931
Watercolour on paper, 11-1/2 x 15-3/8 in. (29.2 x 39.1 cm)

INSCRIPTION: Signed and dated l.r., *Jack Humphrey 1931.*

PROVENANCE: Purchased from the artist; Douglas M. Duncan, Toronto; Gift from the Douglas M. Duncan Collection, 1970.

EXHIBITION: Ottawa, NGC, 5 March – 4 April 1971, *Gift from the Douglas M. Duncan Collection and the Milne-Duncan Bequest,* no. 97.

The National Gallery of Canada, Ottawa (16463)

76

Jack Humphrey 1901 – 1967
Charlotte 1939
Oil over tempera on canvas, 24 x 19-7/8 in. (61.0 x 50.5 cm)

INSCRIPTION: Signed l.r., *Jack Humphrey.*

PROVENANCE: Purchased from the artist (AGT, 1940); Gift from the Albert H. Robson Memorial Subscription Fund, 1940.

EXHIBITIONS: Toronto, AGT, 11 October – 11 November 1940, *Lowrie Warrener, Goodridge Roberts, Eric Goldberg, Jack Humphrey,* [no cat. no.]; Andover, Addison Gallery of American Art, Phillips Academy, 18 September – 8 November 1942, *Aspects of Contemporary Painting in Canada,* no. 33, repr. p. 49; New Haven, Yale University Art Gallery, 11 March – 16 April 1944, *Canadian Art 1760 – 1943,* [no cat. no.]; Toronto, AGT, January 1945, *The Development of Painting in Canada 1665 – 1945,* no. 221, repr. p. 47; Paris, Musée d'Art Moderne, 18 November – 28 December 1946, *Exposition internationale d'art moderne* (sponsored by UNESCO), no. 15; Toronto, AGT, October – November 1949, *Fifty Years of Painting in Canada,* no. 81, repr. p. 14; Toronto, AGT, October 1951 – March 1952, *Exhibition of Paintings* (Travelling Exhibition), no. 9; Winnipeg, The Winnipeg Art Gallery, 30 September – 30 October 1956, *Portraits Mirror of Man,* no. 53; Stratford (Ontario), Festival Arena, 11 June – 12 September 1964, *Faces of Canada,* [no cat. no.]; Fredericton, The Beaverbrook Art Gallery, 1966 – 1967, *Jack Humphrey/A Retrospective Exhibition,* no. 17; Toronto, AGO, 1972, *The Timeless Image* (Travelling Exhibition), no. 18.

BIBLIOGRAPHY: Douglas G.W. McRae, *The Arts and Crafts of Canada* (1944), p. 46 repr.; Andrew Bell, 'The Art Gallery of Toronto,' *Canadian Art,* vol. v, no. 4 (Spring – Summer 1948), p. 169 repr.; AGT, *Painting and Sculpture* (1959), p. 81 repr.; *Bradfield AGO* (1970), p. 200, repr., repr. in colour p. 545.

Art Gallery of Ontario, Toronto (2549)

77

Jack Humphrey   1901 – 1967
Edith White   1939
Oil over tempera on masonite, 24 x 20 in. (61.0 x 50.8 cm)

INSCRIPTION: Signed u.r., *Jack Humphrey.*

EXHIBITION: The Maritime Art Association, 1939 – 1940, *Paintings by Artists of the Maritime Provinces* (Travelling Exhibition), no. 23, repr.

Mrs Jack Weldon Humphrey, Saint John

*78

Miller Brittain   1913 – 1969
Master McCullough   1939
Oil on masonite, 20 x 16 in. (50.8 x 40.6 cm)

INSCRIPTION: Signed l.r., *MGB.*

PROVENANCE: Acquired from the artist.

EXHIBITIONS: Montreal, AAM, 9 March – 2 April 1939, *56th Spring Exhibition*, no. 50; New York, World's Fair, 1 August – 15 September 1939, *Canadian Group of Painters*, no. 6; Toronto, AGT, April 1941, *Miller Brittain, Adrien Hébert, J.W.G. Macdonald, Bernard Middleton*, [no cat. no.] (as *Boy in Blue Sweater*); Saint John, The New Brunswick Museum, 1970 – 1971, *Miller Brittain Privately Collected Works*, no. 11 (as *Boy in Blue Sweater*).

The Honourable Milton Gregg and Erica Deichmann Gregg, Fredericton

79

Miller Brittain   1913 – 1969
Longshoremen   1940
Oil on masonite, 20 x 25 in. (50.8 x 63.5 cm)

INSCRIPTION: Signed and dated l.l., *MGB/40.*

PROVENANCE: Purchased from the estate of the artist per
Griffiths Galleries, Vancouver, 1970.

EXHIBITIONS: Toronto, AGT, April 1941, *Miller Brittain,
Adrien Hébert, J.W.G. Macdonald, Bernard Middleton,* [no
cat. no.] (as *Longshoremen No. 2*); Vancouver, Griffiths
Galleries, 8 – 28 February 1970, *Miller Gore Brittain
1913 – 1969,* [no cat. no.], repr.

There are three other studies of longshoremen from this
period: *Three Longshoremen* (1939, carbon pencil and
eraser and wash on paper; 15 x 12 in., 38.1 x 30.5 cm) in
the collection of Memorial University, St. John's;
Longshoremen (1938, oil glazes on masonite, 22-1/4 x 18
in., 56.5 x 45.7 cm) and *Longshoreman* (c. 1937, ink and
coloured chalk on paper; 12 x 9 in., 30.5 x 22.9 cm) both
in The New Brunswick Museum, Saint John.

The National Gallery of Canada, Ottawa (15916)

80

Marc-Aurèle Fortin   1888 – 1970
Landscape at Hochelaga   c. 1931
Oil on paper board, 19-3/4 x 26-9/16 in. (50.2 x 67.5 cm)

ORIGINAL TITLE: *Paysage à Hochelaga*

INSCRIPTION: Signed l.r., *M.A. Fortin.*

PROVENANCE: Purchased from the artist, 1937.

EXHIBITIONS: Quebec, Musée de la Province de Québec,
3 – 31 May 1944, *Exposition de Marc-Aurèle Fortin,* A.R.C.A.,
Adrien Hébert, R.C.A., *Henri Hébert,* R.C.A., *Edwin Headley
Holgate,* R.C.A., no. 2; Arvida, Comité des Arts et Métiers
d'Arvida, 18 – 28 October 1946, *Un siècle d'art canadien,*
no. 37; Baie-Comeau, Centre Sportif, August 1951,
Un siècle et demi d'art canadien, no. 26.

Musée du Québec, Quebec (A 37-23P)

81

André Biéler b. 1896
Corpus Christi Procession, Sainte-Adèle   1936
24 x 28 in. (61.0 x 71.1 cm)

ORIGINAL TITLE: *Fête-Dieu à Sainte-Adèle*

INSCRIPTION: Signed and dated l.r. centre, *A. Biéler 1936.*

PROVENANCE: Gift of Mr & Mrs Walter Klinkhoff, Montreal, 1969.

The Sir George Williams Art Galleries and Collection of Art, Concordia University, Montreal

*82

André Biéler b. 1896
Before the Auction   1936
Oil on pressed board, 44 x 48 in. (111.8 x 121.9 cm)

INSCRIPTION: Signed and dated l.l., *A. Biéler '36.*

PROVENANCE: Acquired from the artist.

EXHIBITIONS: London, Royal Institute Galleries, 8 – 29 May 1937, *Exhibition of Paintings Drawings and Sculpture by Artists of the British Empire Overseas*, no. 18; Liverpool, Walker Art Gallery, 16 October 1937 – 8 January 1938, *63rd Autumn Exhibition*, no. 482; Toronto, CNE, 26 August – 10 September 1938, no. 120, repr.; Montreal, AAM, 9 March – 2 April 1939, *56th Spring Exhibition*, no. 35; Kingston, Agnes Etherington Art Centre, Queen's University, 1970 – 1971, *André Biéler 50 Years: A Retrospective Exhibition 1920 – 1970*, no. 19.

BIBLIOGRAPHY: Douglas G.W. McRae, *The Arts and Crafts of Canada* (1944), p. 53 repr.; Gertrude Gaylord, 'There's a Painting for Every Home,' *Canadian Homes and Gardens,* vol. XXIII (October 1946), p. 55 repr.

Dr and Mrs Albert Fell, Kingston

83

André Biéler   b. 1896
Gatineau Madonna   1940
Tempera on pressed board, 36 x 41-1/2 in. (91.4 x 105.4 cm)

INSCRIPTION: Signed l.r., *André Biéler.*

PROVENANCE: Purchased from the artist, 1945.

EXHIBITIONS: Toronto, AGT, 11 October – 11 November 1940, *61st RCA*, no. 14, repr.; Ottawa, NGC, 1941, *RCA Travelling Exhibition*, no. 5; Rio de Janeiro, Museu Nacional de Belas Artes, November – December 1944, *Pintura Canadense Contemporanea*, no. 3; Kingston, The Agnes Etherington Art Centre, Queen's University, 4 October – 3 November 1963, *A Retrospective Exhibition of the Work of André Biéler*, no. 33 repr. (incorrectly measured: '41-1/2 x 36 in.'); Kingston, The Agnes Etherington Art Centre, Queen's University, 1970 – 1971, *André Biéler 50 Years: A Retrospective Exhibition 1920 – 1970*, no. 23 (incorrectly measured: '41-1/2 x 36 in.').

BIBLIOGRAPHY: *Canadian Review of Music and Art*, vol. I, no. 2 (March 1942), p. 19 repr.; Marius Barbeau, *Painters of Quebec* (1946), p. 27 repr.; Graham C. McInnes, *Canadian Art* (1950), repr.; 'André Biéler,' *Encyclopedia Canadiana* (1957), vol. I, p. 386 repr.; *Hubbard NGC* (1960), p. 18, repr. (incorrectly measured: '41-1/2 x 36 in.').

The National Gallery of Canada, Ottawa (4610)

*84

Jean Paul Lemieux   b. 1904
Landscape in the Eastern Townships   1936
Oil on masonite, 22 x 29-3/4 in. (55.9 x 75.6 cm)

ORIGINAL TITLE: *Paysage des Cantons de l'Est*

INSCRIPTION: Signed and dated l.r., *JEAN PAUL LEMIEUX/'36.*

PROVENANCE: Purchased from the artist, 1938.

EXHIBITIONS: Montreal, AAM, April 1943, *8ᵉ Salon des Anciens de l'École des Beaux-Arts*, no. 64; Toronto, AGT, January 1945, *The Development of Painting in Canada 1665 – 1945*, no. 187, repr. p. 41; Arvida, Comité des Arts et Métiers d'Arvida, 18 – 28 October 1946, *Un siècle d'art canadien*, no. 47, repr. p. 3; Baie-Comeau, Centre Sportif, August 1951, *Un siècle et demi d'art canadien*, no. 35, repr.; Montreal, MMFA, 15 September – 11 October 1967, *Jean Paul Lemieux*, no. 9.

BIBLIOGRAPHY: Marius Barbeau, *Painters of Quebec* (1946), p. 39 repr.; Guy Robert, *Jean Paul Lemieux* (1968), p. 23 repr.

Musée du Québec, Quebec (A38-26P)

85

Jean Paul Lemieux   b. 1904
Lazarus   1941
Oil on masonite, 39-3/4 x 32-7/8 in. (101.0 x 83.5 cm)

ORIGINAL TITLE: *Lazare*

INSCRIPTION: Signed and dated l.l., *JEAN PAUL LEMIEUX/1941.*

PROVENANCE: Purchased from the artist, 1941 (AGT, 1941).

EXHIBITIONS: Toronto, AGT, October – November 1941, *Charles Goldhamer, Jean Paul Lemieux, Peter Haworth, Tom Wood,* [no cat. no.]; Paris, Musée d'Art Moderne, 18 November – 28 December 1946, *Exposition internationale d'art moderne* (sponsored by UNESCO), no. 17; Toronto, AGT, 14 August – 22 September 1963, *Religious Art, A Loan Exhibition,* no. 12, repr. pl. IV; London (Ontario), London Public Library and Art Museum, 1964, *Surrealism in Canadian Painting,* no. 50; London (Ontario), The Art Gallery of London, 1 – 26 February 1966, *Jean Paul Lemieux,* no. 3 repr.; Ottawa, NGC, 15 May – 15 September 1967, *Three Hundred Years of Canadian Art,* no. 259, repr.; Montreal, MMFA, 15 September – 11 October 1967, *Jean Paul Lemieux,* no. 13, repr. p. 27.

BIBLIOGRAPHY: AGT, *Accessions 1941,* repr.; Graham C. McInnes, 'Can Lusty Nationalism Foster Best in Art?', *Saturday Night,* vol. LX, no. 26 (3 March 1945), p. 5 repr.; Marius Barbeau, *Painters of Quebec* (1946), p. 35 repr.; Canada, Department of Citizenship and Immigration, *The Arts in Canada* (1957), p. 101; AGT, *Painting and Sculpture* (1959), p. 80 repr.; 'Canadian Painting in the Twentieth Century: An Introduction,' *Winds of Change* (1961), repr. in colour pl. 7; Robert H. Hubbard, *The Development of Canadian Art* (1963), p. 115; George Wallace, 'A Review of Two Exhibitions of Religious Art,' *Canadian Art,* vol. XX, no. 6 (November – December 1963), p. 331 repr.; J. Russell Harper, *Painting in Canada* (1966), p. 333 repr.; Elizabeth Kilbourn, ed., *Great Canadian Painting* (1966), p. 60 repr. in colour; Guy Robert, *Jean Paul Lemieux* (1968), p. 31, repr. p. 29; *Bradfield AGO* (1970), p. 241, repr., repr. in colour p. 545.

Art Gallery of Ontario, Toronto (2574)

86

Jori Smith   b. 1907
Mlle Rose   1936
24-1/8 x 18-1/8 in. (61.3 x 46.0 cm)

INSCRIPTION: Signed and dated u.r., *Jori Smith/'36.*

PROVENANCE: Purchased from the artist, 1937.

EXHIBITIONS: Montreal, The Arts Club, February 1937, [*Group Exhibition*] (no cat.); Toronto, AGT, January 1945, *The Development of Painting in Canada 1665 – 1945,* no. 209.

BIBLIOGRAPHY: Donald W. Buchanan, 'Le Musée de la Province de Québec,' *Canadian Art,* vol. VI, no. 2 (Christmas 1948), p. 73 repr.

Musée du Québec, Quebec (A 37-2P)

---

*87

Stanley Cosgrove   b. 1911
Madeleine with Short Hair   1939
Oil on masonite, 10 x 9 in. (25.4 x 22.9 cm)

ORIGINAL TITLE: *La Madeleine aux cheveux courts*

INSCRIPTION: Signed and dated l.l., *COSGROVE 39.*

PROVENANCE: Acquired from the artist, 1939.

EXHIBITIONS: Quebec, École des Beaux-Arts de Québec, 21 October – 4 November 1939, *Exposition Stanley Cosgrove*, no. 49; Montreal, AAM, April 1940, *6ᵉ Exposition des Anciens de l'École des Beaux-Arts*, no. 25; Quebec, Galerie Municipale, 26 April – 3 May 1941, *Première exposition des Indépendants*, no. 9 (as *La Madeleine*); Montreal, AAM, April 1943, *8ᵉ Salon des Anciens de l'École des Beaux-Arts*, no. 27 (as *La Madeleine aux cheveux coupés*); Montreal, AAM, 7 – 30 October 1944, *Paintings and Drawings by Stanley Cosgrove*, no. 46.

BIBLIOGRAPHY: Dennis Reid, *A Concise History of Canadian Painting* (1973), p. 207, repr. p. 208 (as *Madeleine*).

Jules Bazin, Montreal

*88

John Lyman   1886 – 1967
Haying by the Lake   1933
18 x 22 in. (45.7 x 55.9 cm)

INSCRIPTION: Signed l.r., *Lyman.*

PROVENANCE: Presented by Mr Thornton Grier, 1939.

EXHIBITIONS: New York, Valentine Gallery, 14 – 28 May [1936], *Paintings by John Lyman*, no. 6 (as *Hayfield by the Lake*); Montreal, W. Scott & Sons, 6 – 20 February 1937, *Exhibition of Paintings by John Lyman*, no. 36 (as *Hayfield*); Montreal, Faculty Club, McGill University, 2 April 1939, *Exhibition of Works by John Lyman*, no. 14; St. Catharines (Ontario), Rodman Hall Arts Centre, 1 – 28 May 1962, *Sixteen Quebec Painters*, [no cat.]; Montreal, MMFA, 5 – 29 September 1963, *John Lyman*, no. 40 repr.

BIBLIOGRAPHY: 'Lyman of Canada Has New York Exhibit,' *The Art Digest*, vol. X, no. 17 (1 June 1936), p. 39 repr. (as *Canadian Landscape*); Paul Dumas, 'Lyman,' *Le Quartier Latin* (17 December 1943), p. III repr.; MMFA, *Catalogue of Paintings* (1960), p. 26

This is one of a series of landscapes entitled 'Variations on the Lake.' Another work in this series, entitled *Reflections in a Mountain Lake* (oil on canvas; 17-1/4 x 25 in., 43.8 x 63.5 cm) ,was sold at Montreal, Christie, Manson & Woods (Canada) Ltd., 24 October 1974, lot 108 (repr. in cat.).

The Montreal Museum of Fine Arts (939.700)

89

John Lyman   1886 – 1967
The Card Game   c. 1935
25-1/2 x 32-1/4 in. (64.8 x 81.9 cm)

ORIGINAL TITLE: *Le jeu de cartes*

INSCRIPTION: Signed l.r., *Lyman.*

PROVENANCE: Purchased from Dominion Gallery, Montreal, 1966.

EXHIBITION: London, The Tate Gallery, 1938, *A Century of Canadian Art*, no. 141 (as *Joueuses de Cartes*).

BIBLIOGRAPHY: Guy Robert, *L'Art au Québec depuis 1940* (1973), p. 57, repr.

The National Gallery of Canada, Ottawa (14902)

90

John Lyman   1886 – 1967
Jori Smith in Costume   1936
20 x 22 in. (50.8 x 55.9 cm)

INSCRIPTION: Signed l.l., *Lyman.*

PROVENANCE: Acquired from the artist.

EXHIBITIONS: New York, Valentine Gallery, 14 – 28 May [1936], *Paintings by John Lyman*, no. 22 (as *Costume 1890*); Montreal, W. Scott & Sons, 6 – 20 February 1937, *Exhibition of Paintings by John Lyman*, no. 22 (as *Costume 1890*); Dallas, Greater Texas and Pan American Exposition, Dallas Museum of Fine Arts, 12 June – 31 October 1937, *Art of the Americas*, no. 70 (as *Costume 1890*); Montreal, Faculty Club, McGill University, 2 April 1939, *Exhibition of Works by John Lyman*, no. 5 (as *Portrait of Jori Smith in Costume*); Joliette, Seminaire de Joliette, 11 – 14 January 1942, *Exposition des maîtres de la peinture moderne*, no. 14 (as *Costume 1890*); Montreal, MMFA, 5 – 29 September 1963, *John Lyman*, no. 45 (dated 1940); Montreal, École française d'été, McGill University, 1969, *Deux cents ans de peinture québecoise*, no. 47b.

BIBLIOGRAPHY: 'John Lyman, Canadian Painter, Shows Oils,' *The Art News*, vol. XXXIV, no. 34 (23 May 1936), p. 9 repr. (as *Costume 1890*); Robert Ayre, 'Art,' *The Montrealer* (February 1937), repr. (as *Costume 1890*); Paul Dumas, 'Lyman,' *Le Quartier Latin* (17 December 1943), p. III repr. (as *Portrait of Jori Smith in Costume*).

Maurice Corbeil, Montreal

91

John Lyman   1886 – 1967
Woman with White Collar   c. 1936
Oil on board, 24-1/8 x 17-3/8 in. (61.3 x 44.1 cm)

ORIGINAL TITLE: *Femme au collet blanc*

INSCRIPTION: Signed u.l., *Lyman.*

PROVENANCE: Purchased from Dominion Gallery, Montreal, 1958.

EXHIBITIONS: New York, Valentine Gallery, 14 – 28 May [1936], *Paintings by John Lyman,* no. 21 (as *Helen*); Montreal, W. Scott & Sons, 6 – 20 February 1937, *Exhibition of Paintings by John Lyman,* no. 21; Montreal, Sun Life Building, National Produced in Canada Exhibition, November 1937, *Art Exhibition,* no. 28; Montreal, Faculty Club, McGill University, 2 April 1939, *Exhibition of Works by John Lyman,* no. 6 (as *Portrait of Mrs. L. C. Marsh*); Montreal, Les Philosophes de Sainte-Croix, 4 – 14 March 1945, *John Lyman/Goodridge Roberts,* no. 11 (as *Femme au Col Blanc*).

BIBLIOGRAPHY: Graham C. McInnes, 'Contemporary Canadian Artists No. 5 – John Lyman,' *The Canadian Forum,* vol. XVII, no. 197 (June 1937), p. 94, repr. p. 95; Maurice Gagnon, *Peinture Moderne* (1943), p. 77, repr. fig. 30 (as *Portrait de Helen Marsh*); Zoé Biéler, 'Lyman, Pursuit of Perfection Has Made Him An Outstanding Artist And Critic,' Montreal *Standard* (12 August 1944), repr. (as *Portrait of Mrs. Leonard P. Marsh*); Paul Dumas, *Lyman* (1944), p. 22, repr. pl. 18 (as *Portrait de Madame Helen M.*); Paul Duval, 'John Lyman Helps Younger Artists To Experiment,' *Saturday Night,* vol. LXII, no. 48 (2 August 1947), p. 2 repr. (as *Helen*); Paul Duval, *Four Decades* (1972), p. 88 repr. (dated: 'c. 1942'); Dennis Reid, *A Concise History of Canadian Painting* (1973), pp. 203 – 204, repr. colour pl. XXVIII.

The National Gallery of Canada, Ottawa (6942)

*92

John Lyman   1886 – 1967
Lassitude   c. 1937
Oil on plywood, 24 x 34 in. (61.0 x 86.4 cm)

INSCRIPTION: Signed l.l., *Lyman.*

PROVENANCE: Acquired from the artist, 1944.

EXHIBITIONS: Montreal, W. Scott & Sons, 6 – 20 February 1937, *Exhibition of Paintings by John Lyman,* no. 2; Toronto, AGT, November 1937, *Canadian Group of Painters,* no. 95; Ottawa, NGC, 1938, *Canadian Group of Painters,* no. 46; Montreal, Faculty Club, McGill University, 2 April 1939, *Exhibition of Works by John Lyman,* no. 8; Montreal, AAM, 1939, *Summer Exhibition by Contemporary Montreal Artists,* no. 26; Montreal, Dominion Gallery, 18 March – 1 April 1944, *John Lyman 1913 – 1943,* [no. cat.]; Montreal, Cercle Universitaire de Montréal, 1953, *Peinture canadienne moderne,* [no cat.].

BIBLIOGRAPHY: Paul Dumas, *Lyman* (1944), p. 23, repr. pl. 7.

Private collection

*93

Goodridge Roberts   1904 – 1974
Ottawa Valley   1933
Watercolour on paper, 20-7/8 x 25-1/2 in. (53.0 x 64.8 cm)

INSCRIPTION: Signed l.r., *G. Roberts.*

PROVENANCE: Purchased from the artist, 1941.

EXHIBITIONS: New York, World's Fair, 10 June – 31 July 1939, *CSPWC,* no. 78; Philadelphia, The Pennsylvania Academy of the Fine Arts, 19 October – 23 November 1952, *The Philadelphia Water Color Club 50th Annual International Exhibition,* no. 538; Berlin, German Industries Fair, 1953, [no cat.]; Stratford (Ontario), Shakespearean Festival, 1954, [no cat. avail.].

BIBLIOGRAPHY: *Hubbard NGC* (1960), p. 261, repr.

Painted during the summer of 1933 just off the Montreal Road on the outskirts of Ottawa.

The National Gallery of Canada, Ottawa (4573)

94

Goodridge Roberts   1904 – 1974
Ontario Landscape in a Red Light   1936
Oil on plywood, 20 x 24 in. (50.8 x 61.0 cm)

INSCRIPTION: Signed l.r., *G. Roberts.*

PROVENANCE: Acquired from the artist.

EXHIBITIONS: Montreal, The Arts Club, February 1941, [*Goodridge Roberts*], [no cat.]; Montreal, AAM, 1 April – 1 May 1942, *Landscapes by Goodridge Roberts,* [no cat. no.] (as *Red Landscape*); Montreal, Dominion Gallery, 27 March – 8 April 1943, *Goodridge Roberts,* [no cat.]; Ottawa, NGC, 1969 – 1970, *A Retrospective Exhibition/Goodridge Roberts,* no. 10, repr.

Painted along the Montreal Road on the outskirts of Ottawa, September 1936, after the artist moved from Kingston to Montreal.

Dr and Mrs Raymond Boyer, Montreal

*95

Goodridge Roberts   1904–1974
Marian   1937
33 x 25 in. (83.8 x 63.5 cm)

INSCRIPTION: Signed l.r., *G. Roberts.*

PROVENANCE: Mr and Mrs Gérald Rhéaume, Montreal (c. 1945 – c. 1958).

EXHIBITIONS: Montreal, Sun Life Building, National Produced in Canada Exhibition, November 1937, *Art Exhibition*, no. 42 (as *Marian Roberts*); New York, World's Fair, 1 August – 15 September 1939, *Canadian Group of Painters*, no. 50 (as *Marian Roberts*); Quebec, Galerie municipale, 26 April – 3 May 1941, *Première exposition des Indépendants*, no. 42; Montreal, Henry Morgan & Company, from 16 May 1941, *Peinture moderne*, no. 39; Montreal, Dominion Gallery, 27 March – 8 April 1943, *Goodridge Roberts*, [no cat.]; Montreal, Les Philosophes de Sainte-Croix, 4 – 14 March 1945, *John Lyman/Goodridge Roberts*, no 24 (as *Portrait*); Venice, 1952, *XXVI Biennale di Venezia*, [Canada], no. 14 (as *Ritratto*); Ottawa, NGC, 1953, *Exhibition of Canadian Painting to Celebrate the Coronation of Her Majesty Queen Elizabeth II*, no. 61, repr.; Brussels, Exposition universelle et internationale, Palais des Beaux-Arts, 13 May – 1 June 1958, *Art contemporain au Canada*, [no cat. no.]; Montreal, MMFA, 8 September – 2 October 1960, *Eleven Artists in Montreal 1860 – 1960*, no. 81, repr. (dated: '1938'); London, The Tate Gallery, February – March 1964, *Canadian Painting 1939 – 1963*, no. 2, repr.; Ottawa, NGC, 15 May – 15 September 1967, *Three Hundred Years of Canadian Art*, no. 251 repr. (dated: '1939'); Ottawa, NGC, 1969 – 1970, *A Retrospective Exhibition/Goodridge Roberts*, no. 21, repr. (dated '1938'); Ottawa, NGC, 1973, *Painters of Quebec: The Maurice and Andrée Corbeil Collection*, no. 67, repr. (dated '1938').

BIBLIOGRAPHY: Jacques de Tonnancour, *Roberts* (1944), repr. pl. 7 (dated '1939'); Donald W. Buchanan, *The Growth of Canadian Painting* (1950), repr. pl. 50; Julian Park, ed., *The Culture of Contemporary Canada* (1957), repr. pl. XIII; Robert H. Hubbard, *The Development of Canadian Art* (1963), p. 117, repr. pl. 203 (dated '1939'); Guy Viau, *Modern Painting in French Canada* (1967), p. 30 repr. (incorrectly as in the collection of The National Gallery of Canada).

This painting was submitted to the jury for the *Exhibition of Paintings Drawings and Sculpture by Artists of the British Empire Overseas* in March 1937 (Jury List no. 225).

Maurice Corbeil, Montreal

96

Goodridge Roberts   1904 – 1974
Standing Nude   1938
47 x 24-1/2 in. (119.4 x 62.2 cm)

INSCRIPTION: Signed l.r., *G. Roberts*.

EXHIBITIONS: Montreal, AAM, 17 March – 10 April 1938, *55th Spring Exhibition*, no. 97; Montreal, Dominion Gallery, 18 October – 3 November 1945, *Exhibition of Paintings by Goodridge Roberts*, no. 23 (as *Young Girl*); West Palm Beach (Florida), The Norton Gallery and School of Art, 2 – 28 January 1948, *Six Canadian Painters*, no. 25; Paris, Galerie R. Creuze, 7 – 30 December 1954, *Oeuvres de Goodridge Roberts*, no. 70; Southern Ontario Circuit, 1957, *Figure Paintings*, [no cat.]; Ottawa, Robertson Galleries, March 1958, *G. Roberts*, [no cat.]; Ottawa, NGC, 1969 – 70, *A Retrospective Exhibition/Goodridge Roberts*, no. 19, repr.

Private collection

97

Philip Surrey   b. 1910
The Boardwalk   c. 1938
26 x 34-1/2 in. (66.0 x 87.6 cm)

INSCRIPTION: Signed l.r., *Surrey*.

PROVENANCE: Purchased, 1951.

EXHIBITIONS: Montreal, AAM, 9 March – 2 April 1939, *56th Spring Exhibition*, no. 313; Montreal, AAM, 1939, *Summer Exhibition by Contemporary Montreal Artists*, no. 48; Toronto, AGT, October – November 1939, *André Biéler, Henri Masson, Louis Muhlstock, Philip Surrey*, [no cat. no.]; Montreal, L'Art français, 13 – 30 October 1945, *Exhibition of Oil Paintings, Gouaches and Drawings by Philip Surrey*, no. 2; Federation of Canadian Artists, Quebec Region, February – August 1948, *Current Trends in Montreal Painting* (Travelling Exhibition for Western Canada), no. 23; Montreal, Musée d'Art Contemporain, 28 October – 28 November 1971, *Philip Surrey/Le peintre dans la ville*, no. 1.

BIBLIOGRAPHY: Jacques de Roussan, 'Le peintre des reflets de la ville,' *Vie des Arts*, no. 31 (Summer 1963), p. 28 repr.; Robert Ayre, 'The City and the Dream of Philip Surrey,' *Canadian Art*, vol. XXI, no. 5 (September – October 1964), p. 284 repr.; Jacques de Roussan, *Philip Surrey* (1968), repr.

This work was shipped to The National Gallery of Canada, 31 January 1939.

Musée du Québec, Quebec (A 51-168 P)

*98

Philip Surrey   b. 1910
Sunday Afternoon   1939
20 x 24 in. (50.8 x 61.0 cm)

INSCRIPTION: Signed and dated u.l., *SURREY / 1939.*

EXHIBITIONS: Montreal, AAM, 9 March – 2 April 1939,
56th Spring Exhibition, no. 314; New York, World's Fair,
1 August – 15 September 1939, *Canadian Group of Painters,*
no. 58; Ottawa, Contempo Art Studios, 14 – 28 February
1942, *Exhibition of oils and gouaches by Philip Surrey,* [no
cat.]; Federation of Canadian Artists, Quebec Region,
February – August 1948, *Current Trends in Montreal
Painting* (Travelling Exhibition for Western Canada),
no. 24.

BIBLIOGRAPHY: John Lyman, 'Art,' *The Montrealer* (1 April
1939), repr.

Painted from memory of a *veillée* at Saint-Hilarion which
the artist attended with Jean Palardy and Jori Smith in
October 1938.

Philip Surrey, Montreal

99

Philip Surrey   b. 1910
The Red Portrait   1939
24 x 22 in. (61.0 x 55.9 cm)

INSCRIPTION: Signed l.r. centre, *SURREY.*

EXHIBITION: Montreal, AAM, January – 4 February 1940,
The Eastern Group, [no cat.].

Commenced in the artist's apartment at 3434 Sainte-
Famille Street after 1 October 1939. Portrait of the artist's
wife.

Philip Surrey, Montreal

100

Fritz Brandtner   1896 – 1969
Men of 1939   1939
Coloured ink on paperboard, 13-1/4 x 10-1/4 in. (33.7 x 26.0 cm)

INSCRIPTION: Signed and dated centre l.r., *f. brandtner 39.*
Signed l.l., *f. brandtner*

PROVENANCE: The estate of the artist.

EXHIBITION: New York, World's Fair, 18 September – 31 October 1939, *Canadian Society of Graphic Art*, no. 12.

Slightly altered at a later date.

Kastel Gallery, Montreal

*101

Fritz Brandtner   1896 – 1969
The Riders   1939
Watercolour on paper, 18-5/8 x 24-3/8 in. (47.3 x 61.9 cm)

INSCRIPTION: Signed and dated l.r., *f. brandtner 39.*

PROVENANCE: Purchased, 1940.

EXHIBITIONS: Toronto, AGT, April 1939, *CSPWC*, [no cat. no.]; New York, World's Fair, 10 June – 31 July 1939, *CSPWC*, no. 16; (?) Elmira (N.Y.), Arnot Art Gallery, March 1946, *Canadian Water Color*, no. 23; Boston, Museum of Fine Arts, 14 July – 25 September 1949, *Forty Years of Canadian Painting*, no. 8, repr. p. 29; Toronto, AGT, October – November 1949, *Fifty Years of Painting in Canada*, no. 74.

BIBLIOGRAPHY: 'Canadian Art Show For The New York World's Fair,' *Saturday Night*, vol. LIV, no. 32 (10 June 1939), p. 17 repr.; Donald W. Buchanan, 'Canada,' *The Studio*, vol. CXXV (April – May 1943), p. 124 repr.; Andrew Bell, 'The Art Gallery of Toronto,' *Canadian Art*, vol. V, no. 4 (Spring – Summer 1948), p. 168 repr.; Andrew Bell, 'Contemporary Canadian Water-Colours,' *The Studio*, vol. CXLIII (April 1952), p. 111 repr.; *Bradfield AGO* (1970), p. 40, repr. p. 41.

A small watercolour version of this work is in the collection of Robert Ayre, Montreal.

Art Gallery of Ontario, Toronto (2541)

*102

Fritz Brandtner 1896 – 1969
Abstraction 1936
Ink, gouache, and charcoal on paper, 17-3/8 x 23-3/8 in. (44.1 x 59.4 cm)

INSCRIPTION: Signed and dated l.r., *f. brandtner 1936.*

PROVENANCE: The estate of the artist; Kastel Gallery, Montreal; Purchased, 1970, Harriette J. MacDonnell Bequest.

EXHIBITION: Montreal, Sir George Williams University, 1971 – 1972, *Fritz Brandtner 1896 – 1969,* no. 21.

The Montreal Museum of Fine Arts (970.1700)

103

Marian Scott b. 1906
Escalator 1937
30 x 21 in. (76.2 x 53.3 cm)

INSCRIPTION: Signed l.r., *M. SCOTT* and *M* and *D* in monogram.

EXHIBITION: Montreal, Sun Life Building, National Produced in Canada Exhibition, November 1937, *Art Exhibition,* no. 16.

BIBLIOGRAPHY: Graham C. McInnes, 'Contemporary Canadian Artists No. 10 – Marian Scott,' *The Canadian Forum,* vol. XVII, no. 202 (November 1937), p. 274, repr. p. 275.

There are three versions of this subject. One is in the collection of King Gordon, Ottawa.

McCready Galleries Inc., Toronto

*104   *105

Marian Scott b. 1906   **Louis Muhlstock b. 1904**
Tenants c. 1940   *Sainte-Famille Street* 1939
Oil on board, 25 x 16-1/2 in. (63.5 x 41.9 cm)   25-1/2 x 29-1/2 in. (64.8 x 74.9 cm)

INSCRIPTION: Signed l.l., M. SCOTT.   INSCRIPTION: Signed and dated l.r., *Muhlstock / 1939.*

PROVENANCE: J.S. McLean, Toronto.   PROVENANCE: Purchased from the artist per T. Eaton Co.,
                                                       Toronto, 1945.
EXHIBITIONS: Boston, Grace Horne Galleries, 26 May –
14 June 1941, [*Marian Scott*], repr. on invitation; Toronto,   EXHIBITION: Toronto, AGT, October – November 1939,
AGT, February 1942, *Canadian Group of Painters*, no. 104,   *André Biéler, Henri Masson, Louis Muhlstock, Philip Surrey,*
repr.; Andover, Addison Gallery of American Art,   [no cat. no.].
Phillips Academy, 18 September – 8 November 1942,
Aspects of Contemporary Painting in Canada, no. 62, repr.   Another version, *Sainte-Famille Street (Wet Day)* (1939,
p. 11 (dated: 'c. 1941 – 42'); Washington, Phillips Memor-   oil on canvas; 26 x 30 in., 66.0 x 76.2 cm) is in the collec-
ial Gallery, 17 January – 15 February 1943, *Aspects of*   tion of Mrs I.H. Weldon, Toronto. See Robert Ayre,
Contemporary Canadian Painting, no. 14; New Haven,   'The New Muhlstock,' *Canadian Art*, vol. IX, no. 4
Yale University Art Gallery, 11 March – 16 April 1944,   (Summer 1952), p. 142 repr.
Canadian Art 1760 – 1943, [no cat. no.] (dated 'c. 1941 –
42'); Ottawa, NGC, 1952, *Paintings and Drawings from the*   University College, University of Toronto
Collection of J.S. McLean, no. 83.

BIBLIOGRAPHY: A. Biéler, 'On the Canadian Group of
Painters,' *Maritime Art*, vol. 2, no. 4 (April – May 1942),
p. 123 repr.

A related work, *Stairway* (1940, oil on canvas; 29 x 20 in.,
73.7 x 50.8 cm) is in the collection of The Montreal
Museum of Fine Arts (942.749).

Canada Packers Limited

106

Louis Muhlstock   b. 1904
Open Door of Third House, Groubert Lane, Montreal   c. 1939
30 x 26 in. (76.2 x 66.0 cm)

INSCRIPTION: *Verso, Third Door Groubert Lane Op. 2.*

EXHIBITION: Toronto, AGT, 1950, *Canadian Group of Painters,* no. 65.

A related work, *Leduc Lane, Three Doors (c. 1939),* is in the collection of the artist.

Louis Muhlstock, C.G.P., Montreal

*107

Alexandre Bercovitch   1893 – 1951
The Artist's Family   1934
26-1/4 x 24-3/4 in. (66.7 x 62.9 cm)

INSCRIPTION: Dated and signed l.l., *1934 / A. Bercovitch.*

PROVENANCE: By succession to Mrs Ninel Schuman (née Bercovitch).

EXHIBITIONS: Montreal, AAM, 21 March – 14 April 1935, *52nd Spring Exhibition,* no. 40; Toronto, AGT, March 1936, *64th OSA,* no. 20, repr.; London, Royal Institute Galleries, 8 – 29 May 1937, *Exhibition of Paintings Drawings and Sculpture by Artists of the British Empire Overseas,* no. 6; Liverpool, Walker Art Gallery, 16 October 1937 – 8 January 1938, *63rd Autumn Exhibition,* no. 6.

BIBLIOGRAPHY: Graham C. McInnes, 'Art of Canada,' *The Studio,* vol. CXIV (August 1937), p. 64 repr.

Mrs Ninel Schuman, New York

108

Eric Goldberg   1890 – 1969
Tossa del Mar   c. 1934
21 x 29 in. (53.3 x 73.7 cm)

INSCRIPTION: Signed l.l., *Eric Goldberg.*

PROVENANCE: Purchased from the artist with the William G. Cheney Fund, 1939.

EXHIBITION: Montreal, Dominion Gallery, 23 October – 3 November 1943, *Eric Goldberg,* [no cat.].

BIBLIOGRAPHY: Rafael Benet, 'Tossa, Babel de les Arts,' *Art* (Barcelona), vol. II, no. 1 (October 1934), fig. 40 (repr. of unfinished painting); MMFA, *Catalogue of Paintings* (1960), p. 16.

Tossa del Mar is a Mediterranean port and artists' colony near Gerona in Spain where, *c.* 1934, the Goldbergs spent a month.

The Montreal Museum of Fine Arts (939.681)

109

Paul-Émile Borduas   1905 – 1960
Portrait of Maurice Gagnon   1937
19-5/8 x 17-5/8 in. (49.9 x 44.8 cm)

ORIGINAL TITLE: *Portrait de Maurice Gagnon*

INSCRIPTION: Signed and dated u.l., *Borduas / 1937*

PROVENANCE: Acquired from the artist; Mrs Maurice Gagnon; Purchased from Mr Gilles Gagnon, 1969.

EXHIBITIONS: Quebec, Galerie municipale, 26 April – 3 May 1941, *Première Exposition des Indépendants,* no. 3; Montreal, Henry Morgan & Company, from 16 May 1941, *Peinture moderne,* no. 3.

BIBLIOGRAPHY: Guy Robert, *Borduas* (1972), p. 34 repr.; Dennis Reid, *A Concise History of Canadian Painting* (1973), p. 209, repr. p. 210.

A poem by François Hertel, 'Sur un portrait de notre hôte M. Maurice Gagnon,' dedicated to 'M. Borduas et Gagnon,' n.d., is among the Borduas papers (no. 132).

The National Gallery of Canada, Ottawa (15794)

66.   PARASKEVA CLARK, *Self-Portrait* (1933)

Selected Bibliography

A / General

Abell, Walter. 'The Limits of Abstraction.' *The American Magazine of Art*, vol. 28, no. 12 (December 1935), pp. 735 – 740.

Representation and Form. New York: Charles Scribner's Sons, 1936. Reprinted Westport, Conn.: Greenwood Press, 1971.

'Form Through Representation.' *The American Magazine of Art*, vol. 29, no. 5 (May 1936), pp. 303 – 310.

'Co-operative Art in the Maritimes.' *Saturday Night*, vol. LII, no. 32 (12 June 1937), p. 7.

'Some Canadian Moderns.' *Magazine of Art*, vol. 30, no. 7 (July 1937), pp. 422 – 427.

'Art and Democracy' in André Biéler and Elizabeth Harrison, eds. *The Kingston Conference. Conference of Canadian Artists.* Kingston, 1941, pp. 22 – 33.

'Canadian Aspirations in Painting.' *Culture*, vol. III (1942), pp. 172 – 182.

'Neighbours to the North.' *Magazine of Art*, vol. 35, no. 6 (October 1942), pp. 209 – 211.

Alford, John. 'Trends in Canadian Art.' *University of Toronto Quarterly*, vol. XIV, no. 2 (January 1945), pp. 168 – 180.

Ayre, Robert. (Occasional articles in *Saturday Night* from November 1937; articles in Montreal *Gazette* from January 1935; articles in *The Canadian Forum* from December 1933 to August 1935; articles in Montreal *Standard* from 1939.)

'Murals in Our Public Buildings.' *Saturday Night*, vol. LV, no. 30 (25 May 1940), p. 2.

Barbeau, Marius. *Painters of Quebec.* Toronto: The Ryerson Press, 1946.

Breithaupt, Paul T. 'History of the Art Students' League.' *Etcetera*, vol. 1, no. 1 (September 1930), pp. 28 – 30; vol. 1, no. 2 (October 1930), pp. 28 – 30; vol. 1, no. 3 (November 1930), pp. 30 – 33.

Brooker, Bertram, ed. *Yearbook of the Arts in Canada, 1928 – 1929.* Toronto: The Macmillan Company of Canada Limited, 1929.

Yearbook of the Arts in Canada, 1936. Toronto: The Macmillan Company of Canada Limited, 1936.

Brown, Eric. 'Canada's National Painters.' *The Studio*, vol. CIII (June 1932), pp. 311 – 323.

'New Art on the Horizon.' *The Christian Science Monitor*, Weekly Magazine Section (13 January 1937), p. 8.

Buchanan, Donald W. (Articles in *The Canadian Forum* from December 1934 to October 1936.)

James Wilson Morrice. Toronto: The Ryerson Press, 1936.

'The Story Of Canadian Art.' *Canadian Geographical Journal*, vol. XVII, no. 6 (December 1938), pp. 273 – 294.

'Variations in Canadian Landscape Painting.' *University of Toronto Quarterly*, vol. X, no. 1 (October 1940), pp. 39 – 45.

'The Gentle and the Austere: A Comparison in Landscape Painting.' *University of Toronto Quarterly*, vol. XI, no. 1 (October 1941), pp. 72 – 77.

'Canada.' *The Studio*, vol. CXXV (April 1943), pp. 122 – 125.

Canadian Painters from Paul Kane to the Group of Seven. Oxford, London: Phaidon Press, 1945.

The Growth of Canadian Painting. London, Toronto: William Collins & Son, 1950.

Buckman, Edward. 'With Canadian Pioneers.' *Magazine of Art*, vol. 30, no. 9 (September 1937), pp. 568 – 571, 586, 588.

Cameron, Janice, Frances Ferdinands, Sharon Snitman, Madli Tamme, and Annetta Wernick. *Eclectic Eve.* n.p. [1973].

Chauvin, Jean. *Ateliers.* Montreal, New York: Louis Carrier & Cie., 1928.

Duval, Paul. *Canadian Water Colour Painting.* Toronto: Burns and MacEachern, 1954.

Four Decades. The Canadian Group of Painters and their Contemporaries – 1930–1970. Toronto, Vancouver: Clarke, Irwin & Company Limited, 1972.

A Vision of Canada. The McMichael Canadian Collection. Toronto, Vancouver: Clarke, Irwin & Company Limited, 1973.

Fairley, Barker. 'Canadian Art: Man vs. Landscape.' *The Canadian Forum*, vol. XIX, no. 227 (December 1939), pp. 284, 286.

Friedman, Martin L. *The Precisionist View in American Art* (exhibition catalogue). Minneapolis: Walker Art Center, 1960.

Gagnon, Clarence. 'L'Immense Blague de l'Art Moderniste,' *Amérique française* (September 1948), pp. 60 – 65; (December 1948), pp. 44 – 48; (March 1949), pp. 67 – 71; (June 1949), pp. 30 – 33.

Gagnon, Maurice. (Articles in *La Revue Moderne*, February – September 1937.)

Peinture Moderne. Montreal: Éditions Bernard Valiquette, 1940.

Peinture Moderne. Revised ed. Montreal: Valiquette, 1943.

Sur un état actuel de la peinture canadienne. Montreal: Société des Éditions Pascal, 1945.

Gauvreau, Jean-Marie. 'L'artisanat dans la province de Québec,' *Le Canada* (16 – 20 February 1937.)

Girard, Henri. (Articles in *La Revue Moderne* from 1929 to 1933; articles in *Le Canada* from 1937.)

'L'École du Meuble.' *La Revue Moderne*, vol. 21, no. 4 (August 1939), p. 11.

Hamel, Émile-Charles. (Articles in *Le Jour* from 1937.)

Harper, J. Russell. *Canadian Paintings in Hart House.* Toronto: Art Committee of Hart House, University of Toronto, 1955.
Painting in Canada: A History. Toronto: University of Toronto Press, 1966.

Harvey, Jean-Charles. (Articles in *Le Jour* from September 1937.)

Hubbard, Robert H., ed. *An Anthology of Canadian Art.* Toronto: Oxford University Press, 1960.
The Development of Canadian Art. Ottawa: Queen's Printer, 1963.

Jones, Hugh G. and Edmond Dyonnet. 'History of the Royal Canadian Academy of Arts ' (Montreal?). Typed by T.A. Dickson, 1934.

Lewis, Wyndham. 'Canadian Nature and Its Painters,' in Walter Michael and C.J. Fox, eds. *Wyndham Lewis on Art. Collected Writings 1913 – 1956.* New York: Funk & Wagnalls, 1969, pp. 425 – 429.

Mellen, Peter. *The Group of Seven.* Toronto, Montreal: McClelland and Stewart Limited, 1970.

Morisset, Gérard. 'À l'École du Meuble.' *La Revue Populaire,* vol. 30, no. 8 (August 1937), pp. 9, 55.
Coup d'œil sur les arts en Nouvelle-France. Quebec: Presses de Charrier et Dugal Limitée, 1941.

Morris, Jerrold. *The Nude in Canadian Painting.* Toronto: New Press, 1972.

McInnes, Graham C. 'The World of Art.' *Saturday Night.* (A weekly art column, except summers, from April 1935 to April 1939. Numerous articles from April 1939.)
(Articles in *The Canadian Forum* from February 1936 to March 1939.)
'Canadian Critic Proclaims Independence of the Dominion's Art.' *The Art Digest,* vol. x no. 11 (1 March 1936), pp. 10 – 11.
'New Horizons in Canadian Art.' *New Frontier,* vol. 2, no. 2 (June 1937), pp. 19 – 20.
'Art and Propaganda.' *New Frontier,* vol. 2, no. 3 (July – August 1937), pp. 17 – 18.
'Art of Canada.' *The Studio,* vol. cxiv (August 1937), pp. 55 – 75.
A Short History of Canadian Art. Toronto: Macmillan Company of Canada Limited, 1939.
'The Canadian Artist and His Country.' *The Geographical Magazine,* vol. xvi, no. 8 (December 1943), pp. 396 – 407.
Canadian Art. Toronto: The Macmillan Company of Canada Limited, 1950.
'The Decline of Genre.' *Canadian Art,* vol. ix, no. 1 (Autumn 1951), pp. 10 – 14.

Finding a Father. London: Hamish Hamilton, Limited, 1967.

Ostiguy, Jean-René. *Un siècle de peinture canadienne 1870 – 1970.* Quebec: Les Presses de l'Université Laval, 1971.

Parizeau, Marcel. 'Peinture Canadienne d'Aujourd'hui.' *Amérique française,* vol. ii, no. 2 (October 1942), pp. 8 – 18.

Prévost, Roland. 'M. Gérard Morisset.' *La Revue Populaire,* vol. 28, no. 4 (April 1935), p. 5.

Reid, Dennis. *The Group of Seven* (exhibition catalogue). Ottawa: The National Gallery of Canada, 1970.
A Concise History of Canadian Painting. Toronto: Oxford University Press, 1973.

Ringbom, Sixten. 'Art in "The Epoch of the Great Spiritual" Occult Elements in the Early Theory of Abstract Painting.' *Journal of the Warburg and Courtauld Institute,* vol. 29 (1966), pp. 386 – 418.

Robert, Guy. *L'Art au Québec depuis 1940.* Montreal: Les Éditions La Presse, 1973.

Scott, Charles H. 'A Short Art History of British Columbia.' *Behind the Palette.* Vancouver: Vancouver School of Art, 1946 – 1947.

Stewart, Roderick. *Bethune.* Toronto: New Press, 1973.

Viau, Guy. *Modern Painting in French Canada.* Quebec: Department of Cultural Affairs, 1967.

Vivash A.T. 'Trade Unions for Artists.' *New Frontier,* vol. 2, no. 1 (May 1937), pp. 22 – 23.

B/Artists

NOTE: *For certain artists only major sources and articles not in other bibliographies are noted.*

ALEXANDRE BERCOVITCH

Reinblatt, Moe. 'Aleksandre Bercovitch 1893 – 1951.' *Canadian Art*, vol. VIII, no. 3 (Spring 1951), pp. 110 – 111.

ANDRÉ BIÉLER

McInnes, Graham C. 'Contemporary Canadian Artists, no. 4 – André Biéler.' *The Canadian Forum*, vol. XVII, no. 196 (May 1937), pp. 56 – 57.

Biéler, André. 'National Aspects of Contemporary American and Canadian Painting.' In R.G. Trotter, A.B. Corey, W.W. McLaren, eds. *Conference on Canadian-American Affairs Held at Queen's University, Kingston, Ontario, June 14 – 18, 1937: Proceedings.* Boston, New York, Montreal, London: Ginn and Company, 1937, pp. 134 – 136.

Biéler, André and Elizabeth Harrison, eds. *The Kingston Conference. Conference of Canadian Artists.* Kingston, 1941.

'On the Canadian Group of Painters.' *Maritime Art*, vol. 2, no. 4 (April – May 1942), pp. 118 – 123, 136.

'The Kingston Conference – Ten Years Afterwards.' *Canadian Art*, vol. VIII, no. 4 (Summer 1951), pp. 150 – 152.

Le Grand, Albert. 'André Biéler.' *Arts et Pensée*, vol. 2 no. 8 (March – April 1952), pp. 36 – 39.

Ayre, Robert. 'Introduction.' *A Retrospective Exhibition of the Work of André Biéler* (exhibition catalogue). Kingston: The Agnes Etherington Art Centre, Queen's University, 1963.

Smith, Frances K. *André Biéler 50 Years: A Retrospective Exhibition 1920 – 1970* (exhibition catalogue). Kingston: Agnes Etherington Art Centre, Queen's University, 1970. Contribution by Ralph Allen.

'A Canadian Artist in the Market Place: André Biéler.' *Canadian Antiques Collector*, vol. 6, no. 2 (February 1971), pp. 6 – 9.

Chassé, Pierre-E. 'Biéler.' *Vie des Arts*, no. 64 (Autumn 1971), pp. 54 – 57.

PAUL-ÉMILE BORDUAS

Gagnon, Maurice. 'Paul-Émile Borduas . . . Peintre montréalais.' *La Revue Moderne*, vol. 18, no. 11 (September 1937), pp. 10 – 11.

Élie, Robert. 'Borduas.' *Le Quartier Latin*, vol. XXVI, no. 11 (17 December 1943), p. IV. *Borduas.* Montreal: L'Arbre, 1943.

Borduas, Paul-Émile. *Projections libérantes.* Montreal: Mithra-Mythe, 1949. Reprinted in Guy Robert, *Borduas*, 1972. An annotated edition published in *Études françaises*, vol. VIII, no. 3 (August 1972), pp. 245 – 305, with 'Borduas l'homme et l'œuvre (repères chronologiques)' by Nicole Boily, pp. 309 – 329.

'Quelques pensées sur l'œuvre d'amour et de rêve de M. Ozias Leduc.' *Canadian Art*, vol. X, no. 4 (Summer 1953), pp. 158 – 161, 168. Reprinted in *Ozias Leduc et Paul-Émile Borduas.*

'Paul-Émile Borduas nous écrit au sujet de Ozias Leduc.' *Arts et Pensée*, vol. 3, no. 18 (July – August 1954), pp. 177 – 179. Reprinted in *Ozias Leduc et Paul-Émile Borduas.*

Turner, Evan H. *Paul-Émile Borduas 1905 – 1960* (exhibition catalogue). Montreal: The Montreal Museum of Fine Arts, 1962. Contributions by John Lyman ('Borduas and the Contemporary Arts Society'), Guy Viau ('La Démarche du Peintre'), Paul-Émile Borduas ('Refus Global').

Robert, Guy. *Borduas.* Quebec: Les presses de l'Université du Québec, 1972.

Ozias Leduc et Paul-Émile Borduas, Conférences J.A. de Sève 15 – 16. Montreal: Les Presses de l'Université de Montréal, 1973. Contributions by Jean-Éthier Blais ('Ozias Leduc'), Françoise Le Gris ('Chronologie des rapports entre Ozias Leduc et Paul-Émile Borduas'), François Gagnon ('Trois textes de Paul-Émile Borduas sur Ozias Leduc').

FRITZ BRANDTNER

Ayre, Robert. 'Art-Expressionist in Montreal.' *New Frontier*, vol. 1, no. 2 (May 1936), pp. 29 – 30.

'Artists in Canada – Fritz Brandtner,' *Canadian Stage Screen and Studio*, vol. 1, no 4, March 1937, pp. 39 – 41.

Frye, Helen Kemp. 'Fritz Brandtner.' *The Canadian Forum*, vol. XVIII, no. 215 (December 1938), pp. 272 – 273.

Harper, J. Russell. *Fritz Brandtner 1896 – 1969 / A Retrospective Exhibition* (exhibition catalogue). Montreal: Sir George Williams University, 1971.

MILLER BRITTAIN

McInnes, Graham C. 'Contemporary Canadian Artists No. 11 – Miller Brittain.' *The Canadian Forum*, vol. XVII, no. 203 (December 1937), pp. 312 – 313.

Nicol, Pegi. 'Miller Brittain.' *Maritime Art*, vol. 1, no. 4 (April 1941), pp. 14 – 18.

Brittain, Miller. 'A Note by the Artist.' *Northern Review*, vol. 2, no. 6 (August – September 1949), p. 20.

Lord, J. Barry. 'Miller Brittain's Saint John Hospital Cartoons.' *Artscanada*, vol. XXIV, nos 6 – 7 (June – July 1967).

Andrus, Donald F.P. *Drawings and Pastels c. 1930 – 1967 by Miller Gore Brittain* (exhibition catalogue). Fredericton: Creative Art Centre, University of New Brunswick, 1968.

BERTRAM BROOKER

Brooker, Bertram. 'The Seven Arts.' (A weekly art

column published in the Southam newspapers from
October 1928 to November 1930.)
'Nudes and Prudes.' In William Arthur Deacon and
Wilfred Reeves, eds. *Open House*. Ottawa: Graphic
Publishers Limited, 1931, pp. 93 – 106.
'Art and Society.' In *Yearbook of the Arts in Canada,
1936*. Toronto: The Macmillan Company of Canada
Limited, 1936, pp. xiii – xxviii.
Lee, Thomas R. 'Bertram Brooker 1888 – 1955.' *Cana-
dian Art*, vol. xiii, no. 3 (Spring 1956), pp. 286 – 291.
Reid, Dennis. *Bertram Brooker 1888 – 1955*. Ottawa:
The National Gallery of Canada, 1973. Includes
bibliography.

EMILY CARR
Barbeau, Marius. 'The Canadian Northwest Theme
for Modern Painters.' *The American Magazine of Art*,
vol. xxiv, no. 5 (May 1932), pp. 331 – 338.
Mortimer-Lamb, H. 'A British Columbia Painter.'
Saturday Night, vol. xlviii, no. 10 (14 January 1933), p. 3.
Emily Carr / Her Paintings and Sketches (exhibition cata-
logue). Toronto: Oxford University Press, 1945.
Contributions by Ira Dilworth ('Emily Carr, Bio-
graphical Sketch') and Lawren Harris ('The Paintings
and Drawings of Emily Carr').
Carr, Emily. *Growing Pains, The Autobiography of Emily
Carr*. Toronto: Oxford University Press, 1946.
Turpin, Marguerite. *The Life and Work of Emily Carr
(1871 – 1945) A Selected Bibliography*. Vancouver:
School of Librarianship, The University of British
Columbia, 1965.
Carr, Emily. *Hundreds and Thousands. The Journals of
Emily Carr*. Toronto, Vancouver: Clarke, Irwin &
Company Limited, 1966.
Hembroff-Schleicher, Edythe. *m.e. A Portrayal of Emily
Carr*. Toronto: Clarke, Irwin & Company Limited,
1969. Includes correspondence from Emily Carr.
Shadbolt, Doris. *Emily Carr: A Centennial Exhibition*
(exhibition catalogue). Vancouver: The Vancouver
Art Gallery, 1971. Includes bibliography.
'Emily Carr: Legend and Reality.' *Artscanada*, vol.
xxviii, no. 3 (June – July 1971), pp. 17 – 21.
Carr, Emily. *Fresh Seeing. Two Addresses by Emily Carr*.
Toronto, Vancouver: Clarke, Irwin & Company
Limited, 1972.
Humphrey, Ruth. 'Letters from Emily Carr.' *University
of Toronto Quarterly*, vol. xli, no. 2 (Winter 1972),
pp. 93 – 150.
Tippett, Maria. ' "A Paste Solitaire in a Steel Claw
Setting": Emily Carr and Her Public.' *B.C. Studies*, no.
20 (Winter 1973 – 1974), pp. 3 – 13.
Contemporaries of Emily Carr in British Columbia

(exhibition catalogue). Burnaby, B.C.: Simon Fraser
Gallery, Simon Fraser University, 1974.

PARASKEVA CLARK
Clark, Paraskeva. 'Come Out From Behind the Pre-
Cambrian Shield.' *New Frontier*, vol. 1, no. 12 (April
1937), pp. 16 – 17.
McInnes, Graham C. 'Contemporary Canadian Artists
No. 7 – Paraskeva Clark.' *The Canadian Forum*, vol.
xvii, no. 199 (August 1937), pp. 166 – 167.
'The Artist Speaks: A Statement by Paraskeva Clark,'
Canadian Review of Music and Art, vol. iii, no. 9 – 10
(October – November 1944), pp. 18 – 20.
Bell, Andrew. 'The Art of Paraskeva Clark.' *Canadian
Art*, vol. vii, no. 2 (Christmas 1949), pp. 42 – 46.
Sabbath, Lawrence. 'Artist in Action Series: 3, Paraskeva
Clark with Lawrence Sabbath.' *Canadian Art*, vol.
xvii, no. 5 (September 1960), pp. 291 – 293.

CHARLES COMFORT
Comfort, Charles. 'The Painter and His Model.' In
William Arthur Deacon and Wilfred Reeves, eds.
Open House, Ottawa: Graphic Publishers Limited,
1931, pp. 213 – 218.
Jackson, H.M. *Charles Comfort / The Man and the
Artist*, n.p. (Christmas 1935. New Year 1936).
Comfort, Charles. 'Where I Stand on Spain.' *New
Frontier*, vol. 1, no. 8 (December 1936), p. 13.
McInnes, Graham C. 'Contemporary Canadian
Artists No. 3 – Charles F. Comfort.' *The Canadian
Forum*, vol. xvii, no. 195 (April 1937), pp. 18 – 19.
Comfort, Charles. 'Observations on a Decade 1938 –
48: Canadian Painting, Sculpture and Print Making.'
Journal Royal Architectural Institute of Canada, vol. 25,
no. 1 (January 1948), pp. 3 – 9.
Glover, Patricia E. *Charles Fraser Comfort Fifty Years*
(exhibition catalogue). Winnipeg: The Winnipeg Art
Gallery, 1973.

STANLEY COSGROVE
Leber, Germain. 'Stanley Cosgrove peintre audacieux.'
La Revue Moderne, vol. 26, no. 3 (July 1944), pp. 7, 22.
Girard, Henri. 'Stanley Cosgrove.' *Amerique française*,
vol. 4 (October 1944), pp 34 – 39.
Sabbath, Lawrence. 'Artist in Action Series: 6, Stanley
Cosgrove with Lawrence Sabbath.' *Canadian Art*,
vol. xviii, no. 2 (March – April 1961), pp. 114 – 116.
Gagnon, François. 'Cosgrove et la Critique d'Art
Officielle,' *Vie des Arts*, no. 60 (Autumn 1970), pp.
12 – 17.

LEMOINE FITZGERALD
Harris, Lawren. 'LeMoine FitzGerald – Western
Artist.' *Canadian Art*, vol. iii, no. 1 (October – Novem-
ber 1945), pp. 10 – 13.

Ayre, Robert. 'Lionel LeMoine FitzGerald 1890 – 1956.' *Canadian Art,* vol. xiv, no. 1 (Autumn 1956), pp. 14 – 16.

Eckhardt, Ferdinand. 'The Technique of L.L. Fitz-Gerald.' *Canadian Art,* vol. xv, no. 2 (April 1958), pp. 114 – 119, 149.

L.L. FitzGerald 1890 – 1956 / A Memorial Exhibition (exhibition catalogue). Winnipeg: The Winnipeg Art Gallery, 1958.

MARC-AURÈLE FORTIN

Chauvin, Jean. 'Marc-Aurèle Fortin.' In *Ateliers,* Montreal, New York: Louis Carrier & Cie., 1928, pp. 146 – 159.

Laberge, Albert. 'Marc-Aurèle Fortin.' In *Journalistes, Écrivains et Artistes,* Montreal: Édition privée, 1945, pp. 173 – 182.

Ostiguy, Jean-René. 'Marc-Aurèle Fortin.' *Vie des Arts,* no. 23 (Summer 1961), pp. 26 – 31.

Marc-Aurèle Fortin (exhibition catalogue). Ottawa: The National Gallery of Canada, 1964.

Jouvancourt, Hugues de. *Marc-Aurèle Fortin.* Montreal: Lidec, Inc., Collection Panorama, 1968.

Bonneville, Jean-Pierre. *M.A. Fortin* (exhibition catalogue). Verdun: Verdun Cultural Center, 1968.

ERIC GOLDBERG

Lyman, John. 'Art.' *The Montrealer* (15 April 1938).

Viau, Guy. 'Propos d'un rapin: Eric Goldberg, peintre pour plaire.' *Le Quartier Latin,* vol. xxvi, no. 6 (12 November 1943), p. 5.

LAWREN P. HARRIS

Harris, Lawren P. 'Our "Middle-Men" of the Arts.' *The Canadian Forum,* vol. xx, no. 231 (April 1940), p. 18.

Rombout, L. 'Lawren Harris, Profile of a Painter.' *The Atlantic Advocate* (December 1964), pp. 55 – 59, 61.

Smith, Ernest W. *Lawren P. Harris 37 / 72* (exhibition catalogue). Halifax: The Dalhousie Art Gallery, 1972.

LAWREN S. HARRIS

Harris, Lawren S. 'Different Idioms in Creative Art.' *Canadian Comment,* vol. 2, no. 12 (December 1933), pp. 5 – 6, 32.

Rudhyar, Dane. 'The Birth of the Transcendental Movement and Its Manifestations in Music and the Modern Dance.' *The New Mexico Daily Examiner,* Magazine Section (21 August 1938), p. 3.

Morang, Alfred. 'The Transcendental Painting Group, Its Origin, Foundation, Ideals and Works.' *The New Mexico Daily Examiner,* Magazine Section (21 August 1938), p. 3.

Transcendental Painting. Santa Fe, New Mexico: American Foundation for Transcendental Painting, Inc., 1940.

Smith, Sydney. 'The Recent Abstract Work of Lawren Harris.' *Maritime Art,* vol. 2, no. 3 (February – March 1942), pp. 79 – 81.

Carr, Emily. 'Lawren Harris.' In *Growing Pains,* Toronto: Oxford University Press, 1946, pp. 340 – 352.

Key, Sydney, ed. *Lawren Harris Paintings 1910 – 1948* (exhibition catalogue). Toronto: The Art Gallery of Toronto, 1948. Contributions by A.Y. Jackson ('Lawren Harris, A Biographical Sketch') and Sydney Key ('The Paintings').

Frye, Northrop. 'The Pursuit of Form.' *Canadian Art,* vol. vi. no. 2 (Christmas 1948), pp. 54 – 57.

Harris, Lawren. 'An Essay on Abstract Painting.' *Journal Royal Architectural Institute of Canada,* vol. xxvi, no. 1 (January 1949), pp. 3 – 8. Reprinted in *Canadian Art,* vol. vi, no. 3 (Spring 1949), pp. 103 – 107, 140.

McNairn, Ian, ed. *Lawren Harris Retrospective Exhibition, 1963* (exhibition catalogue). Ottawa: The National Gallery of Canada, 1963. Contributions by Paul Duval ('From Nature to Abstraction 1921 – 1931') and William Hart ('Theory and Practice of Abstract Art 1932 – 1948').

Reid, Dennis. 'Lawren Harris.' *Artscanada,* vol. xxv, no. 5 (December 1968), pp. 9 – 16.

Harris, Bess and R.G.P. Colgrove, eds. *Lawren Harris.* Toronto: The Macmillan Company of Canada Limited, 1969.

See also Dennis Reid, *A Bibliography of the Group of Seven,* Ottawa: The National Gallery of Canada, 1971.

PRUDENCE HEWARD

Holgate, Edwin H. 'Prudence Heward.' *Canadian Art,* vol. iv, no. 4 (Summer 1947), pp. 160 – 161.

Memorial Exhibition/Prudence Heward 1896 – 1947 (exhibition catalogue). Ottawa: The National Gallery of Canada, 1948.

Duval, Paul. 'Art and Artists/Prudence Heward Show.' *Saturday Night,* vol. lxiii, no. 29 (24 April 1948), p. 29.

EDWIN HOLGATE

Chauvin, Jean. 'Edwin Holgate.' In *Ateliers,* Montreal, New York: Louis Carrier & Cie, 1928, pp. 18 – 27.

Carrier, Louis. 'Edwin Holgate.' In *Les Casoars,* Montreal: n.p., 1928, pp. 21 – 23.

Holgate, Edwin H. 'Some Comments on Wood Engraving in Canada.' *The McGill News* (March 1933), pp. 23 – 26.

Archer, Thomas. 'Montreal Letter: The Art of Holgate.' *Saturday Night,* vol. xlviii, no. 23 (15 April 1933), p. 7.

See also Dennis Reid, *A Bibliography of the Group of Seven,* Ottawa: The National Gallery of Canada, 1971.

YVONNE McKAGUE HOUSSER
'Paris – The Magnet.' *Quality Street* (April 1926), pp. 9 – 10, 24, 29.
Frye, Helen Kemp. 'Yvonne McKague Housser.' *The Canadian Forum*, vol. XVIII, no. 212 (September 1938), pp. 176 – 177.

JACK HUMPHREY
Abell, Walter. 'Jack Humphrey – Painter.' *The Canadian Forum*, vol. XVI, no. 185 (June 1936), pp. 16 – 18.
'Jack Weldon Humphrey.' *Maritime Art*, vol. 1, no. 2 (December 1940), pp. 12 – 16.
'The Artist Speaks. A Statement by Jack W. Humphrey.' *Canadian Review of Music and Art*, vol. III, nos. 3 – 4 (April – May 1944), pp. 27 – 29.
Humphrey, Jack. 'A Note by the Artist.' *Northern Review*, vol. 2, no. 5 (April – May 1945), pp. 21 – 24.
Rombout, Louis. 'Jack Humphrey.' *Canadian Art*, vol. XXIII, no. 2 (April 1966), pp. 35 – 37.
Harper, Russell. 'A Painter in the Maritimes.' In *Jack Humphrey, A Retrospective Exhibition* (exhibition catalogue). Fredericton: Beaverbrook Art Gallery, 1966.

A.Y. JACKSON
Jackson, A.Y. 'Modern Art No "Menace".' *Saturday Night*, vol. XLVIII, no. 6 (17 December 1932), p. 3.
Robson, Albert H. *A.Y. Jackson*. Toronto: The Ryerson Press, 1938.
Key, Sydney. *A.Y. Jackson Paintings 1902 – 1953* (exhibition catalogue). Toronto: The Art Gallery of Toronto, 1953. Contribution by Arthur Lismer ('A.Y. Jackson').
Jackson, A.Y. *A Painter's Country. The Autobiography of A.Y. Jackson*. Toronto, Vancouver: Clarke, Irwin & Company Limited, 1958. Paperback edition, 1964; Centennial Edition, 1967.
Sabbath, Lawrence. 'Artist in Action Series: 2, A.Y. Jackson with Lawrence Sabbath.' *Canadian Art*, vol. XVII, no. 4 (July 1960), pp. 240 – 241, 243 – 244.
Groves, Naomi Jackson. *A.Y.'s Canada*. Toronto, Vancouver: Clarke, Irwin & Company Limited, 1968.
See also Dennis Reid, *A Bibliography of the Group of Seven*, Ottawa: The National Gallery of Canada, 1971.

JEAN PAUL LEMIEUX
Lemieux, Jean Paul. 'Notes sur quelques toiles de Pellan.' *Le Jour*, vol. 1, no. 35 (14 May 1938) p. 3.
'Aperçu sur la peinture contemporaine.' *Le Jour*, vol. 1, no. 40 (18 June 1938), p. 2.
'La peinture chez les canadiens français.' *Le Jour*, vol. 1, no. 44 (16 July 1938), p. 3.
'Notes sur le dessin.' *Le Jour*, vol. 2, no. 3 (1 October 1938), p. 2.
Corbeil, Gilles. 'Jean Paul Lemieux, peintre intimiste.'

Arts et Pensée, vol. 3, no. 4 (November – December 1953), pp. 36 – 41.
Picher, Claude and Marcel Cadieux. 'Jean Paul Lemieux.' *Canadian Art*, vol. XVII, no. 5 (September 1960), pp. 264 – 273.
Iberville-Moreau, Luc d'. *Jean Paul Lemieux* (exhibition catalogue). Montreal: The Montreal Museum of Fine Arts, 1967.
Robert, Guy. *Jean Paul Lemieux la poétique de la souvenance*. Quebec: Éditions Garneau, 1968.
Dumas, Paul. 'Rencontre avec Jean Paul Lemieux.' *L'Information Medicale et Paramedicale* (17 June 1969).

ARTHUR LISMER
Lismer, Arthur. 'The World of Art.' *Canadian Comment* (a monthly column from February 1932 to August 1933). Various articles from September 1933 to July 1936.
'Art and Education in the Southern Dominions.' *The Curtain Call*, vol. 9, no. 2 (November 1937), p. 8.
Hunter, E. Robert. 'Arthur Lismer.' *Maritime Art*, vol. 3, no. 5 (July – August 1943), pp. 137 – 141, 168 – 169.
Key, Sydney. *Arthur Lismer Paintings 1913 – 1949* (exhibition catalogue). Toronto: The Art Gallery of Toronto, 1950. Contribution by Lawren Harris ('Arthur Lismer').
McLeish, John A.B. *September Gale. A Study of Arthur Lismer of the Group of Seven*. Toronto, Vancouver: J.M. Dent & Sons (Canada) Ltd., 1955. Paperback edition 1973.
See also Dennis Reid, *A Bibliography of the Group of Seven*, Ottawa: The National Gallery of Canada, 1971.

JOHN LYMAN
Lyman, John. 'Canadian Art.' *The Canadian Forum*, vol. XII, no. 140 (May 1932), pp. 313 – 314.
'From Monet to Matisse.' *Bridle & Golfer* (December 1934), pp. 18 – 19, 38.
'Renoir and His Contemporaries.' *The Montrealer* (March 1936).
'The School of Paris.' *The Montrealer* (October 1936), pp. 18 – 20.
'Art.' *The Montrealer* (a monthly art column from November 1936 to September 1937. Bi-monthly from October 1937 to 15 May 1939, except summers. Monthly from November 1939 to December 1940).
Ayre, Robert. 'Art.' *The Montrealer* (February 1937).
McInnes, Graham C. 'Contemporary Canadian Artists No. 5 – John Lyman.' *The Canadian Forum*, vol. XVII, no. 197 (June 1937), pp. 94 – 95.
Lyman, John. 'Painting in Quebec.' *Journal Royal Architectural Institute of Canada*, vol. XVIII, no. 4 (April 1941), p. 69.

Dumas, Paul. 'Lyman.' *Le Quartier Latin*, vol. XXVI, no. 11 (17 December 1943), pp. III, VIII. Reprinted in *Aujourd'hui*, no. 54 (March 1944), pp. 24 – 32.

Lyman. Montreal: L'Arbre, 1944.

Lyman, John. *Morrice*. Montreal: L'Arbre, 1945.

Shaw, Neufville. 'John Lyman.' *Northern Review*, vol. 1, no. 2 (February 1946), pp. 19 – 24.

Corbeil, Gilles. 'John Lyman, Peintre.' *Arts et Pensée*, vol. 3, no. 15 (January – February 1954), pp. 75 – 83.

Lyman, John. 'Extraits de non-journal.' *Arts et Pensée*, vol. 3, no. 17 (May – June 1954), pp. 138 – 139.

'Adieu, Matisse.' *Canadian Art*, vol. XII, no. 2 (Winter 1955), pp. 44 – 46.

Sabbath, Lawrence. 'Artist in Action Series: 4, John Lyman with Lawrence Sabbath.' *Canadian Art*, vol. XVII, no. 6 (November 1960), pp. 372 – 374.

Lawson, Edward P. *John Lyman* (exhibition catalogue). Montreal: The Montreal Museum of Fine Arts, 1963. Contribution by Gilles Corbeil ('John Lyman').

Viau, Guy. 'John Lyman.' *Vie des Arts*, no. 33 (Winter 1963 – 1964), pp. 26 – 31.

John Lyman (exhibition catalogue). Quebec: Le Musée du Québec, 1966. Introduction by Philip Surrey.

J.W.G. MACDONALD

British Columbia College of Arts Limited, Illustrated Prospectus 1934 – 1935, Vancouver: Sun Publishing Company Limited, (1934).

Corriveau, L. de B. 'The Art of James W.G. Macdonald.' *Canadian Review of Music and Art*, vol. III, nos 1 – 2 (February – March 1944), pp. 25 – 27.

Bates, Maxwell. 'Jock Macdonald, Painter-Explorer.' *Canadian Art*, vol. XIV, no. 4 (Summer 1957), pp. 151–153.

Nicholson, Carolyn and Judi Francis. 'J.W.G. Macdonald The Western Years.' Burnaby: The Burnaby Art Gallery, 1969, Typescript.

Pollock, R. Ann, and Dennis Reid. *Jock Macdonald* (exhibition catalogue). Ottawa: The National Gallery of Canada, 1969. Includes bibliography.

PEGI NICOL MACLEOD

Nicol, Pegi. 'The Passionate Snow of Yesteryear.' *The Canadian Forum*, vol. XVI, no. 183 (April 1936), p. 21.

McInnes, Graham C. 'Contemporary Canadian Artists No. 8 – Pegi Nicol.' *The Canadian Forum*, vol. XVII, no. 200 (September 1937), pp. 202 – 203.

Memorial Exhibition / Pegi Nicol MacLeod 1904 – 1949 (exhibition catalogue). Ottawa: The National Gallery of Canada, 1949.

Buchanan, Donald W. 'Pegi Nicol MacLeod 1904 – 49.' *Canadian Art*, vol. VI, no. 4 (Summer 1949), pp. 158 – 162.

Harper, J. Russell. 'Pegi Nicol MacLeod: A Maritime Artist.' *The Dalhousie Review*, vol. 43, no. 1 (Spring 1963), pp. 40 – 50.

DAVID MILNE

Buchanan, Donald W. 'An Artist Who Lives in the Woods.' *Saturday Night*, vol. L, no. 4 (1 December 1934), p. 2.

'David Milne.' *The Canadian Forum*, vol. XV, no. 173 (February 1935), pp. 191 – 193.

Jarvis, Alan. 'Notes on Two Canadian Artists.' *The Undergraduate* (1936), pp. 35 – 37.

Exhibition of Little Pictures by David B. Milne (exhibition catalogue). Toronto: Mellors Galleries, 1936.

McInnes, Graham C. 'Contemporary Canadian Artists No. 9 – David Milne.' *The Canadian Forum*, vol. XVII, no. 201 (October 1937), pp 238 – 239.

Milne, David. 'From Spring Fever to Fantasy.' *Canadian Art*, vol. II, no. 4 (April – May 1945), pp. 162 – 165. Reprinted in *Canadian Art*, vol. XV, no. 1 (January 1958), pp. 16 – 19.

Frye, Northrop. 'David Milne: An Appreciation.' *Here and Now*, vol. 1, no. 2 (May 1948), pp. 47 – 58. Reprinted in Northrop Frye, *The Bush Garden/Essays on the Canadian Imagination*. Toronto: Anansi Press Ltd., 1971, pp. 203 – 206.

Milne, David. 'Feeling in Painting.' *Here and Now*, vol. 1, no. 2 (May 1948), pp. 57 – 58.

Buchanan, Donald W. 'David Milne as I Knew Him.' *Canadian Art*, vol. XI, no. 3 (Spring 1954), pp. 89 – 92.

Jarvis, Alan. *David Milne* (exhibition catalogue). Ottawa: The National Gallery of Canada, 1955. Includes 'The Colour Dry-Point' by David Milne, originally published in *Canadian Art*, vol. IV, no. 4 (Summer 1947), pp. 144 – 147.

Moon, Barbara. 'Genius in hiding: David Milne.' *Maclean's Magazine*, vol. LXXIV (17 June 1961), pp. 14 – 17, 48 – 50.

Jarvis, Alan. *David Milne*. Toronto: McClelland and Stewart Limited, 1962.

Silcox, David P. *David Milne 1882 – 1953* (exhibition catalogue). Kingston: The Agnes Etherington Art Centre, Queen's University, 1967. Includes bibliography.

David Milne (1882 – 1953) (exhibition catalogue). Montreal: Galerie Godard Lefort, 1971.

LOUIS MUHLSTOCK

Saint-Denys Garneau, Hector de. 'Chronique des beaux-arts: Louis Muhlstock.' *La Relève*, vol. 2, no. 5 (January 1936), pp. 158 – 160.

McInnes, Graham C. 'Louis Muhlstock Painter of People.' *New World* (March 1941).

Ayre, Robert. 'Louis Muhlstock.' *Northern Review*, vol. 2, no. 4 (January – February 1949), pp. 15 – 20.

'The New Muhlstock.' *Canadian Art*, vol. ix, no. 4 (Summer 1952), pp. 140 – 143.

Repentigny, Rodolphe de. 'Louis Muhlstock.' *Vie des Arts*, no. 16 (Autumn 1959), pp. 10 – 15.

Sabbath, Lawrence. 'Artist in Action Series: 1, Louis Muhlstock with Lawrence Sabbath.' *Canadian Art*, vol. xvii, no. 4 (July 1960), pp. 216 – 223.

LILIAS TORRANCE NEWTON

'Canadian Women in the Public Eye/Lilias T. Newton.' *Saturday Night*, vol. xlii, no. 52 (12 November 1927), p. 35.

GOODRIDGE ROBERTS

Neumann, Ernst. 'Canadian Artists of Today: Wm. Goodridge Roberts.' *New Frontier*, vol. 1, no. 4 (July 1936), p. 30.

Tonnancour, Jacques de. 'Sur Goodridge Roberts, un peintre authentique.' *La Relève*, vol. 5, no. 7 (April 1941), pp. 216 – 221. Reprinted in *Amérique francaise*, vol. 1, no. 5 (April 1942), pp. 32 – 37.

Harrison, Allan. 'Roberts.' *Le Quartier Latin*, vol. xxvi, no. 11 (17 December 1943), p. vi.

Tonnancour, Jacques de. 'Roberts.' *Le Quartier Latin*, vol. xxvi, no. 11 (17 December 1943), p. vi.

Roberts. Montreal: L'Arbre, 1944.

Ayre, Robert. 'Goodridge Roberts.' *Canadian Art*, vol. iii, no. 2 (January – February 1946), pp. 48 – 51.

Shaw, Neufville. 'Goodridge Roberts – 1949.' *Northern Review*, vol. 3, no. 1 (October – November 1949), p. 27.

Boulanger, Rolland. 'Esquisses . . . Goodridge Roberts.' *Arts et Pensée*, vol. 1, no. 3 (May 1951), pp. 74 – 79.

Roberts, Goodridge. 'From This Point I Looked Out.' *Queen's Quarterly* (Autumn 1953), pp. 316 – 331. Reprinted in James Borcoman, *Goodridge Roberts*, pp. 185 – 196.

Borcoman, James. *Goodridge Roberts* (exhibition catalogue). Ottawa: The National Gallery of Canada, 1969. Contributions by Robert Ayre ('A Biographical Sketch'), Alfred Pinsky ('A Study of the Work'), and Goodridge Roberts ('From This Point I Looked Out').

SARAH ROBERTSON

Jackson, A.Y. 'Sarah Robertson, 1891 – 1948.' *Canadian Art*, vol. vi, no. 3 (Spring 1949), pp. 125 – 126.

Memorial Exhibition/Sarah Robertson 1891 – 1948 (exhibition catalogue). Ottawa: The National Gallery of Canada, 1951.

ANNE SAVAGE

Sherman, Leah. *Anne Savage/A Retrospective* (exhibition catalogue). Montreal: Sir George Williams University, 1969.

CARL SCHAEFER

McInnes, Graham C. 'Contemporary Canadian Artists, No. 1 – Carl Schaefer.' *The Canadian Forum*, vol. xvi, no. 193 (February 1937), pp. 18 – 19.

Buchanan, Donald W. 'Carl Schaefer Canadian Painter.' *The Studio*, vol. cxxiii (February 1942), p. 49.

Johnston, George. 'Carl Schaefer – Artist and Man.' *Queen's Quarterly*, vol. lxi, no. 3 (Autumn 1954), pp. 345 – 352.

'Carl Schaefer.' *Canadian Art*, vol. xvii, no. 2 (March 1960), pp. 66 – 71, 99.

'Carl Schaefer interviewed by Joy Carroll.' *Canadian Art*, vol. xxii, no. 3 (May – June 1965), pp. 38 – 40.

Harper, J. Russell. *Carl Schaefer Retrospective Exhibition / Paintings from 1926 to 1969* (exhibition catalogue). Montreal: Sir George Williams University, 1969. Contributions by George Johnston ('Carl Schaefer, A Short Appreciation') and Carl Schaefer ('Personal Reminiscences'). Includes bibliography.

MARIAN SCOTT

McInnes, Graham C. 'Contemporary Canadian Artists No. 10 – Marian Scott.' *The Canadian Forum*, vol. xvii, no. 202 (November 1937), pp. 274 – 275.

Forsey, Harriet R. 'Womankind.' *The Canadian Forum*, vol. xvii, no. 204 (January 1938), p. 366.

Selye, Hans and Marian Scott. 'Art and Science.' *Canadian Art*, vol. i, no. 1 (October – November 1943), pp. 17 – 19, 36 – 37.

Exhibition of Paintings by Marian Scott (exhibition catalogue). Montreal: Dominion Gallery, 1954. Three mimeographed sheets.

JORI SMITH

McInnes, Graham C. 'Contemporary Canadian Artists No. 6 – Jori Smith and Jean Palardy.' *The Canadian Forum*, vol. xvii, no. 198 (July 1937), pp. 130 – 131.

PHILIP SURREY

Roussan, Jacques de. 'Le peintre des reflets de la ville.' *Vie des Arts*, no. 31 (Summer 1963), pp. 24 – 29.

Ayre, Robert. 'The City and the Dream of Philip Surrey.' *Canadian Art*, vol. xxi, no. 5 (September – October 1964), pp. 284 – 287.

Roussan, Jacques de. *Philip Surrey*. Montreal: Lidec, Inc., Collection Panorama, 1968.

Barras, Henri. *Philip Surrey Le peintre dans la ville* (exhibition catalogue). Montreal: Musée d'art contemporain, 1971. Contributions by Guy Viau and Gilles Corbeil.

FREDERICK VARLEY

Duval, Paul. 'Art and Artists/Vigorous Veteran of Canadian Art – Frederick Horsman Varley.' *Saturday Night*, vol. lx, no. 15 (16 December 1944), p. 35.

C / Collectors

Buchanan, Donald W. 'The Paintings and Drawings of F.H. Varley.' *Canadian Art*, vol. VII, no. 1 (Autumn 1949), pp. 2 – 5.

F.H. Varley Paintings 1915 – 1954 (exhibition catalogue). Toronto: The Art Gallery of Toronto, 1954. Contributions by Arthur Lismer ('The Twenties'), J.W.G. Macdonald ('Vancouver') and R.H. Hubbard ('An Approach to Varley').

Carpenter, Edmund. 'Varley's Arctic Sketches.' *Canadian Art*, vol. XVI, no. 2 (May 1959), pp. 93 – 100.

Carpenter, Edmund S., Frederick H. Varley, and Robert Flaherty. *Eskimo*. Toronto: University of Toronto Press, 1959.

Porter, McKenzie. 'Varley.' *Maclean's Magazine*, vol. LXXII, no. 23 (7 November 1959), pp. 30 – 33, 62, 64 – 66, 71.

Kincaid, Sheila. *Varley / The Middle Years* (exhibition catalogue). Burnaby: Burnaby Art Gallery, 1974. Contributions by Chris Varley ('Introduction') and Dave Brock ('Fred's Furnace').

See also Dennis Reid, *A Bibliography of the Group of Seven*, Ottawa: The National Gallery of Canada, 1971.

CHARLES S. BAND

Paintings and Drawings from the Collection of Mr. and Mrs. C.S. Band (exhibition catalogue). Ottawa: The National Gallery of Canada, 1953. Introduction by Arthur Lismer.

Band, Charles S. 'I Collect What I Like.' *Mayfair* (April 1955), pp. 27 – 29, 57 – 60.

'Charles S. Band.' *Canadian Art*, vol. XVIII, no. 3 (May – June 1961), pp. 158 – 161.

DOUGLAS M. DUNCAN

Bell, Andrew. 'Design for an Art Angel – Douglas Duncan and the Picture Loan Society.' *Canadian Art*, vol. IX, no. 4 (Summer 1952), pp. 149 – 151.

'Douglas Duncan.' *Canadian Art*, vol. XVIII, no. 3 (May – June 1961), pp. 166 – 169.

Théberge, Pierre. *Gift from the Douglas M. Duncan Collection and the Milne-Duncan Bequest* (exhibition catalogue). Ottawa: The National Gallery of Canada, 1971. Contributions by Norman J. Endicott ('Douglas Moerdyke Duncan: A Memoir') and Alan Jarvis ('Douglas Duncan').

Cameron, Stanley. 'Douglas M. Duncan (1902 – 1968), Uncommon Collector.' *Canadian Antiques Collector*, vol. 6, no. 6 (July – August 1971), pp. 14 – 17.

Jarvis, Alan, ed. *Douglas Duncan. A Memorial Portrait*. Buffalo, Toronto: University of Toronto Press, 1974.

J.S. McLEAN

Dacre, Douglas. 'The Butcher with a Poet's Soul.' *Maclean's Magazine*, vol. LXIV (1 October 1951), pp. 18 – 19, 61 – 63, 65 – 66.

Paintings and Drawings from the Collection of J.S. McLean (exhibition catalogue). Ottawa: The National Gallery of Canada, 1952. Introduction by A.Y. Jackson.

McLean, J.S. 'On the Pleasures of Collecting Paintings.' *Canadian Art*, vol. X, no. 1 (Autumn 1952), pp. 2 – 7.

VINCENT MASSEY

Massey, Vincent. 'Art and Nationality in Canada.' *Transactions of the Royal Society of Canada*, 3rd. ser., vol. XXIV (1930), pp. LIX-LXXII.

What's Past is Prologue. Toronto: Macmillan Company of Canada, 1963.

McPherson, Hugo. 'The Resonance of Batterwood House.' *Canadian Art*, vol. XXI, no. 2 (March – April 1964), pp. 96 – 103.

Hubbard, R.H. *Vincent Massey Bequest / The Canadian Paintings* (exhibition catalogue). Ottawa: The National Gallery of Canada, 1968.

96. GOODRIDGE ROBERTS, *Standing Nude* (1938)

Index

Photograph Sources

Credits

COLOUR PHOTOGRAPHS:
Clarke, Irwin & Company Limited, Toronto: cat. no. 15;
The National Gallery of Canada, Ottawa: cat. nos. 45,
49, 66, 96; Ron Vickers, Toronto: cat. no. 26.

BLACK AND WHITE PHOTOGRAPHS:
The National Gallery of Canada, Ottawa, except for the
following: Walter Abell, reproduced courtesy Paraskeva
Clark, R.C.A., Toronto: fig. no. 10; Art Gallery of Ontario,
Toronto: cat. nos. 5, 8, 18, 34, 57, 72 76, 85, 101; Lloyd
Bloom, Hamilton: cat. nos. 14, 15, 25, 71; Mrs F.
Brandtner, Montreal: fig. nos. 7, 13; Brigdens Photography, Winnipeg: cat. no. 46; John Evans, Ottawa: cat. no.
84; Tod Greenaway, Vancouver: cat. nos. 11, 54, 60;
Jennifer Harper, Montreal: cat. nos. 1, 16, 20, 36, 90, 92,
98, 99, 100, 106; Harvey Studios, Fredericton: cat. nos. 23,
74, 78; Ian Hodkinson, Kingston: cat. no. 82; Mrs Jack
Humphrey, Saint John: fig. no. 12; H.U. Knight, reproduced courtesy the Archives of the City of Victoria: fig.
no. 4; Levy Studios Ltd., Toronto: cat. no. 103; MacKen-
zie Studios, New Glasgow, N.S.: cat. no. 9; The McMichael
Canadian Collection, Kleinburg: cat. no. 10; The Montreal Museum of Fine Arts, Montreal: fig. no. 3; cat. nos.
88, 102, 108; Musée du Québec, Quebec: cat. nos. 80, 86,
97; Daniel M. Newman, Windsor: cat. no. 24; Eric
Pollizer, New York: cat. no. 107; Otto Reppen, T.D.F.,
Toronto: cat. nos. 22, 26, 35, 61; Carl Schaefer, Toronto:
fig. no. 8; Concordia University, Montreal: cat. no. 81;
Hazen Sise, reproduced courtesy Public Archives of
Canada, Ottawa: fig. no. 11; Gabor Szilasi, Montreal: cat.
no. 87; Robert Title, Toronto: cat. no. 59; The Vancouver
Art Gallery, Vancouver: cat. nos. 29, 30, 31, 32, 33, 38;
J. Vanderpant, reproduced courtesy Mrs. A. Vanderpant
Ackroyd and Mrs. C. Vanderpant Shelley, Vancouver:
fig. nos. 1, 5, 6; Ron Vickers, Toronto: cat. nos. 3, 6, 28,
37, 40, 47, 69, 104, 105; George Wilkins Photography Ltd.,
Toronto: cat. no. 64; The Winnipeg Art Gallery, Winni-
peg: cat. no. 44.

Design: Hugh Michaelson
Printing: The Hunter Rose Company, Toronto